CREATIVE APPROACHES TO WRITING CENTER WORK

Research and Teaching in Rhetoric and Composition
Michael M. Williamson and *Peggy O'Neill series editors*

Basic Writing as a Political Act: Public Conversations About Writing
and Literacies
  Linda Adler-Kassner & Susanmarie Harrington
Culture Shock and the Practice of Profession: Training the Next Wave
in Rhetoric and Composition
  Virginia Anderson & Susan Romano
The Hope and the Legacy: The Past Present and Future of "Students' Right"
to Their Own Language
  Patrick Bruch & Richard Marback (eds.)
Market Matters: Applied Rhetoric Studies and Free Market Competition
  Locke Carter (ed.)
In Search of Eloquence: Cross-Disciplinary Conversations on the Role of Writing
in Undergraduate Education
  Cornelius Cosgrove & Nancy Barta-Smith
Creative Approaches to Writing Center Work
  Kevin Dvorak & Shanti Bruce
Teaching/Writing in the Late Age of Print
  Jeffrey Galin, Carol Peterson Haviland, & J Paul Johnson (eds.)
Collaborating(,) Literature(,) and Composition: Essays for Teachers and Writers
of English
  Frank Gaughan & Peter H. Khost
Professing Literacy in Composition Studies
  Peter N. Goggin
Rhetoric in(to) Science Inquiry: Style as Invention in the Pursuit of Knowledge
  Heather Graves
Judaic Perspectives in Rhetoric and Composition Studies
  Andrea Greenbaum & Deborah H. Holdstein
Basic Writing in America: The History of Nine College Programs
  Nicole Pepinster Greene & Patricia J. McAlexander
Revision Revisited
  Alice S. Horning
Multiple Literacies for the 21st Century
  Brian Huot, Beth Stroble, & Charles Bazerman (eds.)
Classroom Spaces and Writing Instruction
  Ed Nagelhout & Carol Rutz
Toward Deprivatized Pedagogy
  Becky Nugent & Diane Calhoun Bell
Unexpected Voices
  John Rouse & Ed Katz
Directed Self-Placement: Principles and Practices
  Dan Royer & Roger Gilles (eds.)
Dead Letters: Error in Composition, 1873-2004
  Tracy Santa
Who Can Afford Critical Consciousness?: Practicing a Pedagogy of Humility
  David Seitz
Composing Feminism(s): How Feminists Have Shaped Composition Theories
and Practices
  Kay Siebler

CREATIVE APPROACHES TO WRITING CENTER WORK

edited by

Kevin Dvorak
St. Thomas University

Shanti Bruce
Nova Southeastern University

HAMPTON PRESS, INC.
CRESSKILL, NJ 07626

Printed in the United States of America

Library of Congress Cataloging-in-Publication Data

Creative approaches to writing center work / edited by Kevin Dvorak, Shanti
Bruce.
    p. cm. -- (Research and teaching in rhetoric and composition)
  Includes bibliographical references and indexes.
  ISBN 978-1-57273-838-6 -- ISBN 978-1-57273-839-3 (pbk.)
  1. English language--Rhetoric--Study and teaching. 2. Report writing--Study
and teaching. 3. Creative writing (Higher education) 4. Writing centers.
5.
Tutors and tutoring. I. Dvorak, Kevin, 1974- II. Bruce, Shanti.
  PE1404.C68 2008
  808'.0420711--dc21

                       2008038175

Cover art: Robert V. Bruce

Hampton Press, Inc.
23 Broadway
Cresskill, NJ 07626

"All the freaky people make the beauty of the world."

~Michael Franti

CONTENTS

ACKNOWLEDGMENTS

We would like to thank the contributing authors for taking chances in their centers and sharing their innovative ideas.

We would also like to thank Nick Mauriello for believing in this project.

INTRODUCTION

Where: A coffeehouse in the Shadyside section of Pittsburgh.

When: Friday night, late October.

It's brisk outside. People are walking the streets wearing Halloween costumes, popping in and out of bars, apartments, and townhomes. And there's a good crowd in this coffeehouse. To our front: a gentleman writing in a rather large, college-bound notebook. On his table for one: two cups, one filled with coffee, the second with water; one large white binder and some kind of granola snack half-eaten and half-wrapped. He's wearing headphones, looking out the window, and writing. A woman sits behind him, her back to us—we can see the monitor of her laptop. She has an open word processing document and another that looks like a .pdf file. Behind her is a bulletin board covered in announcements for, among others, poetry readings, writing groups and book clubs, and yoga classes. To her left, an overcrowded table of five, all recent patrons, chat loudly in a language we do not speak. One table to their left, another gentleman writes—furiously, too, we might add—and has what looks like a large coffee. To his right: one male, two females, one laptop. Next table: two conversationalists. Next: one male, one female—scrub-wearing med students—and a thick textbook. Next: two more pure conversationalists. Then, us: two participant observers, one laptop, one coffee, one latte (extra froth), one half-eaten chocolate chip cookie, two mouths talking, four ears listening, two hands typing (at a time), four eyes noticing.

Nine tables in a public setting—six actively engaged in writing (three solo, three collaborative), three engaged in active conversation. The most intriguing of the bunch, to us, is the table of three working on a laptop. It looks as if two of them are writing music. The document they have appears to be sheet music, and they keep leaning in and away from the screen. They sit back occasionally, talk, point to the screen, and lean in again. She touch-

es the keyboard; he noddingly smiles. Our thoughts? This would be a perfect snapshot for every writing center's home page.

    We set out that late-fall night looking for good coffee, good conversa-
tion, and good writing. What we also happened upon was a reaffirmation
of a conversation we'd had multiple times before: that coffeehouses and
writing centers have much in common, and that, in many ways, coffeehouses resemble writing centers—places where people gather to combine
work and play, where creative literacy activities flourish, and where coffee
(hopefully) flows. We discussed how many of our writing center colleagues
were practicing in their centers many of the creative activities we were seeing at coffeehouses, such as spoken word nights and writing groups, and
decided to celebrate a few of their many creative—original, imaginative,
inspired, artistic, and innovative—approaches to writing center work by
compiling their ideas in a collection that could be shared and discussed
across the profession.

THE VALUE OF CREATIVITY

In addition to simply celebrating the fine work of our colleagues, we
believed strongly that there was great value in sharing these creative
approaches to writing center work. We hoped that this collection might
help counter the institutionalization of writing centers that Riley (1994)
predicted in his essay, "The Unpromising Future of the Writing Center." He
warned that writing centers could become stale, institutional. For when a
field has created its own body of research and its own body of literature,
once handbooks and manuals have been published and proliferate a cen-
tralized way of "doing things," a field can become institutionalized. Stale.

    Gardner and Ramsey (2005) also approached this subject, discussing
the impact stagnation can have on writing center work and how it is important to constantly re-examine and re-identify writing center missions.
Rather than allowing our work to become too institutionalized in the face
of meeting more multicultural demands, Ramsey and Gardner suggested
that "what we need . . . is a theoretical perspective that more productively
centers us in the university even as we offer space for difference" (p. 26).
This collection intends to do just that. It intends to offer writing center
practitioners possibilities for avoiding stagnation, for complicating the status quo. After all, if the populations we work with are ever-changing, our
pedagogical styles and administrative methods should change as well. Not
only do the student populations we work with change, but so do the types
of institutional problems that writing centers face. One semester, a writing
center might be faced with university-wide budget cuts; the next semester,

a writing center might be faced with a potential, and unfavorable, re-location due to space constraints or the development of a new academic program. Regardless, the types of challenges writing centers face on a regular basis are reason enough to realize that directors and tutors should be proactive in their innovative approaches to writing center work.

We asked contributors to share how they incorporated creativity into their writing center environments. We asked them to consider the role of play—its positives and potential pitfalls. We invited them to share their ideas and experiences, and we put little constraints on them, valuing the local and the anecdotal as much as the formally researched. The results prove, to us, that writing centers can include creativity and serious play alongside serious work—or better still—can put play to work, seriously.

ORGANIZATION OF THE BOOK

Creative Approaches shares ways writing centers have incorporated creative activities into their routines and encourages readers to imagine ways to develop their own creative approaches that reach their unique campus communities. We hope this book inspires readers to complicate their visions of what writing centers can be. We hope readers consider these approaches, modify them to fit their local contexts, and create new approaches to writing center work that will further writing center innovations.

We intend to assist those writing center practitioners who wish to meet the challenge of re-envisioning their work by exploring questions such as:

- How do creativity and play enhance—and complicate—writing center work?
- How do creative approaches to staff education enrich learning environments? How can these approaches help build strong relationships among staff members?
- How can administering creative community outreach programs help a writing center strengthen its ethos on campus and in larger literacy communities?

The collection is organized into three parts. Part I explores the connections between writing center work, creativity, and play, both encouraging and questioning the effects they can have on writing center environments. Part II provides creative approaches to pedagogical practices involved in tutor education programs and tutoring sessions. And, Part III introduces readers to various creative outreach activities.

PART I—EXPLORATIONS IN CREATIVITY

While taking a creative approach to tutor training and hosting activities such as creative writing workshops or spoken word nights might sound like good ideas, writing center practitioners should be aware that what seems like a good idea to some might prove to be uncomfortable for others. Thus, Part I – Explorations in Creativity examines some of the pros and cons of creativity and play in writing centers. The authors in this part consider the following questions: What does creativity mean to writing centers? What are the potential ramifications of introducing play into writing center culture? How might looking at creativity in writing centers through a multicultural lens change our perceptions of this seemingly innocent concept? Why do creative physical spaces matter? Why might we want to combine literacy learning and creativity?

Boquet and Eodice begin this collection by trying to "advance a definition of creativity for WCs that is, well, creative" (p. 6). They suggest that the concept of the writing center itself was a creative response to two academic contexts: a developing understanding of the effectiveness of one-to-one tutoring and a growing class of academically underprepared students who benefited from individualized instruction. The result of this creative response, though, was a common one: success bred codification, leading to conformity and uniformity. Let this, then, be Warning #1: a successful creative approach can end up a stagnant practice. Creativity is something that has to constantly be revisited, reevaluated, and readjusted. Creativity has to remain open to . . . being creative.

Scott L. Miller continues in Chapter 2 by exploring the relationship between work and play in the writing center. He suggests that many writing center scholars are ambivalent toward play and introduces Warning #2: while play may be mostly constructive, it can also be destructive to a learning environment. And so it is that the positive outcomes that attract academics to play do not always outweigh the potential negatives.

In Chapter 3, Denny examines issues regarding the impact creativity—and even our conversations about implementing creativity into writing centers—can have on a writing center's culture. Denny questions what creativity means and explores how this practice might disrupt and/or foster traditionally oppressive institutional practices in relation to various demographics within a total student population. Denny's thesis may leave many writing center folk feeling uneasy. Warning #3: "creative pedagogy that ignores the ubiquitous dynamics of social and cultural division risks blindness to re-inscription of bitter practices of racism, sexism and class bias in America" (p. 56). It is this deeper insight into the potential dynamic of a creative environment that is crucial to the success of an innovative writing center.

In Chapter 4, Owens discusses constructing creative physical spaces. According to Owens, writing centers exist somewhere on a "closet-to-centerpiece continuum." He says that their location on this continuum often shows their level of institutional importance. A writing center located in the basement of an underused academic building might struggle to develop a positive institutional identity in ways a writing center located in the heart of a brand new library might not. Regardless of placement on the continuum, Owens challenges directors and tutors to use their spaces creatively.

sj Miller completes Part I by revisiting an issue Boquet and Eodice raise in their opening chapter: what happens when creativity becomes normalized? Miller uses thirdspace theory as a solution to this conundrum and invites readers to conceptualize "literativity": a combination of literacy teaching/learning and creativity. Miller describes how students might benefit from engaging in literativity and how writing centers might incorporate it into their missions.

PART II—CREATIVITY AND TUTORING WRITING

Part II focuses on the pedagogical work of writing centers, from tutor education to tutoring sessions. The chapters are arranged so that readers consider tutor education first, the tutoring session second, and post-session reflection last. The authors in this part tackle the following questions: What are the benefits of using creative activities in tutor education programs? How might using toys in tutoring sessions meet student needs and learning styles? What tools do tutors need to work with creative writers, and how might these same tools benefit academic writers? And finally, how might encouraging tutors to draw images of their sessions bring about important learning opportunities?

Zimmerelli opens Part II with a common scenario: a tutor education course during the first week of the fall semester. As the course progresses, the instructor is disappointed to find that the serious tone she has set in the course has emerged in the tutors' one-to-one sessions. She realizes that the tone of the educational setting influences the tutors' styles, so she decides to incorporate playful activities into the course in order to lighten the mood and establish "a sense of 'peerness' . . . that is at the heart of peer tutoring" (p. 100). Zimmerelli details these unique tutor training activities in Chapter 6.

In Chapter 7, McGlaun explains that tutors and writers "could well benefit from the introduction of guided play into tutor training, especially if that play is productive, a conduit for learning, what Ostrom (1997) calls 'plerk': a fusion of 'work-and-play' that is more than the sum of the two parts" (p. 117). In an effort to "plerk" and infuse stale role-playing activities with new life and meaning, she used her theatre experience to guide her tutors through the process of writing, directing, and acting in role-playing skits that "would allow them to have fun and be creative at the same time that they were interrogating and modeling effective tutoring strategies" (p. 119). The process and the scripts are detailed in this chapter.

In Chapter 8, Verbais explains how he came to use toys to help students during tutoring sessions. He found that "using toys in a WC environment can, in many ways, introduce a tactile learner to various writing concepts. A tactile learner can touch and manipulate toys that might relate to parts of speech, or play with a toy such as a stress ball, which might help stimulate creativity during a session" (p. 138). Incorporating toys into difficult sessions, he suggests, might be a way for tutors to assist students struggling to move forward with their writing. Verbais explains the positives and also explores the potential drawbacks of this method.

Since the primary focus of most writing centers is to work with academic writers, many practitioners often feel intimidated by the thought of having to work with creative writers. In Chapter 9, Ostrom offers advice to tutors working with creative pieces and explains that these methods are easily transferable to academic tutoring sessions.

After hours of training sessions and tutoring sessions, there comes a time for practitioners to gather together and reflect on past experiences and learn from them. In Chapter 10, Geller describes drawing activities she uses with her tutors during staff meetings that often bring about important discussion topics. Patterns can emerge from these drawings that enable practitioners to bring to light various aspects of tutoring that often go unnoticed.

PART III—THE "CREATIVE" WRITING CENTER

Part III treats readers to stories from centers that have used creative thinking to re-envision their writing center missions. Collectively, the authors in this part answer the following question: How might the writing center play a more active role in the literacy development of students, faculty, and the larger campus community?

Goldberg opens Part III by discussing ways in which the Stanford Writing Center has employed the Burkean Parlor metaphor to send "a message to all students—from the research writer preparing an abstract, to the creative writer composing a poem, to the junior statesperson rehearsing a speech—that it has something to offer each" (p. 179). The Stanford Writing Center supports students' creative endeavors by facilitating "Writers'

Nights," which include various activities such as readings sponsored by campus literary magazines and writing groups; a Parents' Weekend Celebration of Writing that brings parents and students together; nights of one-act plays and original songs and music; and poetry slams, among others. This piece is packed with ideas for those wishing to offer far more than traditional tutoring sessions.

Reid continues this section of dynamic writing center offerings by detailing the creative writing "playshops" she developed for writers wishing to engage in games designed to generate ideas and texts in a community of writers. Her practical presentation of the games she has titled "Carnival Ticket Haikus," "Wheel of Fortune Cookie," and "Surrealist Question and Answer" allows inspired readers to immediately facilitate them at their own institutions.

In Chapter 13, Fels reminds readers that the writing center can be a place for teachers as well as students. She says that "directors and tutors know well the value of writing conferences," but, she asks, "how many times are teachers invited to share and talk about *their* writing?" (p. 211). In this chapter, Fels explains how her high school writing center in St. Louis reached out to educators and provided them with a space to gather and grow together as writers.

In Chapter 14, Pennington and Miank share how the Lansing Community College Writing Center staff answered an administrative and academic challenge with a creative solution. In order to help a great number of students preparing final writing portfolios, their center developed "Portfolio Pandemonium Midnight Madness," a night in which writing center tutors and the college's professors pulled together to simultaneously work on portfolios, eat pizza, and build community. From this, the authors learned first-hand that "sometimes the most profound benefits are born out of taking a creative approach to solving practical dilemmas" (p. 233).

In Chapter 15, Severino and Coggins Mosher share the University of Iowa Writing Center's approach to fostering creative expression by explaining their "Invitations to Write," in which students respond to prompts, and Voices, the center's in-house publication. The authors view these programs "as expressions of [their center's] unique identity and contribution to the WC world" (p. 238). In this chapter, they detail these activities and encourage other centers to consider adapting versions of them.

Boczkowski, Randall, Render, and Sinovic conclude this collection on creative approaches to WC work by telling the story of the Columbia College Chicago Writing Center's Never-ending Story, an ongoing text composed by incoming freshman during orientation. The Never-ending Story "is a manuscript of disparate colors, styles, and print (or handwriting). . . . As the contributors . . . take part in a perpetual, collaborative narrative, the different entries form an amalgamation of creativity and community" with the writing center at the heart of it all (p. 262). This experience draws many new freshmen into the WC, provides them with a unique, communal writing experience, and helps the WC develop a positive ethos on campus.

CONCLUSION

As it turned out, our night in the coffeehouse was only one of many instances in which WC folks looked around and asked "What would happen if we introduced even more fun and creativity into our writing center work?" In fact, over the course of the last few years, we have been a part of a growing conversation about creativity in WCs. Writing Center practitioners, be it at professional conferences or on e-mail listservs, have been asking each other what types of creative approaches they take in their WCs to make their work and learning environments more productive. These approaches lend themselves to all levels of WC work from administrating to training tutors to tutoring writers. We hope directors and tutors who are intrigued by pressuring the accepted notions of what WCs can and should be, and who are in search of ways to infuse their centers with creativity and fun, will find *Creative Approaches to Writing Center Work* to be not only an invaluable resource, but also an inspirational one.

REFERENCES

Gardner, P., & Ramsey, T. (2005). The polyvalent mission of writing centers. *The Writing Center Journal, 25*(1), 25-42.

Riley, T. (1994). The unpromising future of writing centers. *The Writing Center Journal, 15*(1), 20-33.

PART I

Explorations in Creativity

1 ————————————

CREATIVITY
IN THE WRITING CENTER

A Terrifying Conundrum

Elizabeth H. Boquet and Michele Eodice

> . . . *let us do what creative writers have done for centuries when faced with a terrifying conundrum: let us go outside and smoke cigarettes in the snow.*
>
> —David Starkey

Gertrude Stein: "A rose is a rose is a rose."

How about this: A rose is/
       A rose is/
       A rose.

Us: Creativity is . . .
   Creativity is . . .

How about this: Creativity Is.

Compulsory writing on creativity. The irony is not lost on us.

This: "Trading Spaces." The first session, Summer Institute 2005, designed to get us to show off our writing centers in a poster session.

    Scissors, gluesticks, Pepto-Bismol posters. The pressure's on. Photo montages and stick-figure layouts. Slideshows and white space, I-don't-have-one-yet insecurities. Egos laid bare on the walls for the week.

"So," we tell our writing response group, "we're working on this piece about creativity in writing centers."

Day by day, corner by corner, the posters bow to the prairie heat and humidity, spines curving in search of terra firma, gravity taking its toll.

Our writing response group bows too. Institutional gravitas. Online presence, outcomes assessment, external funding. All of this, they smile, and you want us to be creative too?

Are you a writer who . . .[1]
. . . finds 50 things to do with pasta?
. . . pinches a penny till it squeals?

Or maybe you're a writing center director who . . .
. . . composes a foolproof annual report,
. . . pens a bulletproof letter of recommendation,
. . . crafts a flawless observation of a colleague's teaching.

"You already are creative," we said. And, in a smaller voice, "Aren't you?" Our writing group members shook their heads, cast their eyes downward. "Well, not really," they admitted.

Us: Creativity Is.

Better yet, maybe you're a little bit country and a little bit rock and roll, crafting those reports while the pasta water sets to boil. Maybe you're both and all these things. Maybe you don't value any of them appropriately for their creative potential yet. We're here to encourage you to reconsider.

If we were to ask you about your own creative expressions, what would you say? Consider yourself asked. How did you respond? Did you, like the members of our Summer Institute 2005 writing response group, deny that you are creative? If we were to prompt you, would you, as they did, recall youthful experiments painting with oils, playing musical instruments, writing poetry? Maybe more recently you could recall the garden you've shaped into being or the built-in bookshelves you put up in your living room. Too often we convince ourselves that evidence of our own creativity is extra-curricular and, as such, somehow *doesn't quite count*. Certainly, one of the purposes of this volume is to convince you otherwise. In fact, we would argue that the daily work in our writing centers (WC) not only reveals creativity, it requires it. Even more than that, to lead our WC staff members to their fullest creative potential, we must be mindful of the relationship between creative work and academic work in our own lives, and we must work with our staffs—and, by extension, with writers—to bring this relationship into the realm of conscious awareness and consideration.

One of the legacies of the process movement in composition has been a demystification of The Writer, the guy (how uncreative!) who sits in a room, alone, producing whole books out of the air and sending them off to **"The daily work in our writing centers not only reveals creativity, it requires it."** be published. The cultural mythos of the solitary artist is pervasive: Creative types are not like us. They are eccentric, passionate. They have edgy thoughts; they lead risky lives. And we don't always understand them or their work. Yet we persist in saying to students, despite their own self-image and enough years of school-sponsored writing to dull a 21st-century Hemingway: You are already a writer. Through careful teaching and structured response, we encourage them to believe us and we come to believe it ourselves.

We see striking parallels to this concept of creativity and creative individuals in our conversations with others about creativity in writing center work. In this chapter, we invite readers to think about creativity more broadly, to think of creative acts not simply as a fun thing or two to do but as built into the fabric of an identity (whether it be an individual's identity or a WC's). Throughout this volume we call for enhancing the creative potential of WC work. But just as calling oneself a writer does not mean one is finished learning to write, recognizing our own creative potential and contributions does not mean we are done considering the issue. In fact, it probably means we are just beginning. As Picasso once said, "I am always doing that which I cannot do in order that I may learn how to do it."2

CREATIVITY IS. . . .?

The addition of free-standing WCs to institutional infrastructures in the late 20th century could be seen as a creative act, requiring the recognition of the value of an alternative learning environment. Likewise the addition (and in many cases the substitution) of peer tutors in centers previously staffed by faculty.3 Such moves appear rooted as much in pragmatic concerns, however, as in legitimate philosophical and educational principles— a direct response to limited resources, trends in remediation, and a growing enthusiasm for peer-to-peer learning. As WCs became embedded in their institutions in fairly traditional, curricular ways, Daniel Lochman (1980) noted that the inevitable followed: they "soon developed procedures and goals according to standards . . . and expectations and methods became increasingly standard and norm-creating" (p. 12). For example, most of the textual products associated with WCs are actually "tutor-training" handbooks designed to school our students in a particular model of peer tutoring. What were ad hoc methods of working with writers one-to-one became accepted (or unacceptable) models for an increasingly standardized, curricularized form of interaction. Tutors no longer just sit down with writers; they sit, instead, in particular ways (next to them, for example, rather than across from them) or in particular places (on a comfortable couch or at a round table rather than at a square one). They don't simply demonstrate interest in a writer's work. Instead they ask questions in a specific manner, with appropriate degrees of frequency and with an acceptable level of response from the writer herself. As we see it, the more recent conscious addition of creativity as integral to a writing center's mission is a reaction to the perhaps inevitable assimilation of writing center work into our schooled cultures. To counter the centripetal force of traditional models of instruction, writing centers have begun to seek ways to continually *re-create* themselves, almost daily, as dynamic sites for learning.

We would like to advance a definition of creativity for WCs that is, well, creative. Maybe we could demonstrate it in an original way, display our definition with visual, musical, or sensual media; we could convert our text-based genre (a written definition in a printed book) into another form, enacting our thesis with an innovative and inspired colorful, jazzy, postmodern dance.

But, for now, the same old, same old, words on a page, in black and white: "Creativity is a central source of meaning in our lives . . . most of the things that are interesting, important, and human are the results of creativity" (Csikszentmihalyi, 1996, p. 1). For this explanation, we appeal, however, not to Webster's or (more traditionally, perhaps) to the Oxford English Dictionary or (slightly more hip) to Wikipedia. We turn instead to an author who has fairly standard academic preparation . . . with a twist: Mikhail Csikszentmihalyi, a psychologist whose work straddles that suspect border between scholarly and non-scholarly, a dilemma to which WC workers, themselves familiar with the insider/outsider dichotomy, can relate.

Two things attract us to Csikszentmihalyi's view of creativity: first, his assertion of the centrality of creativity; next, his systems approach to creativity. For Csikszentmihalyi, creativity is not an add-on, not something folks do only when time and weather permit. And it is also not something they do alone. Out with this romantic vision of the guy in the garret to whom we alluded earlier. To take his place, a dynamic understanding of creativity as "result[ing] from the interaction of a system composed of three elements: a culture that contains symbolic rules, a person who brings novelty into the symbolic domain, and a field of experts who recognize and validate the innovation" (p. 6). If we apply that tripartite explanation to our own work, we could understand the WC as "a culture that contains symbolic rules," more than we could list here, rules that grow out of a presumed shared philosophy or way of understanding the work (having the writer hold the pen to signal textual ownership, for example, or banning no-shows after two missed appointments because other writers could benefit from the WC's limited resources). We certainly see people who "[bring] novelty into the symbolic domain" every time a writer walks in the door or a new tutor is welcomed into the fold or a new dean or director is hired. And finally, you, our readers, represent one of Csikszentmihalyi's third elements. Others in that "field of experts who recognize and validate the innovation" might include the tutors and the writers themselves, as well as interested and invested parties at our various universities.

With these three elements, WCs have the conditions under which creativity may be fostered, but simply possessing these characteristics is not enough. Creativity itself, according to Csikszentmihalyi, "is a process by which a symbolic domain in the culture is *changed*" (p. 8, emphasis added). Changed. If we view our institution as a symbolic domain—a site that confers a value that is highly symbolic in our culture: education—then a WC could become one of the creative forces that contributes to changing this symbolic domain. We might bring about change through our everyday work: Notice how that math professor is now constructing her assignments to invite student writers to reflect on their learning; notice how that writer is willing to defer immediate gratification and take a little cognitive journey with that peer tutor; notice how the dean now talks about international students, not as problems, but as gifts. Our presence, our creative gestures, move others to change.

Change-environments (like WCs) must encourage in their participants a desire for discovery, a talent for flexibility, an interest in difference, risk, and ambiguity.

As creative leaders, we must work to engage people who thrive on the challenge of the new (a characteristic of creative people, as noted in Csikszentmihalyi's studies) and who tie their motivation to loving the work more than what the work produces. These elements, along with Csikszentmihalyi's definition of creativity as "a process," lead to a characterization of creativity that aligns the concept quite closely with our own scholarly tradition in writing center theory and composition studies, work that is as much (if not more) about the process as it is about the product.

. . . WRITING CENTER PLERK?[4]

If we agree that we have the conditions in our WCs to foster creativity (as we have outlined them here) and if we agree that a key goal of WC work is to change the symbolic domain through the ways we work with the participants in the environment, then the next thing we need is a framework for thinking about how those goals might be accomplished. We are not, after all, advocating change simply for change's sake, an all-bets-are-off philosophy of WC work. In the rest of this chapter, we draw on Frank Barrett's work to propose a framework for thinking about writing centers as examples of Csikszentmihalyi's creative change-environments.

In his article "Creativity and Improvisation in Jazz and Organizations: Implications for Organizational Learning," Barrett (1998) listed seven principles of jazz improvisation that are transferable to a learning organization like a WC:

1. Provocative competence: deliberate efforts to interrupt habit patterns.
2. Embracing errors as a source of learning.
3. Shared orientation toward minimal structures that allow maximum flexibility.
4. Distributed task: continual negotiation and dialogue toward dynamic synchronization.
5. Reliance on retrospective sense-making.
6. "Hanging out": Membership in a community of practice.
7. Taking turns soloing and supporting.

We examine each of these principles in turn, briefly summarizing Barrett's explanation and then exploring their relevance to WC work.

Provocative Competence: Deliberate Efforts To Interrupt Habit Patterns

In order to enrich jazz as a musical form and in order to enhance performance in a learning organization, Barrett (1998) called for a deliberate interruption of habits. Habits form when we rely on what we perceive to be successful routines. Successful routines, in and of themselves, may not necessarily be bad, but they can lead to a "competency trap," occasions when actions become "automatic and not even accessible to ordinary recollection and analysis . . . long after [we] have ceased to be able to provide an account of their purposes" (p. 608).

Those of us who work in WCs might easily recognize that part of our job is to disrupt the habit patterns of the writers with whom we work, but we might not recognize so readily the competency trap into which we ourselves have fallen. According to Barrett, all habits are worth disrupting so that our work can remain fresh and imaginative. Cruising on autopilot—whether as writers, tutors, or jazz musicians—thwarts meta-analysis and risk taking, requisite conditions for advancing creative approaches to learning. In conversations with writers, tutors insert a "Why did you decide to include this point here?" or a "How do you think these two ideas are connected?" in an effort to reveal that decisions are being made and, on reflection, can also be altered. As deliberately as we expect writers to work, we need to work just as hard to interrupt our own habit patterns and achieve provocative competence; and doing so is a fresh challenge for WC staff.

Tutors are recruited, educated, and evaluated based on a relatively common set of values and instructions. To some extent, we might consider these tacit agreements to be standards, and standards are not always terrible ideas. Competence is not a dirty word. Good teaching, like good jazz playing, "is very complex and the result of a relentless pursuit of learning and disciplined imagination" (p. 606). But we like Barrett's notion of provocation. He doesn't chuck the idea of competence; he pokes and prods it. Good teachers, like good musicians, "are highly committed to self-renewal, having had to create their own learning opportunities" (p. 606). Across the country, tutors are taught to build rapport to start, then zoom in on higher order concerns, defer the lower order concerns, and ask facilitative questions along the way. We might think of these as the stock phrases, the allowable chord progressions, of tutoring. Once internalized, this habit pattern can afford to be interrupted; and, when tutors are given opportunities to stretch and play with this pattern, sessions can become richer for everyone.

For example, in a recent conversation with Anne Ellen Geller, former director of the WC at Clark University, about staff education strategies, Geller recalled that a tutor mentioned "stepping over the line" with a student (in terms of the amount of help she offered). The other tutors nodded in guilty recognition. The standard advice might be to identify where that moment was in the session and to talk about how to avoid such moments from here on out. But Geller took what we consider to be a more creative approach: She and her tutors agreed that, before their next staff meeting, they would all, deliberately and consciously, step over the line with a student at least once, noticing all they could about that moment for discussion and reflection.

The staff's decision demonstrates the first element of Barrett's framework: Geller deliberately disrupted what may be a standard directorial habit pattern—the one designed to "solve" the problem on the spot—in order to create space for inquiry while the tutors must disrupt the "Whoa, can't go there" habit long enough to break free of the competency trap. Together, they provide support and structured guidance for each other as they venture into this new territory, and their director signals trust and confidence in their abilities to undertake this unorthodox task, one that asks the tutors "to imagine alternative possibilities heretofore unthinkable" (Barrett, 1998, p. 610).

Embracing Errors as a Source of Learning

In the example just presented, Geller and her staff take what could be construed as a "mistake" and, in musical terms, they ride with it. They see where it leads. They repeat it until it starts to make sense. This decision brings us to Barrett's second principle.

Error is a condition of creativity. Barrett wrote: "Jazz bands . . . see error as inevitable and something to be assimilated and incorporated into the performance" (p. 610). Mistakes are not coded as failures but as musical opportunities: "Any event or sound, including an error, becomes a possible springboard to prime the musical imagination, an opportunity to re-define the context so that what might have appeared an error becomes integrated into a new pattern of activity" (p. 610). As we continually work against fix-it shop metaphors to describe our work, we need to conceive of error "as a very important source of learning" (p. 610). When error begins to drive our WC sessions, we can, like jazz musicians, "turn these unexpected problems into . . . opportunities" (p. 610).

Here again, in our field, it would seem we have been more forgiving of our students in this regard than we have been of ourselves. The field of composition studies has embraced error as a sign of growth in writing ever since Mina Shaughnessy published her landmark *Errors and Expectations* in 1977 and Joseph Williams followed with "Phenomenology of Error" in 1981. Although WCs have certainly offered their fair share of grammar modules and programmed instruction, many of which placed an extreme focus on surface-level correctness, current scholarship in WCs aligns the field with second-language acquisition theory and developmental psychology in its treatment of error. As a result, staff education texts teach tutors to work with students on patterns of error, shifting discussions away from random error; and WCs directors spend much time talking with faculty about meaningful error, about the demoralizing effects of red-inked error hunts.

Our tutors, however, still worry about making mistakes, and discussions of error in our field invariably position students as the only people in an educational setting who are likely (or are allowed) to make them. Less is said about other participants in the interaction—tutors and directors—embracing their own errors as a source of learning. (See, e.g., Tassoni & Thelin, 2000). To do so, we would need to adopt what Ted Gioia has called an "'aesthetic of imperfection,' an acknowledgement that learning is something that often happens by trial and error, by brave efforts to experiment outside of the margin" (p. 611). Here again, as with our previous point about provocative competence, participants must feel supported in this risk-taking, must be able to trust that judgment will be suspended in order to explore the consequences of their decisions.

For the past year, Beth and her tutors have run a pilot project on the use of iPods in tutoring sessions. Tutors record sessions (with the writer's permission, of course) and edit them down to 5-minute snippets to bring to meetings for discussion and analysis. One session in particular became the focal point of discussions in the center and beyond. In this session, the tutor dominated the exchange and the writer grew increasingly remote and monosyllabic. What is perhaps most interesting about this scenario is that the tutor felt able to bring in a selection that, in effect, made him look inept. He had many sessions to choose from, and he is a talented, skilled tutor. His decision, then, to reveal this session to the rest of the group (and later to audience members at a technology conference on campus) speaks volumes about him; but it also says something very important, we think, about the WC in which he works.

Shared Orientation Toward Minimal Structures That Allow Maximum Flexibility

Linking this jazz principle to the work of an organization means, for Barrett (1998), learning to "balance autonomy and interdependence": "Modest structures value ambiguity of meaning over clarity, preserve indeterminacy and paradox over excessive disclosure" (p. 611). When musicians come together to jam, they share a common language, even if they have never before met each other. They understand song structure, they know the basic chords, and they possess an understanding of how (in general) these structures can be transformed. This knowledge allows them to converse with each other through music, to make familiar musical terrain unfamiliar and still bring it back home again, to use their common scaffold to build something new within the group, something that could only have been made by these particular people at this particular time.

In WCs, we too have basic structures that guide our work: our shared understanding of the value of one-to-one instruction, the mission statements of our various colleges and universities, the goals and objectives of our individual centers. Valuing ambiguity and preserving indeterminacy are risky administrative practices, to be sure; but we can not expect writers to take risks if we, as tutors and directors, are not willing to peer over the precipice with them. Neither one of us, for example, has a tutoring manual in our WCs, although we have found ourselves strangely in the midst of directorial one-upmanship, conversations where people boast of manuals that reach 10, 25, 50 pages.

Less is more, the two of us believe. Rigid rules are only going to get us into trouble. A statement in a policy manual claiming that a tutor who is late to work three times will be fired, for example, would have led to real problems for one of us, who found herself in the following situation: One of the WC's best tutors wound up with too many commitments one semester, thought she would be able to get herself out of bed for early morning tutoring sessions after pulling Tuesday all-nighters in her role as editor of the campus newspaper, and couldn't admit that she couldn't manage this. She had been late three times. If we have a manual, if we have a non-negotiable rule (as we know a few centers do), now we're up against a wall. Do we fire her to prove a point? Do we make an exception and risk being accused of favoritism? Why have a policy in the first place? We would prefer to recognize the enabling constraints of foundational practices and work from these "root structures" to reach beyond. If we imagine that the song structure of a WC involves a common understanding of how we value the people who walk through our doors, then tutors are also those people, we are all those people. If our foundational principle involves conversational negotiation and collaborative decision making, then we sit with that tardy tutor and we communicate expectations about how to be present with and for others, we remind her how stressful it might be for a student already worried about a due date on a paper to sit and wait for her for 10 minutes. We tell her that one of her strengths is how easily she greets people and sets them at ease. We notice that she can't play to her strengths when she too is rushing in, frazzled, harried and tired. And we work together to find another time, a better time, for her to sit and jam with students. We teach her as we want her to teach others, with the knowledge, as the old jazz saying goes, that we are always only a half-step away from salvation.

Distributed Task: Continual Negotiation and Dialogue Toward Dynamic Synchronization

Barrett explained distributed tasks as having the following characteristics: "shared task knowledge (members monitor progress on an ongoing basis) . . . adequate horizon of observations (they are witnesses to one another's performance); and . . . multiple perspectives . . . (each musical utterance can be interpreted from different points of view)" (p. 613). Barrett described jazz as "an ongoing social accomplishment" in which players are "engaged with continual streams of activity: interpreting others' playing, anticipating based on harmonic patterns and rhythmic conventions, while simultaneously attempting to shape their own creations and relate them to what they have heard" (p. 613). All of this work results in "a remarkable degree of empathic competence, a mutual orientation to one another's unfolding" (p. 613).

In his section on distributed tasks, Barrett invoked familiar theorists—Dewey, Vygotsky, and Csikszentmihalyi—and we are struck, as the two of us read and discuss this part, by how much Barrett's description sounds like tutoring. But Barrett is not interested in the one-to-one aspect of working with others so much as he is interested in the organizational possibilities of these jazzy principles. To apply his work most accurately to our WC settings, we need to look beyond what happens in actual tutoring sessions, which are (in the best-case scenarios) "ongoing social accomplishment[s]" where tutors interpret, anticipate, shape and relate in the ways Barrett suggested. We need to think also about the ways members of a WC staff enter that groove with each other. In what ways do the tutors understand the WC they are creating as having "a shared common rhythm . . . a momentum . . . a life of its own separate from the individual members" (p. 614)?

Both of us have worked in WCs with budgets stretched nearly to the breaking point, centers where we struggled with questions like whether to staff the writing center from 9 a.m. to 9 p.m., with one tutor on duty per hour or, alternatively, to staff it (with the same amount of funding) from 10 a.m. to 4 p.m. with two tutors at all times. Always we would opt for the latter, an administrative decision that privileges tutors' relationships with each other, prioritizes their need to witness each other's performances, to access different points of view.

Like many directors, we recruit tutors from among our committed WC users; we encourage current tutors to continue to bring their own work to the WC; we urge them to eavesdrop on each other's sessions and to step in when the mood strikes. But we also collectively discuss what we as a group gain from this involvement with each other's teaching. We're not hunting for mistakes. We're not even searching for replicability, so that each session begins to sound more and more like the last or the next. We are instead paying attention to the ways in which we teach each other to think about the things we had yet to think about. We might ask the tutors, for example, to make an appointment in the WC before the next staff meeting. During that appointment, we say, pay attention not only to what you're learning about writing from this tutor but also to what you're learning about tutoring.

According to Barrett (1998), "traditional models of organization and group design feature static principles in which fluctuations and change are seen as disruptions to be controlled and avoided. Jazz bands are flexible, self-designed systems that seek a state of dynamic synchronization, a balance between order and disorder" (p. 613). Dynamic synchronization may seem like a contradiction in terms, but synchronization in this case does not necessarily indicate sameness in approach. Instead, it suggests a collaborative "flow" experience (to invoke Csikszentmihalyi again) in order to achieve some dynamic element of working together, a performance in which each instrument in our combo pushes its player and each player pushes her instrument to do more than expected and never in quite the same way twice.

Reliance on Retrospective Sense-Making

Here those of us who work in WCs may find ourselves in our most familiar territory with Barrett. "Retrospective sense-making" might also be called
reflection; and, if there is one thing composition theory has taught us, it is
how to reflect. Flower and Hayes, protocol analyses, meta-cognitive awareness. We are old pros at these. Donald Schön's (1983) "reflective practitioner," the guy who "allows himself to experience surprise, puzzlement, or
confusion in a situation which he finds uncertain or unique" (p. 68). Hey,
we know him! Here's what he does: "He reflects on the phenomenon
before him, and on the prior understandings which have been implicit in
his behaviour. He carries out an experiment which serves to generate both
a new understanding of the phenomenon and a change in the situation" (p.
68).

   Barrett does not, however, call this fifth point of his simply a "reflection" principle.[5] The deliberate use of the term *retrospective sense-making*
highlights a key feature worth discussing: "[R]etrospective sense-making
makes spontaneous action appear purposeful, coherent, and inevitable" (p.
615). Retrospective sense-making, then, carries with it a sense of intention-
ality that the term reflection does not connote. In music, Barrett explained
the principle working in this way:

> The improviser can begin by playing a virtual random series of notes,
> with little or no intention as [sic] how it will unfold. These notes
> become the materials to be shaped and worked out, like pieces of a
> puzzle. The improviser begins to enter into a dialogue with her mate-
> rial: prior selections begin to fashion subsequent ones as themes are
> aligned and reframed in relation to prior patterns. (p. 615)

For us, Barrett's point about retrospective sense-making relates most
directly to his point about minimal structures allowing for maximum flexibility. An organization focused on retrospective sense-making does not rely
primarily on manuals, on do's and don'ts, on immutable rules distributed
in advance. In the WC, as much as we might all wish for a clear sense of
how the day will unfold, we know instead that "members often need to
apply resourcefulness, cleverness, pragmatism in addressing concerns. They
often have to play with various possibilities, re-combining and re-organiz-
ing, to find solutions by relating the dilemma they face to the familiar context that preceded it" (p. 615). Retrospective sense-making, then, is an
active process, one that calls on people not only to reflect back on what
took place but to make it meaningful for both the individual and, as we discuss in the next point, for the WC as a whole.

"Hanging Out": Membership in a Community of Practice

A commitment to "hanging out" is one that jazz musicians and WC staff members share. Our WCs may be better lit than most jazz clubs, the liquid refreshments may be less intoxicating, our seating options perhaps a bit plusher, but we value informal, unprogrammed learning in many of the same ways. Barrett wrote, "Learners need access to experienced practitioners, through formal and informal meetings, conversations, stories, myths, rituals, etc." (p. 616). By participating in such informal networks, learners tap into and become part of "a community memory." New dimensions are added to the concept of retrospective sense-making when actions and decisions are explored collectively, when experienced participants and newcomers are all part of the conversation.

WC folk have long claimed "community" as a descriptor for the affiliation of staff members that runs the gamut, from undergraduate peer tutors to professional staff, from career administrators to untenured faculty, from community college to university to high school and more, stateside and abroad. While the use of the term community to characterize these groupings has been questioned (Boquet, p. 26), Barrett's addition of the idea of practice offers a productive constraint. A community of practice, as Etienne Wenger (1998) defined it in his book, provides opportunities for people to "develop, negotiate, and share" (p. 48) their worldviews. In so doing, participants in these communities, over time, arrive at spoken and unspoken decisions regarding their common interests. Like jam sessions, communities of practice are highly interactional (taking us back to Csikszentmihalyi), overlapping and intersecting. A quick scan of our various WC conference programs—regional and international—shows a community of practice ahead of its time in breaking down divisions between novice and expert, sowing the seeds for maximizing the creative potential of our varied communities of practice, locally and globally. Barrett noted that at first "novices discover they need to know certain 'standard' tunes," much as our new tutors seek steps to follow in each session (p. 616). But the trust they gain from community membership allows them to "guide each other through various learning experiences, borrowing ideas from one another" (p. 616).

We especially like the double-entendre of "hanging out" as it relates to the work called for by us and others in this volume. Engaging in risky behaviors, pursuing the unknown, can certainly leave us feeling as though we are hanging out (on a limb) or worried that we will be hung out (to dry). Hanging out—in a back room, or around a coffee pot, or (virtually) in a blog or collaborative journal—is a start to building the support networks we all need to feel emboldened to take chances now and then.

Taking Turns Soloing and Supporting

As Barrett (1998) linked jazz sessions with organizational practices, he sees a "widespread, yet overlooked" phenomenon: taking turns (p. 616). Jazz bands, Barrett pointed out, tend not to have leaders, per se. Instead, leadership of the band rotates, resulting in a model in which each member has "an opportunity to develop a musical idea while others create space for this development to occur" (p. 616). Members of the band, then, cannot afford to be merely talented soloists. Or, at the very least, it would be a mistake to think that a skillful solo is the result of one person's artistic abilities. Instead, "[t]he role of accompaniment, or 'comping,' is a very active and influential one: it provides a framework which facilitates and constrains the soloist" (p. 616). When comping, players need to engage not only in the retrospective sense-making of which we wrote earlier (e.g., anticipating melodic or rhythmic changes based on recent phrasings); they might also need to assume a bit of a trickster role, "see[ing] beyond the player's current vision, perhaps provoking the soloist in different direction [sic], with accents and chord extensions" (p. 617).

Turn-taking, then, evolves with deep listening, reflection, collaboration and, on many occasions, a good sense of humor—basic ingredients in our tutoring sessions. We expect our tutors to be good listeners in their tutoring sessions, but we have been less careful to articulate the ways turn-taking could be used on an organizational level in our writing centers. Many of our tutors, drawn as they so often are from among our college's best students, are effective soloists and capable leaders. Higher education rewards the star student and the solo artist, too often overlooking the value of a more balanced model, one that affords opportunities not only for leading but also for what Barrett called "a model of followership" (p. 617).

As the two of us discuss Barrett's idea of followership, we think of our own roles in our WCs, places where we follow as much as we lead. This year, for example, Michele has moved to a new job, where she will have (obviously) tutors who are all new to her and, additionally, a whole new center to design. A frustrated architect, she would love nothing more than to sit with the dimensions of the center's assigned space and go to town. Who among us doesn't dream of the opportunity to get the WC's space just right? The first thing Michele did, however, was to turn this task over to the tutors themselves. Make no mistake: She fully intends to weigh in. But her action signals that she expects them to be active participants in the center's redesign. She is no solo artist in this respect, and they will all learn a lot about each other in the process. In one of her first acts as a new director, then, she models for the tutors, who are without doubt trying to figure out what sort of leader she will be, a pretty jazzy style.

. . . HANGING OUT,
HANGING TEN, AND HANGING UP

We began writing this chapter by wondering when and why we started to claim creativity as a fundamental principle in our WCs. Little had been written about the role of creativity in WCs when we accepted our positions as directors in the early 1990s. As stridently as WC folks articulated the unorthodox nature of their academic spaces, the recommended approaches for working with writers and the rationales provided were decidedly traditional. They did not seem, methodologically, to set the space apart. We have written elsewhere (Boquet 2002; Geller, Eodice, Condon, Carroll, & Boquet, 2007) about the deadening effects of staff meetings that feel like just one more class and about the daily occasions we have for creative exchanges in our writing centers. Fortunately for us, just as we began to run up against a few pedagogical walls, we also ran across the work of Nancy Welch (1999), who encouraged us to "reclaim the public dimensions of play" (p. 65) in writing and offered us a framework for doing so.[6]

Drawing on a variety of psychoanalytic approaches (from Freud to Lacan to Winnicott) to consider the role of play in writing center sessions, Welch challenged us, as we have now challenged you, to think of play not as mindless enjoyment but (in more Derridean terms) as play in the wheel—that is, as freedom of movement. So an activity that begins as simply a fun thing to do—for example, a request that tutors each load a song about writing onto the WC's computer—becomes an occasion for extended discussion, debate, consideration as the task gets worked into collective purposes, themes, and goals. In the instance cited earlier, the process, in a nutshell, looks something like this: When one person's song selection resonates with the entire group, it might become the year-long theme for staff education meetings, with activities designed around it, with readings on related topics selected for discussion, with alternate song selections chosen to counter the prevailing sentiment, with poems and artwork found or composed in response, with formal reflections and informal conversations. Some collective sense is arrived at nonsequentially, through the intersections of these explorations alongside and within the work of the tutoring sessions themselves. Such imaginative play, then, doubles as freedom of intellectual movement, taking us back to Derrida, who, according to Alan Aycock (1993), insists that "play is not fixed in finite discourse or structural symmetry or subjective intent: it happens, irresistibly, as a movement elsewhere of the traces of writing in the world" (p. 9).

As we have come to work deeply within the discourses of Welch, Barrett, Wenger, and others, we have learned that creativity in WC work is not optional. Creative practices need not—in fact, should not—be reserved for creative writing assignments in the WC, or shelved entirely in order to meet the "regulatory" demands of institutionally sanctioned writing. As Welch wrote, "This kind of play—and I can't stress this enough—is not some detour in an otherwise one-way road toward assimilation" (p. 61). Creative approaches to WC work are not, in other words, breaks from the real work of the WC. Or, to return to the musical thrust of this chapter, "Improvisation makes the optional a matter of obligation. The improviser can't play only what's required; he's bound to contribute a certain excess. Improvisation marks a line or a partition where excess becomes essence, the incidental becomes requisite, where ornamentation becomes composition" (p. 64).

So creativity is . . . a work in progress *and* work in process. It is not a thing we are (or something many of us are not). Rather, it is a state of being toward which we strive collectively, supported by an overarching understanding of the importance of its role in our work and by clearly articulated goals providing the scaffolding necessary to build and maintain a functioning, creative enterprise.

NOTES

1. This activity appears courtesy of Anne Ellen Geller, who appears later in this volume.
2. This Picasso quote, like dozens of others, has entered our common use without ascription to the original source.
3. The following articles trace the history and origins of writing centers: Boquet (1999), Carino (1995, 1996), and Lerner (1998, 2001).
4. In his essay "Grammar J as in Jazzing Around," Hans Ostrom (1997) coined the term plerk to describe various methods of getting students to both play and work at their writing, to "jazz around" with language. In critiquing Ostrom, whom he claimed stops short of engaging writers in broader cultural and social questions surrounding the synthesis of play and work, Steve Westbrook (2003) took Ostrom's idea even further. Westbrook said we need to elaborate a more thorough and balanced synthesis of playwork, one that encourages students not only to experiment creatively but also to ask themselves what work they are performing when they play with convention-making and -breaking. Thereby, we might prompt them to examine not only the improvisatory art of jazzing around but also the effects and consequences of their jazzing around.
5. Although we understand that writers may understand reflection to be an active process, the term reflection is a static one. We see Barrett's distinction as similar to the distinction between a mirror (which simply returns the image before it) and an eye (which involves complex neural processes seeking to make sense of the image being registered).

6. The following articles are representative of creative approaches to writing center work prior to the publication of Nancy Welch's scholarship: Callahan (1994), Gamboa and Williams (1991), and Nash (1984).

REFERENCES

Aycock, A. (1993). Derrida/Fort-Da: Deconstructing play. *Postmodern Culture, 3–2.*

Barrett, F. J. (1998). Creativity and improvisation in jazz and organizations: Implications for learning. *Organization Science, 9*(5), 605-621.

Boquet, E. H. (1999). Our little secret: A history of writing centers, pre- to post-open admissions. *College Composition and Communication, 50*(3), 463-482.

Boquet, E. H. (2002). *Noise from the writing center.* Logan: Utah State University Press.

Callahan, D. E. (1994). *The effects of variety and complexity of provisioning on the development of constructive play of preschool-age children in writing centers.* Unpublished dissertation, Boston University, Boston.

Carino, P. (1995). Early writing centers: Toward a history. *The Writing Center Journal, 15*(2), 103-116.

Carino, P. (1996). Open admissions and the construction of writing center history: A tale of three models. *The Writing Center Journal, 17*(1), 30-49.

Csikszentmihalyi, M. (1996). *Creativity: Flow and the psychology of discovery and invention.* New York: HarperCollins.

Gamboa, S. H., & Williams. A. W. (1991). Writing centers on the ROPES: Using a wilderness lab for discovery. *The Writing Center Journal, 11*(2), 29-40.

Geller, A. E., Eodice M., Condon F., Carroll M., & Boquet, E. (2007). *The everyday writing center: A community of practice.* Logan: Utah State University Press.

Jarrett, M. (1999). *Drifting on a read: Jazz as a model for writing.* Albany: State University of New York Press.

Lerner, N. (1998). Drill pads, teaching machines, and programmed texts: Origins of institutional technology in writing centers. In E. H. Hobson (Ed.), *Wiring the writing center* (pp. 119–136). Logan: Utah State University Press.

Lerner, N. (2001). Searching for Robert Moore. *The Writing Center Journal, 22*(1), 9-32.

Lochman, D. T. (1986). Play and games: Implications for the writing center. *The Writing Center Journal, 7*(1), 11-19.

Nash, T. (1984). Derrida's "play" and prewriting for the laboratory. In G. A. Olson (Ed.), *Writing centers: Theory and administration* (pp. 182-197). Urbana, IL: NCTE.

Ostrom, H. (1997). Grammar "J" as in jazzing around: The role play plays in style. In W. Bishop (Ed.), *Elements of alternate style* (pp. 75-87). Portsmouth, NH: Heinemann/Boynton Cook.

Schön, D. (1983). *The reflective practitioner: How professionals think in action.* New York: Basic Books.

Shaughnessy, M. (1977). *Errors and expectations: A guide for the teacher of basic writing*. New York: Oxford University Press.

Starkey, D. (2001). *Genre by example: Writing what we teach*. Portsmouth, NH: Boynton/Cook.

Tassoni, J. P., & Thelin, W. H. (Eds.). (2000). *Blundering for a change: Errors, expectations in critical pedagogy*. Portsmouth, NH: Boynton/Cook.

Welch, N. (1999). Playing with reality: Writing centers after the mirror stage. *College Composition and Communication, 51*(1), 51-69.

Wenger, E. (1998). *Communities of practice: Learning, meaning, and identity*. New York: Cambridge University Press.

Westbrook S. (2003). "Plerk," "plabor,"' and a conventional caper: Redefining the work and play of poetry within the discipline of English. *Language and Learning Across the Disciplines, 6*(2), 141-153.

Williams, J. (1981). The phenomenology of error. *College Composition and Communication, 32*, 152-68.

2 ⎯⎯⎯⎯⎯⎯⎯⎯⎯⎯⎯⎯⎯⎯⎯⎯⎯

THEN EVERYBODY JUMPED FOR JOY!
(But Joy Didn't Like That, So She Left)

Play in the Writing Center

Scott L. Miller

How can one count or assess the species and kinds of play that arise, ripen, explode in the writing center? As I write, ripples—sometimes roars—of laughter spill into my office through the open door to the center. It's laughter from a group of tutors jawing away in what they call the "makeout corner," the angle of sofas where they hang out between tutorial sessions. They're probably laughing about the latest entry in the writing center journal—not the august IWCA periodical of that name but rather a ratty, spiral-bound notebook that the tutors themselves have established as a cherished collaborative writing space.[1] (As director, I've never written in it and never will, but I do sneak peeks when no one is looking.) Although a few entries are serious reflections on our work, most entries are salacious, raunchy, insulting, junior-high-schoolish, lewd, and/or violent—and invariably witty, dazzlingly creative, and completely hilarious. In short, our writing center journal is a sort of shadowland, where tutors' other selves come out to play. The writers get to be people in that shadowland that not even they knew they could be, writing in genres and in voices that continuously surprise both the writers and their readers. And yet they also get to be themselves—sharing their cruddy (or excellent) handwriting, their lousy (or astonishingly good) drawing ability, their experiences, their stories, their jokes. Our WC offers a container for all these kinds of creativity, for self-expression, for self-and-other-revelation, for wild experimenting, and the tutors love it. And I love the fact that they love it.

And yet this wild play frightens me too. Some of my fears are immediate: I worry sometimes that a tutor will cross some line in her or his comments in the journal, resulting in a fellow tutor being truly insulted or hurt—a bad thing to have happen, and then lots of other bad things could happen in consequence. I see the danger of one participant being politically incorrect (whatever that might mean in this community), the danger of people hitting each other's sore spots, the danger of regretted over-self-revelation, the danger of somebody getting hit by sharp-edged flying objects, epithets, or poetry. "It always ends in tears," parents and teachers say when play gets rambunctious. And I have other fears: fears that the nice senior ladies who run the book sale across the wall from us might hear all this laughter and indecorous exchange and report us. I fear that a colleague or administrator on the hunt for precious office space might poke his nose in at exactly the wrong/right time, and poof! there goes the WC. Way down deep, I fear my own inner voices that tell me, "must be serious! What do you think you're doing, fostering all this crazy nonsense? Get these people to work." Deepest of all, I guess, I fear my own wildness, and part of me wants to rein it in.

So, ambivalence: that's where I am with respect to play, and that's where I think we in the writing center community are as well. For this chapter, I have chosen a title that's funny (I hope) but that also points to the elusiveness and magic of play, its fleeting nature and its need to be cherished and nurtured. And my title is also meant deliberately to be offensive and suggestive of some of the kinds of danger that might accrue from the kinds of play I and other writers in this volume are discussing. They are the kinds of danger that I have seen myself, in the tutors' ratty notebook, in our creative writing "playshops" (see Julie Reid, Chap. 12, this volume), in our more playful training moments, in the "makeout corner" conversation, and in many "nontraditional" tutorials. Of this I am certain: If it's really play, then somehow it will be dangerous.

But that fact has to be okay, if we are to have play. In this volume about creative approaches to WC work we share a profound faith in play, despite and in part because of its dangers, and I write this chapter in the hope that all of us—myself included—can learn to defend play more vigorously, proudly, and strongly.

> **"Of this I am certain: If it's really play, then somehow it will be dangerous. But that fact has to be okay, if we are to have play."**

Looking to various theoretical perspectives, especially from the fields of cognitive psychology and rhetoric, I argue that there are many good reasons for fostering play in the writing center, that the writing center is in fact a magnificent place for play in the institution, and that in fact we are remiss both if we don't foster such play and if we don't learn how to come to play's defense. Indeed, these fields of study argue unequivocally a point that has become a veritable commonplace among teachers, child therapists, and social psychologists, that "play is the child's work." Indeed, play is essential "work" for all human beings. This good news means that we can proudly claim our institutional roles as briccoleurs, mad-men and -women, tricksters, carnies, festival-producers, people who want to inject a note of fun into the serious work of the academy. When people catch us playing on company time, we needn't be ashamed, blanche, stammer, or lie about what we're doing. We can utter any of many strong justifications for our play. Articulating such justifications is the purpose of this chapter.

PLAY AND THE WRITING CENTER TRADITION

Here I discuss how WC scholarship has approached play, focusing especially on exciting recent work that champions play more or less overtly. Scholars who do so are bucking our larger tradition, I think (and frequently they know it and announce their projects as such). It certainly is not accurate to say that WCs were born out of a spirit of play. Our now respectable corpus of historical studies shows clearly (although not unproblematically, to be sure) that WCs and their precursors, usually called clinics, labs, or even workshops (see Boquet, 1999; Carino, 1995; Kelly, 1980; Moore, 1950), are artifacts of the age of remediation. As the terms might suggest, clinics and labs seem to have been established as anything but romper rooms. At its best, the traditional WC (lab, clinic) model offers the center as a space wherein students can do the work that regular teachers don't have the time or will to support. (I announce at the outset that I recognize the false binary in the work–play dyad and address that issue in the next section of this chapter. However, it is the case that in common parlance the binary carries rhetorical weight, and I take it as axiomatic that I can employ that binary myself when discussing play and its roles within a common tradition.)

Recently, the argument that the WC should be a space for play is one that has come to be made fairly commonly in important WC-related publications. It is not inaccurate to say that a sea-change with respect to notions of play in WCs has washed in with the tide. WC folks, of course, long since have worked to substitute a much more intellectually and emotionally engaging (not to say pedagogically correct) understanding of what WCs are and how they can best help students (here I'm thinking of foundational articles by Bruffee, 1984; North, 1984; and Harris, 1990); and I think that this richer understanding has allowed for play, has opened the territory for overt discussion. As a result, indeed, we WC folk have come to call for WC play quite a lot. See, for instance, the suggestive articles in the special millennial issue of *WCJ* (Spring/Summer, 2000), in which, for instance, Lisa Ede and Andrea Lunsford (2000) enjoin WC folks to get wild: "Take all the advantage that you can of your center's multi-bordered, multi-positioned status at your institution. Be a briccaloer, trickster, inventor" (p. 36). Likewise, Lil Brannon and Stephen North (2000) riff on the WC's "enviable site of teaching," wherein "transformative work" —playful work, I read—might be possible (p. 10).

I would go so far as to say that the very best work in WC studies in the past 5 or 10 years has been about play, covertly when not overtly. This work has been informed largely by what some commentators have called *ludic postmodernism* (see Berlin, 1996, for a cogent overview). Ludic postmodernism embraces the playful performative creativity required to live in the world as it is. When all the world is quite literally a stage, a play-space, it stands to reason that self-fashioning can be exciting and fun, constant and ongoing. Thus, Nancy Grimm (1999), in her wonderful book *Good Intentions: Writing Center Work for Postmodern Times*, braces her landmark argument for the development of a postmodern sensibility in WCs by approvingly quoting Kenneth Gergen, who argued that the postmodern ideal is to "carry the clown on one's shoulders—to always be ready to step out of 'serious character' and locate its pretensions, to parody or ape oneself" (p. 25). To be sure, Grimm's book is a very serious one in total, concerned—sincerely and deeply concerned—with the role that WCs can play in either promoting or retarding social equality. Neither her tone nor her answers are necessarily playful. But following the spirit of Gergen, her positions open the way for play, I argue. For instance, when Grimm argues that, given the postmodern condition and the reality of institutional and structural oppression, "[a] fair writing center practice must be constantly under revision, and the people who work in writing centers must be open to transformation, always ready to question the institution and the culture that positions them to work with people inappropriately characterized as 'needing help'" (p. 111), she is announcing a ludic-postmodernist project, I believe. And in her specific suggestions—replacing the traditional tutor reader with a collection of tutor-written theoretical narratives, endorsing Nancy Welch's object-relations theory-based suggestions for creatively playful approaches to tutoring (see later)—I see many possibilities for playful action in the WC.

Elizabeth Boquet's (equally wonderful) *Noise from the Writing Center* (2002) is, in many senses, quite simply an eloquent call for more playful noise from the center. The centerpiece of the book is her notes from a tutor-training course she observed at Rhode Island College one sabbatical. These notes, which describe a richly creative and (obviously) fun course, are offered with the aim of advancing a "performative pedagogy" in the

WC, one meant to amend, or perhaps even replace, the traditional model of tutor training, which Boquet wishes had more of the stuff of life: "Where is the pleasure? Where is the fun? Where is the place where writer and responder can enter into a groove for that session?" (p. 71). She's making a point here very reminiscent of Grimm, longing for tutor-training materials (and, by implication, a writing center theory and culture) "that prefigure the mutation, potential transformation, and re-organization of our systems of education" (p. 85). It's worth noting that both Boquet's and Grimm's books display ludic postmodernism in their very fabric, with Grimm embracing multiple creative models (gardening, mapmaking, quilt-making) as guides and Boquet "channeling" Jimi Hendrix and finding metaphorical enlightenment by seeking a technical understanding of musical "feedback." Both writers, Boquet especially, strive to embody that postmodern clown in both manner and matter.

A third very important commentator embracing play in the writing center has been Nancy Welch. In her book *Getting Restless: Rethinking Revision in Writing Instruction* (1997) and in essays like "Playing with Reality: Writing Centers After the Mirror Stage" (1999), Welch develops a fascinating and, to my mind, sound justification for play grounded in a sophisticated and critical psychoanalytic theory. Many of Welch's positions are broadly compatible with those of Grimm and Boquet, notably her understanding of the writing center as "a space of critical exile" (Welch, 1997, p. 81) where students can confront and assess the many voices that are speaking within the words they wish to use; her articulation of the WC as a space in which students can "migrate" to new "rationalities" through the process of playful revision; her understanding of writing centers and teacher in-service courses as "potential spaces that foster zestful, support-ive questioning and play" (p. 130); and her general argument in favor of learning to revise "excess-ively." These positions are developed specifically for writing center purposes in her "Playing with Reality" essay, in which she describes her experience helping a blocked writer complete a very academ-ic assignment by inviting her to approach it with a genre she's already used to "playing with": poetry. Welch is distinctive among these commentators for her willingness to argue overtly for a specific understanding of play, one grounded in object-relations theory and the play-therapy approaches of D.W. Winnicott.

Thus, the call for clowning around in WCs has become an important thread of WC scholarship. However, I argue that our scholarly literature betrays a continued ambivalence about play. The very fact that play has been a leitmotif—if not an afterthought—in our more general scholarship suggests as much. Certainly, as noted earlier, most of the history of WC advocacy has promoted WCs as sites of serious work, not serious play. I might argue that even the very play-positive work of Boquet, Grimm, and

Welch offers play with a keen recognition of its dangers. Some of these dangers are the ones I share with them and noted at the outset. More specifically, Boquet, Grimm, and Welch offer play as a revolutionary tool, a vital means whereby one "center" of the institution can militate against the high seriousness, the *religious* seriousness, of academic labor; play can offer counter-hegemonic potential for destabilizing power structures, knocking over stuffed-shirt (and power-laden) subjectivities, and pointing out the parodically ascertained truth (small-T) to all. Play defines and inscribes the radical edge of the work of Boquet, Grimm, and Welch. And play (by implication) is therefore an activity not to be entered into lightly, precisely because of its dangerous implications, for us and for the academy. We fear that, when we play, onlookers will see and understand our nefarious, empire-toppling hidden agenda and react violently toward us. I guess this is the deeper fear beneath the more common fear we have about play, that our constituencies will see our play and shut us down for being noisy wastes of dollars that could so much better go to the serious purposes of the academy. Boquet's book very much finds its impetus from precisely this fear, as it opens with a scary anecdote about a colleague complaining about that playful noise.

And there's also a recognition—also commonly asserted in our professional literature—in the injunction to play that playing in the writing center will only increase our already marginal status.[2] On the one hand, we appreciate that being marginal carries privileges. Brannon and North (2000) made this case best when they argued, "When no one outside writing centers notices or cares, writing centers have created for themselves an enviable site where transformative work might actually be possible" (p. 10). But we also have so much wanted to be central forces in our institutions—radicalizing forces (Grimm, Boquet, and Welch, as above, and John and Tilly Warnock, 1984, et al.) or just forces advocating a more richly informed and accurate vision of what it means to learn how to write (Bruffee, 1984; Lunsford, 1991; North, 1984). Two then-tutors in our WC, Kevin Dvorak and Erin Goldin, thought up our motto, since replicated many times on marketing materials and on the tops of cakes: "We're at the Center of the Universe-city; Where Are You?" I think all WC people understand and appreciate the point buried in these words.

So we live in a contrary site, and we are conflicted. We want to have play, with all of its wild possibilities; but we're afraid of precisely those possibilities, and also afraid that the play will just make us even less relevant than we already are. But whatever the radical potentialities of play, there are more than enough good justifications for play when we need them. In good postmodern fashion, I agree with everything that has been said and overviewed here about play in WCs, and I hope profoundly that WC practitioners can embrace all the pedagogical and political power that play embodies and conveys. However, play in and of itself is not so strange a thing. Everybody does it, for very good reasons. It may be objected that normalizing play in this way de-radicalizes it—and, not to mention, takes a lot of the fun out of it. The position I'm taking is deliberately not to explore play as a politically radical force (although I earnestly support work that does so). The good news and the bad news, I think, is that play (again, in and of itself) is not inherently anything, either radical or conservative. Play is. And it does. Lots of things.

WHAT WE TALK ABOUT WHEN WE TALK ABOUT PLAY

What do we talk about, in general public life, when we talk about play? What does the word mean, where does it come from, and how does it find its rhetorical way into discourse? The purpose of this section is to rest briefly on the ambiguities and ambivalences that accrue around the idea of play, for the purpose of exploring some of these contradictions more deeply. Ultimately, I argue that those contradictions are rooted, ultimately, within the word *play* itself. Many commentators, both in general public discourse and in the academic community, use the word *play* in a loose way, whether advocating or condemning it, and my aim here is to begin to move toward a more precise and analytic language for play (the aim of the next sections). Here, I'll open the conversation where most of us live, the world of common parlance, embarking on some easy deconstructions, and then move backward in time through the word's etymology.

The word *play* is often opposed to another word, *work*, as in the commonplace "Americans work too much; we need to learn to play more, like the Italians (Spaniards, Aussies, etc.)." The commonplace presents work as soul-killing labor foisted on us by a postindustrial, economically oppressive world and play as soul-revivifying reconnection to our "true" "innocent" selves freed of ideological shackles. This notion, rooted of course in our heritage of transcendental romanticism, ultimately gets its power from a Christian worldview, I think, wherein play offers itself as a route back to Eden and work offers itself as clear evidence of our eviction therefrom ("In the sweat of thy face thou shalt eat bread . . ."). But the opposition between work and play is eminently deconstructible. We have probably all held jobs that tried mightily to kill our souls, but we have probably also all had jobs that brought us rich meaning, purpose, and joy (all attributes commonly ascribed to play). We have probably all experienced play that felt like work and work that felt like play. A few terms ago, when I taught an advanced comp class with the theme of work and play, the work–play opposition—

the very raison d'etre of the class—very quickly fell in pieces at our collective feet. It took only a few discussions in class before none of us could really get behind the opposition very heartily at all. I think even in regular WC work (i.e., not the kind that happens in the makeout corner in the interstices of the day's schedule), we see this fact in the WC quite a lot. When tutor and tutee are "playing" with colored markers in an effort to help the tutee organize his paper better (red for key points, green for tangential points), are they working or playing? They are laughing and joking and having a great time, so clearly they're playing (right?). And yet the tutee leaves having done some great work on his paper. Clearly, we can and do play as we work and work as we play.

A more fruitful opposition might be that between *playfulness* and *seriousness*. The appropriate commonplace here would be "kids, playtime is over; it's time to get serious." Perhaps play is not so much a thing, an activity, an object, a noun but rather a quality, a way of being, an attitude, an adjective. A moment's reflection suggests that one can do pretty much anything (write, dig a ditch, engage in a domestic quarrel) more or less playfully or seriously. As my discussion grounded in Richard Lanham's (1976) rhetorical view of play suggests, I think this attitudinal approach to play has some interesting merits. But however useful that approach might prove, it is still vital to assert that calling play merely an attitude offers little in the way of a productive definition for the word. If play were really only an attitude, then clearly we could be born in play and die in play and have nothing but play in between. Furthermore, the notion of play as an attitude raises profound problems for our inquiry: What is an attitude? How do people learn or acquire attitudes? What do they mean? Finally, as Johan Huizinga (1938/1955) and L.S. Vygotsky (1933) concur, the notion of play as an attitude rather obviates the idea of serious play: the look of intense concentration in a kid coming up to bat; the unsmiling thoughtfulness of an artist testing out a new brush; and the careful attention a tutee displays while shuffling word cards to make a found poem. As much as I, like all of us, no doubt, cherish and relish a playful, fun attitude and a great sense of humor, reducing play to lightheartedness alone rather diminishes play and begs more questions than it solves.

We can see already in these observations of common parlance some of the sources of anxiety that the word *play* pretty much inevitably drags in. The first of these anxieties obviously speaks from the point of view of the serious, hard-working aspects of our identities. Certainly, for Americans especially, our national character itself, born and bred in the briar patch of Poor Richard's Protestant work ethic, in many ways militates against play. That fact, no doubt, is certainly the main reason people who champion play still feel as though they're being a bit edgy.

But I think those sources of anxiety are rooted even deeper—in the word itself, as revealed by its etymology. The Oxford English Dictionary lists nearly 20 historical senses of *play* when used as a noun and nearly three dozen verb senses. It is a good old Anglo-Saxon word, originally relating not to fun and recreation specifically but rather to descriptions of physical movement: "Exercise, brisk or free movement or action." It is easy to see how the many modern senses of play are associated with a sense of free motion and activity, with dancing, gamboling, leaping, running—with being physically unimpeded. (And sexual associations have been present in the word for many centuries.) I would even argue that these meanings rooted in physical action are still overtly present in modern language, as the senses of "playing with" an object (a toy, mashed potatoes) or "playing on" a musical instrument would seem to have at least as much provenance in ideas of physical movement as joyful recreation. *Play* is a word that is rooted in the body, that ever-present site of anxiety in Western culture.

And more modern senses of *play* carry other such scary connotations and denotations. The word apparently acquired its predominant Western-cultural sense of "Exercise or action [specifically] for amusement or diversion" sometime before the thirteenth century, and since then many derivations and associative meanings linked to this sense have developed. In writing centers, when we talk about play, I think we talk mostly about two kinds of play: play with words and play with identities. Play of words is defined by the OED as "a playing or trifling with words; the use of words *merely* or mainly for the purpose of producing a rhetorical or fantastic effect" (italics added). The OED's example sentences, beginning with Hume's 1739 *Human Nature* ("To confess . . . that human reason is nothing but a play of words"), all offer disparaging views on verbal play; they all, in fact, are choice artifacts from the history of anti-rhetoricism. The idea of playing with identity emerges from the dramatic senses of *play*, as in "watching a play" or "playing the role of Falstaff"—and these senses of *play* have also been in use for centuries. The long on-again, off-again legality of theatricals in English history illustrates clearly the sense of deep suspicion that arises from this play of identity.

The word *play* then itself suggests some of the ways in which we might be ambivalent about or a little frightened of play in the writing center. Whenever we play, it follows that we are setting in motion several scary possibilities for human life: the possibility that words may not be fixed, clear, univocal; the possibility that people themselves in their identities may not be singular, essential, individual; and the possibility that cherished cultural rules of behavior can be easily and lightly violated. As we have seen, these possibilities are what Grimm (following many compositionists, e.g., Berlin, 1996; Faigley, 1992) called elements of postmodernity—and celebrates and advocates for, following her progressive hopes for writing center work. As ultimately becomes clear, I qualify this notion considerably, arguing instead (with Lanham) that what we often call postmodernism looks an awful lot like what might be called a rhetoric, or one kind of understanding of rhetoric (and none of the above commentators would disagree). These definitions of *play* that call up unstable understandings of language and of the self are indeed radical in the sense that Grimm celebrates. And I would not choose to understate the radical potentialities associated with various kinds of play. I merely point out that all play occurs in a context, and various contexts can use even a radical activity for conservative ends.

There is clearly no doubt that danger is an inherent element of *play* (the word). It would be naive to suggest that this danger can be evaded through analysis and conceptualization alone, but I do think, strongly, that we can learn better how to argue for the kinds of play we wish to nurture in the WC. To do that, we can turn in many directions. The traditions of cognitive psychology and rhetoric offer two such possibilities.

ON THE PLAYING FIELDS OF EATIN'

> Any thinking person can see at a glance that play is a thing on its own, even if his language possesses no general concept to express it. Play cannot be denied. You can deny, if you like, nearly all abstractions: justice, beauty, truth, goodness, mind, God. You can deny seriousness, but not play. (Huizinga, 1938/1955, p. 3)

> ... the category "playful activity" is so loose that it is almost useless for modern psychology. (Schlosberg, 1947, p. 231)

As commentators have noted (see e.g., Carino, 1995), the tradition of cognitive psychology never held a great deal of influence over WC conceptualization and practice. But that tradition did and does continue to dramatically impact many other fields, most notably the fields of education and developmental psychology. For these reasons alone, I believe it is worthwhile for WC folks to be able to talk some of the language of cognitive psychology, a language developed primarily by those two profoundly influential researchers, Jean Piaget and Lev Vygotsky. This section largely addresses the work of these two commentators, beginning by offering a contrasting view, that of the seminal modern student of play, Johan Huizinga. The aim will be to understand some fascinating—yet very different—analytical definitions of *play*.

Piaget and Vygotsky strove to use *play* in scientifically precise (i.e., deductive) senses. By contrast, Huizinga essentially threw up his hands at the task, defining *play* not analytically but rather descriptively. *Play*, he concluded, is that form of human activity having the following characteristics:

1. It is free, voluntary, and intrinsically engrossing: "play . . . is, in fact, freedom" (p. 8).
2. Play is extraordinary. It is a "stepping out of 'real' life into a temporary sphere of activity with a disposition all of its own" (p. 8).
3. Play is disinterested and unserious.
4. Play is delimited: "'played out' within certain limits of time and place" (p. 9).
5. Play creates or requires order—rules of the game.
6. Play creates community.

Consider, for instance, the case of a child playing with her dinner—playing with as opposed to actually eating dinner. For the sake of clarity of argument, let's imagine a child playing a game called "dinnertime." Following Huizinga's descriptive definition, the child would clearly be playing:

- She enters into the game freely and voluntarily by stepping into a new reality (criteria 1 and 2): "I know! Let's play dinnertime!"
- She creates a special place and time, a "playground," outside of "reality" for the game (criterion 4): "The toy chest can be the table, and these Legos can be our food."
- She understands that "really" eating has greater consequence and weight, is more serious (criterion 3): "Billy, don't eat the Lego, we're just playing."
- She follows clearly discernible rules as she plays, oftentimes making rules herself when she needs to (criterion 5): "When you play dinnertime, you get to eat dessert first!"
- She cements bonds of community in her play (criterion 6): "Let's play dinnertime again tomorrow!"

A moment's reflection will show how these criteria fit my example of tutors writing in our writing center journal. The tutors in the "makeout corner" certainly do enter into their play voluntarily, and the play-space most certainly constitutes a "new reality" physically located in a playground (the ratty spiral-bound notebook itself); they certainly understand that "real" reality takes precedence ("playtime's over, Jason, your tutee is here!"); the play follows clear rules that they invent (for instance, at the beginning of each term, every tutor is given a page in the journal called his or her "shrine," in which other tutors comment upon, compliment, and/or rib the tutor in question); and most certainly of all, the tutors build their community through this play—indeed, it's through their writing in the writing center journal that the tutors get to know each other at the beginning of each year. Thus Huizinga's descriptive definition can be called a productive one in a sense. But it is still only a description of what play looks like, a naming of parts, not a deductive explanation of what play really *is*, scientifically speaking.

Huizinga's tack of describing play rather than analytically defining it is a common one followed by many commentators, particularly in the field of education. For instance, in Monighan-Nourot, Scales, and Van Hoorn's (1987) *Looking at Children's Play*, play is ascribed the following characteristics: intrinsic motivation, attention to means rather than ends, nonliteral behavior, and freedom from external rules. And following even more closely on Huizinga, Patrick Biesty (2003), in "Where Is Play?," suggested four additional characteristics to Huizinga's six, characteristics which, taken together, add the concepts of egalitarianism, mutual consent, and what Biesty called the "zeroing" of gravity (his way of explaining the challenge or contest elements in a play-game). All of these definitions serve not so much to define *play* as to identify it, so that, in the same way that Supreme Court Justice Potter Stewart approached pornography (*Jacobellis v. Ohio*, 1964), we can know it when we see it. Most assuredly, I am in sympathy with these approaches. We all know the experience of being "at play," and we all know the experience of suddenly falling out of play, when someone gets hurt, when someone breaks the rules, and so on. Huizinga made hay out of this fact, arguing that such a priori phenomenological data authorize an assertion that there is in fact a thing called play, whether we can ultimately explain it or not. If pressed, I think I would agree with Huizinga that all definitions for play that we might articulate will "leak"; finally, we will have no choice but to call it as we see it.

But Piaget and Vygotsky have at least tried to define *play* analytically. To start with the former: Piaget (1951/1962) argued that "Play is primarily mere functional or reproductive assimilation" (p. 87). Understanding this statement requires an understanding of Piaget's notions of assimilation and accommodation and their roles within schema theory. For Piaget, human development occurs stepwise, with children essentially growing better and better adapted to the requirements of the outside world through a process of attuning their interior landscapes to it. The stages of development are clearly discernible to Piaget, and they occur each time the developing child interiorizes what Piaget called a scheme or schema. A schema, essentially, is an organizing arrangement of knowledge and habits, a way of looking at and interacting with the world. The process of developing new schemas—of growing the mind to a new developmental step, based on seeing and interacting with the outside world—is what Piaget calls accommodation. Assimilation, by contrast, is the process of exercising, gaining familiarity and proficiency in, and in fact enjoying the schemas that one has already incorporated into the ego. Accommodation fundamentally changes or reorients or develops the mind; assimilation enables the child to make use of his or her accommodated mind powerfully and dynamically. Play, for

Piaget, is directly associated and nearly synonymous with assimilation, at least for younger children.

The functional gain for Piaget and for observers of play is that his approach delimits play for the purposes of research. To take an example: A child learning to play baseball (learning the rules of the game, becoming somatically familiar with the required skills of hitting, catching, and running) is, for Piaget, not *playing* per se. Rather, play begins when the child has accommodated him or herself to the schema of baseball and is then able to assimilate the game by "playing" the schema of baseball in an effort to develop skill, agility, fluency, and so on. Hence, a researcher observing such a child at play could meaningfully observe starts and stops of play, could use the term *play* in a very precise sense, distinguished from the "work" (not Piaget's term) of accommodating the mind to the world of the game. As Piaget said, "Play . . . proceeds by a relaxation of the effort at adaptation and by maintenance or exercise of activities for the mere pleasure of mastering them and acquiring thereby a feeling of virtuosity or power" (p. 89). In our playing-with-food example, dining itself, in its rules, its accouterments, its techniques, its substances (edible vs. inedible) constitutes within the ever-developing mind a schema, or a number of interlocking schemas (e.g., TV-dinner dining vs. fine dining). Learning a schema for eating dinner is tricky and takes some serious growing, as any parent can attest. But once that schema is learned, the child wants to assimilate that schema by playing at it: "Let's play dinnertime!" For Piaget, accommodation and assimilation are both acts of intelligence; assimilation is what we do when we explore and play in the world that the process of accommodation creates in our heads.

Assimilation play is readily apparent in many of the kinds of WC play I'm familiar with and, no doubt, in many of the kinds discussed in this book. I think assimilation play happens anytime we invite a tutee or a tutor to use a familiar form, language, or strategy in a new or otherwise challenging way. In one of our WC's Halloween-themed playshops, for instance, I was once asked to rewrite a familiar nursery rhyme from the point of view of the Wolf Man. It was an incredibly fun challenge, and the result was, well, indescribable. (People laughed, I assure you.) In our tutor-training workshops, I always begin the first day by asking the tutors to reflect on their personalities and the work of tutoring within the form of some fun, familiar genre or other—the book-jacket "about the author" blurb one year, an "it was a dark and stormy night" mystery story another year, and, yet another year, a "dear class of 2045" graduation speech. Every year we take the time to read all of these aloud, and it's always the best time of the workshop. (And the learning is rich and palpable, full of wonderful lessons about writing center work that we can later discuss more analytically.) Although Nancy Welch (1999), in her "Playing with Reality" essay, doesn't talk quite this way about how she helped her struggling student write her way into the academy through poetry, I think that one could easily read that drama through the lens of Piagetian assimilation.

Vygotsky (1933) offered a very different view of play. In his one (extraordinarily interesting) commentary on play, he argued that play is grounded in imaginative activity—that play proper only really begins when the imagination blossoms, at preschool age or so. It's no coincidence whatsoever for Vygotsky that the birth of the imagination comes simultaneous with the development of the child's language abilities, for, Vygotsky argued, the imagination is nothing less than the child's realization of the eternal divorce of the signifier from the signified. In concrete terms, imagination (and therefore play) blossoms when humans learn that a stick can be a horse. Thus, for Vygotsky, play is intimately involved with language: with metaphor, symbol, and word-play more generally. Furthermore, like Piaget, Vygotsky offered a clear articulation of the distinction between play and not-play. In regular "non-play" life, Vygotsky argued, meaning is subordinate to things and actions; in non-play life, we have to take the world and its meanings seriously and literally. "Let's have dinner" means filling our stomachs. However, in play, "let's have dinner" becomes divorced from mashed potatoes and silverware. The important feature is no longer the mashed potatoes and silverware (which have in fact been replaced by blocks and tinkertoys) but in fact the meaning of "let's have dinner." That meaning is "played," pantomimed in terms of actions and rules. Objects are subordinated to meaning in that the blocks and tinkertoys (or whatever) replace the real object; and actions are subordinated to meaning in that the meaning of the pantomimed eating actions (abbreviated, hyperbolized, chomp, crunch, smack) becomes the very purpose of the actions. For Vygotsky, all this play is utterly essential to the development of the child, but not exactly for the same reason that Piaget sees. "It is in play," Vygotsky argued, "that the child learns to act in a cognitive, rather than an externally visible, realm, relying on internal tendencies and motives, and not on incentives supplied by external things" (p. 544). This is a thunderous assertion. Essentially, for Vygotsky, play is what enables children to live in the symbol-rich universe of human life.

For WC work, Vygotsky's ideas add a theoretical justification for language-play itself as an intrinsically useful activity. By messing around with words, making them soar from context to context and making strange meanings out of them, we grow in our ability to navigate the waters of the symbolic realm. So, for instance, in the delightful game of Mad-libs, which we in our center use in the early days of each term, when our "mandated," credit-earning tutees come down without paper assignments yet, words are stretched to fit into an established discourse, and the discourse is stretched to fit the new adjectives, nouns, verbs, and adverbs that the student arbitrarily summons forth. Or in creating a haiku from word-tickets (words and phrases scissored out of magazines and taped to carnival tickets), a student settles into the mystery that words are both owned individually and shared communally: The words on the word tickets now exist both still on the tickets and in the poem, which now possesses her meanings. It's easy to foster Vygotskean symbolic play: Any gesture that snips the always thin association between words and their "serious" objects and actions can start it off. Metaphor games especially are excellent strategies: "Okay, your assignment is to critique *The Taming of the Shrew*. Let's play with that word 'critique.' If critiquing were something that occurred in the animal kingdom, for instance, where would we find it and what would it look like?" I use these kinds of questions frequently to help students develop richer concepts and deeper meanings. They often groan when I present the activity, but they get into the fun quickly and see the point even faster.

In all of these commentaries on play, we find incessant paradox—not merely between commentators but even within particular commentaries themselves. Two of these paradoxes seem particularly interesting to me: the paradox of play's purposeful purposelessness and the paradox of play's boundless boundedness. To take the first of these: For Piaget, Vygotsky, and nearly all commentators, play is purposive, functional. Among other things, as we have seen, it helps kids develop and mature. But Huizinga (1938/1955) argued that the soul of play can't be reduced to any instrumental function:

> Most [of the proposed instrumental functions of play] only deal incidentally with the question of what play is *in itself* and what it means for the player. They attack play direct with the quantitative methods of experimental science without first paying attention to its profoundly aesthetic quality. As a rule they leave the primary quality of play as such, virtually untouched. To each and every one of the . . . "explanations" it might well be objected: "So far so good, but what actually is the *fun* of playing? Why does the baby crow with pleasure? Why does the gambler lose himself in his passion? Why is a huge crowd roused to frenzy by a football match?" This intensity of, and absorption in, play finds no explanation in biological analysis. Yet in this intensity, this absorption, this power of maddening, lies the very essence, the primordial quality of play. (pp. 2-3)

The controversy is over the extent to which play is "autotelic," "self-aimed," as J.M. Baldwin (1897/1906, p. 161) argued (see Piaget 1951/1962 for an overview of this debate). There's no question but that play is that activity in which we engage for its own sake. But nor is there any question but that play accomplishes things, produces things. Serious reflection on this paradox shows that we cannot sacrifice one of these poles (purposelessness) in any way for the other (purposefulness).

Play also seems simultaneously to be bounded and unbounded, by rules I mean. All commentators agree with Huizinga that play is "a free activity standing quite consciously outside 'ordinary life'" (p. 13). Normal, "serious" rules do not apply in the playground, where anyone can be anyone else, and anything can stand in for anything other. In this sense, the playground is a space of boundless freedom. And yet all commentators agree also that, within that play space, rigid rules apply. Vygotsky made this point strongly, going so far as to argue that the rules stem from "real" life:

> I think that wherever there is an imaginary situation in play there are rules. Not rules which are formulated in advance and which change during the course of the game, but rules stemming from the imaginary situation. . . . If the child is playing the role of a mother, then she has rules of maternal behavior. The role the child fulfills, and her relationship to the object if the object has changed its meaning, will always stem from the rules, i.e. the imaginary situation will always contain rules. In play the child is free. But this is an illusory freedom. (p. 542)

In contrast to Vygotsky, I argue that the paradox of the boundless boundedness of play resists resolution. Both elements, rule and rule-freedom, seem to be true and real in play.

These two paradoxes teach some vital lessons about fostering play in WCs. The first lesson is simply, if it ain't fun, it ain't play. Most teachers probably know the misery of play-failure, when a learning game they present does not, shall we politely say, find the desired eager reception among the students. The vital corollary Huizinga is pointing to is that the benefits to be gained from play are somehow, mysteriously, entirely imbricated and associated with the fun of it. By implication, any writing center play that seems forced or ill-received is best abandoned; better to resort to grammar exercises in a workbook. The second vital lesson is the absolute requirement of laws within the lawless play-space. Play opens out when we make up rules for the game. Kenneth Burke (1931/1968) called form in literature (e.g., genre) "the arousing and fulfillment of desires" (p. 124) and with respect to play, it's easy to see what he's talking about. In our playshops, when we're asked to write captions for funny photos provided by the playshop leaders, the caption itself constitutes a form, and our desires are fulfilled in witnessing the various witty ways of working within the constraints of that form. To play successfully means to dwell within these two paradoxes, and it follows that play is therefore sort of literally magical: fragile, organic, melding irreconcilables, rooted in the chemistry of communities.

We can use these analytical commentaries on play strategically in our work, in many, many ways. A brief list of the pedagogical aims of play might consist of the following:

- **Play builds community**. All commentators agree on this. Because play intrinsically involves risk and self-display, people who play together come to know one another in intimate ways. They become friends and learn to value one another.

- **Play helps build and sophisticate the mind**. If we accept Piaget's notion of assimilation, play is clearly the mechanism whereby key mental patterns are perfected and habituated (even if it has little role in the initial process of the more foundational processes of *accommodation*). Simply put, play is the tool for getting good at living.

- **Play builds confidence and expertise**. In play, we learn what we are good at, and in playing some more, we get even better at it. We gain a sense of our own power in the world. This too is a key Piagetian assertion.

- **Play socializes**. This assertion is Vygotsky's essential contribution. For Vygotsky, play is the tool whereby we learn to live freely and powerfully in the symbol-rich human world. In learning how to divorce meaning from object and activity, we become people who can see things that aren't there and take seriously realities beyond the phenomenological. Play teaches us what language is and how it works, and this knowledge releases us into the fully human world: ideological, rhetorical, even (one might argue) spiritual.

- **Play reveals character and talent**. Plato himself essentially made the point that teachers and child therapists know very well: to know a child, watch her play. (See Morris, 1998, for a fine overview of Plato's commentaries on play.)

- **Play teaches the possibility of living in paradox**. Perhaps this is my own contribution. By dwelling in the purposeful purposelessness and the bounded boundlessness of play, we come to learn to live in the real world, fraught with all of its contradictions and warring truths. How much less successful would we writing center folks be at living in our contrary, contradictory institutional site if we had not learned how to play?

- **Play teaches a utopian, egalitarian vision of life**. As Biesty argued, play is only really play when all the players are treated fairly and included fully, with free consent of all parties. Any play that involves hurt, that entails "playing with" someone for the sake of wounding him or treating him as a "plaything," cannot really be called play. Play ends when the tears begin.

All of these justifications stand apart from the multitude of intrinsic justifications we might name for play: the joy it brings, the "work" it produces (poems, finger-paintings), the meaning and purpose it brings to life, the magnetic draw it creates on those who see it. People come to our writing center's playshops because they want to hang out with such cool people who can have such a great time—and that justification alone is good enough for me (and, I suspect, good enough for my various institutional constituencies). Given all these good reasons for playing, and given the scarcity of play opportunities in serious places like universities, it should be very clear by this point that play—as an element of what we in this volume are more generally calling "creative approaches" to writing center work—is a fundamental learning tool. At those moments when the writing center turns into a joy-filled funhouse, we need—we *need*, in the face of all those voices that say otherwise—to congratulate ourselves: the play among the tutors and tutees is exactly what they're here to do.

VIVA HOMO RHETORICUS!

There's another justification for play that applies even more directly to writing center contexts, and it arises from the rhetorical tradition. I argue that learning to play rhetorically—by which I mean getting better and better at playing with language, writing wildly, donning and doffing diverse ethos with abandon—is an essential element of learning to become a writer, of learning to live in a world where being *different kinds of writers* is essential for success, happiness, and empowerment. In making this point, I invoke Richard Lanham's vision of a western culture that's always been conflicted about language and about the self (in some contrast, as noted above, to the fairly commonly put forth position that such conflicts are primarily elements of ludic postmodernism as described above).[3] Lanham argued that what he called the rhetorical attitude and the serious attitude have always been with us and always in opposition. He embodied these two attitudes in personae: *Homo seriosus* and *Homo rhetoricus*. *Homo seriosus* is who humans are when we flatter ourselves that we possess "a central self, an irreducible identity" (p. 1). When we are serious, we think that we create and use language to communicate real "facts and concepts about both nature and society" as well as our feelings. Homo seriosus is in a sense puritanical, "pledged to a single set of values" (p. 5). He's deliberately and avowedly unplayful with language.

Homo rhetoricus, on the other hand, delights in language play. In contrast to the serious Puritanism of *Homo seriosus*, *Homo rhetoricus*, Lanham wrote, likes "Protagoras's wonderful answer when asked if the gods exist: 'I do not know whether they exist or not. It is a difficult question and life is too short'" (p. 4). Freed from such ties to Truth, *Homo rhetoricus* "can play freely with language. For him it owes no transcendental loyalties. Rhetorical man will always be an unregenerate punster" (p. 4).

And so *Homo seriosus*, saying exactly what she means, being her essential self, striving for sincerity and clarity in all interactions, stands in inevitable and irrevocable opposition to *Homo rhetoricus*, who speaks the truth that works for the moment, who puts on a different self to fit a new occasion, who strives ever for sexiness, humor, or interest—a Voice That Works. The Academy, founded by that master of the serious attitude, Plato, and emerging from the ultra-serious Christian monastic tradition, is, I argue, on balance a very serious place. And it's getting seriouser. K–12, of course, is in the age of (so-called) No Child Left Behind, which has cemented the focus on high-stakes testing that has been incipient on the American educational scene for years. And the same "accountability" pressures are now universally felt in higher education, where outcomes-based assessments are now mandated by accrediting agencies.[4] In our work in schools, colleges, and universities these days, we're supposed to know exactly what we're doing and be able to prove that we're doing it. There's no play in this understanding of our mission, no "make it up as we go along" spirit, no recognition at all of the fact that knowledge grows and changes, that certainty isn't ever really, that growth—and life itself—happen in the process (a good old word in composition circles that deserves revival, if we pursue a play-focus).[5] These accountability pressures bring a serious overtone to an already serious place.

Given all of these factors, it might seem to be not merely an option but rather incumbent upon us "marginal" writing center folks to use our "marginal" writing center spaces to show students a more complete vision of the world and of how they might use language.

As David Bartholomae (1985) argued so influentially, when students become writers in the Academy, they need to (re)invent it: its language, its modes of arguing, its stylistic quirks and predilections. Such an act of invention would seem to be a highly rhetorical act, and it is. But despite two decades of work in composition calling for new visions of the writer and new understandings of the writing process, most writing that students bring to the WC is in a serious mode, I think. In our WC, we see English students needing to argue "their" opinions about books, movies, TV ads. We see psychology students needing to write and analyze their own dreams. We see political science students needing to make "their" case for or against NAFTA. We see Nursing 480 (Human Sexuality) students needing to describe "their" masturbation rituals (I'm not kidding).[6] The pressure to be serious, to speak one's truth and in so doing be a "real" student, leaves students prone to crushing paradox, profound inner conflict, and acute anxiety.

Here's a good example of these dynamics in action. As director of our WC, I tend to devote much of my own tutoring and workshopping time to SSU's master's-degree candidates, who frequently lack good, sustained mentorship at our profoundly overburdened campus. Many of these students make their ways to the writing center after having struggled for months or years to finish their theses or other culminating projects. Such a student is typically a fully functioning adult who has achieved success in her many years of higher education. She has written many fine papers, and very often she is already a fully functioning professional in her chosen field, whether teaching or business or counseling. But in trying to write a thesis, she has hit a wall. In talking with her, I nearly always find that she has done more than enough reading, that she is already very much an expert on her topic, and that she knows what she wants to say. But now she is stuck: badly beset by writer's block and feeling good at nothing except telling herself what a fraud she is. All the while, in her "professional" interactions, she needs to deny all this uncertainty. Nancy Welch described this painful state of being beautifully: "For . . . graduate students I meet in a campus writing center, learning to write in the academy is a process of increasing orientation, the work of adapting and mirroring, with any sense of misfit, distortion, and excess to be suppressed or excised" (p. 19). There are many impelling reasons behind this painful inner struggle, but I think one chief reason has to do with an interior war being waged between *Homo seriosus* and *Homo rhetoricus*. In writing a thesis, the graduate student is doing rhetorical work, writing like a professional in her field, a Scholar. And knowing that she needs to learn how to sound like a Scholar, she is in fact inventing the idea of "scholar" as she works. But at war with this emerging invention is her serious attitude, which tells her that she is what she is and sounds as she sounds—that these are her ways, and to adopt other ways would mean to irrevocably change her into something else. How can she sound like all those people she knows she needs to sound like—Foucault and Vygotsky and Erving Goffman and Plato and all the rest—and still retain her her-ness? I think this example is only a more acute and visible case of the kind of struggle that all students face as they seek to do the work of the Academy. And the only cure that I know for the pain associated with this struggle is play. In my experience, what our example student needs is to learn to play with words (again). Through the low-stakes, high-yield magic of play, she can in fact navigate the painful waters of her growth into a new professional body and spirit.

I have seen the fruits of this kind of play in the work of students in the writing center, like in the master's thesis of a psychology student who found her way into her project through (literally) scribbling playfully on blank sheets of paper and then hunting for images in the scribble. The activity began as a self-support mechanism and turned into the very subject of her thesis, a thesis which, I know, became a model for later students to emulate. As I described in the introduction, I certainly have seen the fruits of this kind of play in our playshops (again, see Julie Reid's Chapter), in our tutor-training workshops, in my own classes, and in tutorials, where setting in motion some playful rule or other (put your thesis into a haiku, write the paper in the form of a love letter) has somehow "freed" writers into brilliance. And I think our scholarly literature is full of examples like these. Certainly Welch and Boquet illustrate many such examples; and I might even suggest that some of our "negative" illustrative stories, like the one described in Anne DiPardo's (1992) "Whispers of Coming and Going: Lessons from Fannie" might be read as cautionary tales in favor of the right kind of play.

And so, however low the stakes might be for the players, the larger stakes for play in the writing center are very high indeed. Play, I argue, is one of our essential tools for helping people become capable of living fully and successfully as various kinds of writers working in the world. This notion of the high stakes of play is

"Play, I argue, is one of our essential tools for helping people become capable of living fully and successfully as various kinds of writers working in the world."

another element embedded in the history of the word. Huizinga points out that many languages, like ancient Greek, carry a distinction between the general concept of "childish" fun play, denoted in Greek by the word *Paidia*, and the general concept of contest, denoted by the word *agon*—a word familiar to *Homo rhetoricus*, as noted earlier. This is the distinction between the ludic as a fun, stakes-free, life-enriching leisure activity and the ludic as a battle played out in symbolic terms for blood or money or some other kind of real goods. The games of the playground (kickball, monkey-bar-gymnastics) have little larger immediate consequence for the players; the games of Life (buying a member of congress, selling yourself successfully on the job market, wooing your life partner) have profound significance for people and the society in which they live. Some of what we mean when we say that we wish to prepare students for successful citizenship and productive work, it seems to me, boils down to learning how to play these games of life. And so learning how to play with language is an essential element of our core missions in the modern academy.

Given the reality of the world in which we live and work, I am not in the least surprised at the joy with which the tutors and tutees in the writing center I direct (and in the classes I teach, for that matter) approach their writing-play. In that play, in "just playing," the participants are acknowledging their own limitations fully and completely. They suspect (to the point of certainty) that their own personal inventions of the university (and of society and world) are partial, weak, limited, literally sophomoric.

And they know that when they have to engage their work seriously, which means having to step into the persona of *Homo seriosus*, they will engage with only limited and partial success. They can't grow as they know they must without a lot of serious work and play, and they know this; and yet as Bartholomae and Welch articulate so well, so often they need already to pretend that they are serious citizens, fully vested with all the rights and privileges pertaining to adulthood (as in many ways they are). They need to pretend that they have already gotten over all the innocence and incomplete socialization of youth. But in their wild play, students' limitations are given, accepted, and allowed to be. Simultaneously, the students get to relax into rhetorical selves—all of whom are always already partial and incomplete—who play freely in the playground of language. And in that low-stakes, creative play, they create cool stuff like funny poems and new friends and also create new selves and new ways of using words. In short, in their play, they confront the crushing paradoxes of their fraught positions in the academy with the only tool that really helps.

This is a point we can learn to make better to any constituencies that are interested. In inviting a student to play in the writing center, we aren't just giving her a brief vacation from the tyranny of *Homo seriosus* (although I think that's a worthy goal); we are giving her an opportunity to become strategically better at living. We can ask our constituents to come in and listen—listen closely. The play here is good work.

> **"In inviting a student to play in the WC, we are giving her an opportunity to become strategically better at living."**

AND BY THE WAY, VIVA *HOMO SERIOSUS*, TOO

Nothing I have written in this chapter is particularly radical. As I said at the outset, one of my aims here is precisely to approach play from a relatively apolitical position, *so that we can talk that language if we must*. Nor is anything I've said particularly distant from what's often called common sense. The point made in the last section is a not much more erudite way of saying that all work and no play make Jack and Jill not merely dull but also incomplete people. But I do sincerely believe that *Homo seriosus* is rather having her way with *Homo rhetoricus* in the world as we live in it today. The only remedy I—and the writing center players I observe—know of is to live out the potential of *homo rhetoricus* and *Homo ludens*, in low-stakes, fun play for play's sake. We know what feeds our play-personae. They live on a diet consisting of large helpings of silliness accompanied by side dishes of hilarity, gibberish, face-painting, water balloons, Charlie Chaplin, bubblegum-ball ice cream, and a big glass of oulipian poetry. With the commentators noted in the introduction, I believe that the writing center, with its relative freedom from scrutiny, its shifting, ad-hoc educational goals, and its relative pragmatism and by-seat-of-pants aviation, clearly offers itself as the vital place on campus for the miraculous and vital tool, gift, and dessert called play.

With commentators like Welch, Boquet, and Grimm, I think play can be used for radical or progressive purposes, and I certainly laud such usages. But I am not sanguine about the possibilities for play making the whole world into a fairer and more humane place. I do not think that the utopian egalitarianism of the play-space threatens any time soon to make the world come to its senses. Indeed, I would say rather that play promises to remain marginal. This point reiterates one of the fears we hold for play in the writing center—that our play will ensure our marginality. To some degree, I think we will have to accept this bargain, its upsides and its downsides.

For I am not in any way prepared to champion playfulness over seriousness in any larger, (not to say) Platonic sense. Rather, I agree with Lanham that *Homo seriosus* and *Homo rhetoricus* are both vital parts of complete selves, despite the fact of their constant war. A human being without one or the other is an incomplete human being. Here's how Lanham made the point:

> The study of rhetoric . . . teaches . . . that we cannot be freed from it, that it represents half of man [*sic*]. If truly free of rhetoric, we would be pure essence. We would retain no social dimension. We would divest ourselves of what alone makes social life tolerable, of the very mechanism of forgiveness. For what is forgiveness but the acknowledgment that the sinner sinning is not truly himself, plays but a misguided role? If always truly ourselves, which of us shall scape hanging? . . . [T]he central self depends on the social self. . . . The struggle between social and central self is a—literally—self-generating, self-protective force. To free ourselves from rhetoric would be to shut that device down. To recommend such "freedom" invites us to think ourselves divine. (pp. 8–9)

Likewise, to free ourselves from the central self, from the serious parts of ourselves (*even if* that central self is but a certain particularly powerful effect, really, of the rhetorical self, as so many postmodernists argue) would be to leave us with no ground for dignity, no way of being sincere when we wish to be. We can embody both archetypes. True magic happens when the archetypes work in concert. I'm thinking of the hyper-playful poetry of hyper-serious poets, like the Christian poets George Herbert and Gerard Manley Hopkins. These are poets who truly played with language (Huizinga argued that all poetry is grounded in play in any case). And yet in their poetry they confronted what were for them the most serious imaginable questions, like the fate of the soul, the proper humility before creation, and the challenge itself of melding language and spirit. I find their poetry breathtaking in its heroism, its determination to use the rhetorical playground as a tool for finding Truth. Ultimately I think (sentimentally, perhaps) that this heroic quest is what we're here to help students accomplish.

But making both the playfully rhetorical and the unplayful serious selves live fully requires that we nurture both, in a world where the former starves nearly to death much of the time. So I too call for playful noise from the writing center, for divine shenanigans that can teach us how to be better actors as well as better people. And I think we have no reason whatever to do so shamefully, as if behind the back of Authority. Playing makes sense, and making the writing center into a play space is good wisdom.

ACKNOWLEDGMENTS

I offer sincere and deep gratitude to the (then) students who set me to thinking seriously about play in the writing center, most especially Kevin Dvorak and Julie Reid. Kevin was assistant director in the SSU Writing Center during the 2001/02 academic year and entered the job with a keen desire to make our center into the kind of play-space argued for in this essay. Julie, working as a tutor in the center and in coursework with me, conceived the idea of our Parlour Parlour "playshops" (see her essay in this collection) and then very successfully mounted several of these playshops during spring term 2002. My sincere thanks also go to the many tutees and tutors who have participated in our play-activities: watching them at play has taught me more than anything else about play in the writing center. Finally, I'd like to offer special thanks to Dr. Sandee McGlaun for so many formative conversations.

NOTES

1. I'd like to publicly thank the tutors who have taken the lead in institutionalizing our writing center journal, especially Kavita Maitreya Salvado da Rocha.
2. North and Brannon made this point explicitly in their essay in the 20th anniversary edition of *WCJ*. Long before that, John and Tilly Warnock (1984) urged WC practitioners to "remain on the fringes of the academic community, in universities and public schools, to maintain critical consciousness" (p. 22).
3. As mentioned in the literature overview section, I take the term *ludic postmodernism* immediately from James A. Berlin's (1996) *Rhetorics, Poetics, and*

Cultures, wherein, summarizing work by postmodern commentators like David Harvey, Berlin acknowledged the potential excitements of living in a postmodern age: "The [postmodern] urban landscape becomes an invitation for self-fashioning in a domain of unstable subjects, free-floating signifiers, and unstable truths" (p. 65). In this chapter, I deliberately do not invoke commentary of this nature, for several reasons, but primarily simply because I don't think we need to do so in making the case for play in the WC. (I have no quarrel with commentators who do so—indeed, I find such commentaries interesting and exciting.) This chapter on play is not the time or place to explore my point about the essentially rhetorical nature of what are often called elements of the postmodern condition. Obviously, it's a point worthy of serious and extended exploration and that hints at what one might call a possible grounding theoretical concept for writing center work. Commentators in composition like Berlin, Faigley, and others can help writing center practitioners work through these questions.

4. Such is certainly the case at my university. Our current reaccreditation effort will only be successful if, in a few years' time, we prove to our accrediting agency that we have become what's termed in the discourse of accountability a "learning institution"—meaning one that has learned how to police its own results and adapt according to what the surveillance teaches us.

5. Here again in the return to process we find a way in which play is clearly not necessarily radical. I'm thinking of an essay on revision by Toby Fulwiler (1992) in which he offers wildly playful directions to students on ways to revise—by changing points of view, by changing order, and so forth. Perhaps Fulwiler's directions could have politically radical implications, but they're presented really only as instrumental strategies. And I don't really think they necessarily do have radical implications. Rather, they're orchestrated in service of the old revisionist aim of saying better what you mean—what Welch calls "a means to manage unruly voices and rein in excessive texts" (p. 25).

6. This assignment was a famous one on campus, and the nursing professor in question was a highly respected and admired member of the faculty, among students and faculty alike. All the writing assignments in his class were submitted anonymously, identified only by randomized numbers, and the masturbation assignment was only one of several interesting response-paper-type assignments. To be sure, we didn't see a lot of students wanting help on their masturbation papers, but on the rare occasion that we did, it certainly was cause for some chatter in the writing center journal and elsewhere, as one can imagine.

REFERENCES

Baldwin, J. M. (1897/1906). *Social and ethical interpretations in mental development: A study in social psychology*. New York: Macmillan.

Bartholomae, D. (1985). Inventing the university. In M. Rose (Ed.), *When a writer can't write: Studies in writer's block and other composing problems* (pp. 134-65). New York: Guilford Press.

Berlin, J. (1996). *Rhetorics, poetics, and cultures: Refiguring college English studies.* Urbana, IL: NCTE.

Biesty, P. (2003). Where is play? In D. Lytle (Ed.), *Play and educational theory and practice* (pp. 43-55). Westport, CT: Praeger.

Boquet, E. H. (1999). "Our little secret": A history of writing centers, pre- to post-open admissions. *College Composition and Communication, 50*(3), 463-482.

Boquet, E. H. (2002). *Noise from the writing center.* Logan: Utah State University Press.

Brannon, L., & North, S. M. (2000). The uses of the margins. *Writing Center Journal, 20*(2), 7-12.

Bruffee, K. (1984). Collaborative learning and the conversation of mankind. *College English, 46*(7), 635-652.

Burke, K. (1931/1953/1968). *Counter-statement.* Berkeley: University of California Press. (Original work published 1931)

Carino, P. (1995). Theorizing the writing center: An uneasy task. *Dialogue: A Journal for Writing Specialists, 2*(1), 23-27.

DiPardo, A. (1992). Whispers of coming and going: Lessons from Fannie. *Writing Center Journal, 12*(2), 125-144.

Ede, L., & Lunsford, A. (2000). Some millennial thoughts about the future of writing centers. *The Writing Center Journal, 20*(2), 33-37.

Faigley, L. (1992). *Fragments of rationality: Postmodernity and the subject of composition.* Pittsburgh: University of Pittsburgh Press.

Fulwiler, T. (1992). Provocative revision. *Writing Center Journal, 12*(2), 190-204.

Grimm, N. M. (1999). *Good intentions: Writing center work for postmodern times.* Portsmouth, NH: Boynton/Cook.

Harris, M. (1990). What's up and what's in: Trends and traditions in writing centers. *Writing Center Journal, 11*(1), 15-25.

Huizinga, J. (1955). *Homo ludens: A study of the play element in culture.* Boston: Beacon Press. (Original work published 1938)

Kelly, L. (1980). One-on-one, Iowa City style: Fifty years of individualized instruction in writing. *Writing Center Journal, 1*(1), 4-19.

Lanham, R. (1976). *The motives of eloquence.* New Haven, CT: Yale University Press.

Lunsford, A. (1991). Collaboration, control, and the idea of a writing center. *Writing Center Journal, 12*(1), 3-10.

Monighan-Nourot, P., Scales, B., & Van Hoorn, J., with Almy, M. (1987). *Looking at children's play: A bridge between theory and practice.* New York: Teacher's College Press.

Moore, R. H. (1950). The writing clinic and the writing laboratory. *College English, 11*, 388-393.

Morris, S. R. (1998). No learning by coercion: Paidia and *paideia* in Platonic philosophy. In D. P. Fromberg & D. Bergen (Eds.), *Play from birth to twelve and beyond: Contexts, perspectives, meanings* (pp. 109-118). New York: Garland.

North, S. M. (1984). The idea of a writing center. *College English, 46*(5), 433-446.

Piaget, J. (1962). *Play, dreams, and imitation in childhood.* New York: Norton. (Original work published 1951).

Schlosberg, H. (1947). The concept of play. *Psychological Review, 54*(4), 229-231.

Stewart, P. (1963, March). *Concurring opinion*, Jacobellis v. Ohio. Retrieved August 2, 2006, from http://www.law.cornell.edu/supct/html/historics/USSC_CR_0378_0184_ZC1.html.

Vygotsky, L.S. (1933). Play and its role in the mental development of the child. In J. Bruner, A. Jolly, & K. Sylva (Eds.), *Play: Its role in development and evolution* (pp. 537-554). New York: Basic Books.

Warnock, T., & Warnock, J. (1984). Liberatory writing centers. In G. A. Olson (Ed.), *Writing centers: Theory and administration* (pp. 16-23). Urbana, IL: NCTE.

Welch, N. (1997). *Getting restless: Rethinking revision in writing instruction.* Portsmouth, NH: Boynton/Cook Publishers.

Welch, N. (1999). Playing with reality: Writing centers after the mirror stage. *College Composition and Communication, 51*(1), 51-69.

3

WRITING CENTERS AND POLITICS OF COMMUNITY, IDENTITY, AND SOCIAL JUSTICE

Harry C. Denny

Growing up in Iowa, I always knew my family was not well off. My father was fresh out of the army as an enlisted soldier, and entry-level jobs were hard to find. As union-wage meatpacking and manufacturing jobs disappeared, we went through periods when we relied on government assistance, from blocks of cheese to food stamps. My father graduated from a series of security guard positions to asbestos removal (in the dawning days of awareness of its occupational hazards), and he supplemented his income by installing alarm systems for small businesses. From hearing grocery check-out clerks comment on the items we were buying (name brand mac 'n cheese rather than the generic) and seeing my mother avoid eye contact as she tore out USDA coupons from their booklets, I learned that public shame went along with the private awareness of being poor and needing help. Even my grandmother chipped in, working as a domestic after shifts as a hog processor at Oscar Mayer. She would dole out the extra money to help my parents make a loan payment, get food, or buy new school clothes.

In the Mississippi Valley where my Davenport hometown is located, hard times—from the 1970s recessions to the 1980s farm crisis—might have likely forged alliances across the poor and unemployed; instead, bias and stereotypes interfered. My family believed in an odd humility and circumspection: at least other people had it worse than us. We had moved up from the series of trailer courts we started living in. Our tiny ranch house was at least better than the mobile home where many poor Whites lived or the integrated housing projects that were the other options. In our segregated working-class neighborhood, people always talked about it being at least safer than the supposedly crime-infested Black neighborhoods near the river. Strangely enough, Green Acres had its own share of drug use, domestic violence, and petty crime, all of which we assumed was exclusive to where Blacks and Latinos lived but which we chose to ignore in our own backyards. At least, at least, at least. . . . It was a refrain I heard over and over again. Only later in life did I come to understand that identity formations, particularly racial ones, had a long history of dividing, rather than coalescing people.

Despite my family's knee-jerk racism, class bias, and homophobia, they invested me with the sensibility to question, to consider "what if"—they taught me to think creatively, as a means to cope and come to terms with my position in life. Growing up in my neck of Iowa, the western reaches of Rust Belt America, working-class kids had few options in life: scramble for the few remaining union jobs at factories, escape by enlisting in the military, or get to college somehow. I stumbled into the academic world because my family had nurtured a disdain for the futility and grinding inhumanity of line work, and the military, quite frankly, with its policies toward gay people scared me, even if I had not yet come to terms with that aspect of my identity. Life at the University of Iowa was a torrent of dips and turns, from challenging coursework to coming out of the closet. The journey to find myself in college was remarkably similar to experiences more famously documented by Rose (2005), Rodriguez (1983), hooks (1994), Villanueva (2003), and others. We share experiences of making the most of institutional structures and strictures, despite their material reality for most of our peers. Our journeys to academic culture and relative success with it are the odd products of serendipity and (self- /un-)conscious seizing of opportunities (from supportive teachers and personal drive). We epitomize creative response to what society has framed as an otherwise bleak existence; still, our escape from the working class was in some measure a response to a lifestyle (to a life) for which we felt shame.

Although each of us was strategic about using opportunities presented to us, our success was predicated on a degree of luck. Along with this fate, we took risks, not always as the product of self-conscious plotting, but as a result of recognizing possibilities and knowing enough to seize them. Elementary and secondary schools are sites where such providence and opportunism are rife. But they are also spaces where the gap between reality and possibility in our country is stark and documented; they are awash with data and analysis that make this disparity and stratification legible. Education in the United States is advertised as a conduit for meritocracy and social mobility, but volumes of research suggest it actually re-inscribes children's position in society in ways both legible and subtle. That students like me break out of our likely positions in society is a testament, but to what is unclear, since the notion of escape or social mobility presumes a movement away from that which is not necessarily an improvement of anything other than material wealth (although, of course, society teaches us to believe in upward mobility as spiritual and social improvement).

Success as a consequence of the creative use of education to change social and class position becomes even more significant when exploring the reality of stratification in U.S. colleges and universities. One's economic position, gender, and race are among identity markers that are also variables for access to and achievement in education. Although colleges' racial enrollment roughly mirrors the face of the nation, graduation rates reveal inequity (Fig. 3.1). Racial integration is commonplace in urban and coastal sites of public higher education, yet *de facto* segregation still reigns in the south, midwest, and mountain West. Although the racial gap in high school graduation rates has shrunk, it remains wide between whites, African Americans, and Latinos for completing more than 4 years of college education (Fig. 3.1). Women are now numerical majorities on most campuses, but in the workforce, they continue to earn less because gendered social and cultural practices related to child care push them out of the workplace for periods of time significant enough to impact on wage value (Fig. 3.2). Higher education is becoming less financially tenable even as admissions become more inclusive and make access seem democratic. Despite college education being necessary for many entry-level jobs, its impact on wages is marginal, a reality mitigated only by the realization that those with less education have actually lost earning power (Fig. 3.3). Entry into the middle class is increasingly dependent on advanced or graduate education, assuming one pursues a specialized vocation valued in the workforce. For students like me and those from similarly marginalized backgrounds, schooling is both a trap and an escape, each of which requires false consciousness and critical awareness to maintain or overcome.

Today, education faces a market-driven reality, one that requires a creativity to contend with and overcome. Decreasing government spending forces many public institutions to ostensibly privatize and serve corporate interests before student needs, and private colleges and universities must operate in similar ways, currying favor with niche markets, either as service providers for benefactors in need of particular workers or as commodity producers of intellectual property or experiences for students and clients. In *The New York Times*, Sam Dillon analyzes this phenomenon and notes: "The Morrill Act of 1862 granted federal land to states to finance the creation of public universities, and one of their core missions ever since has been to provide services that promote the well-being of communities and states." But this purpose for education is inherently at conflict with dynam-

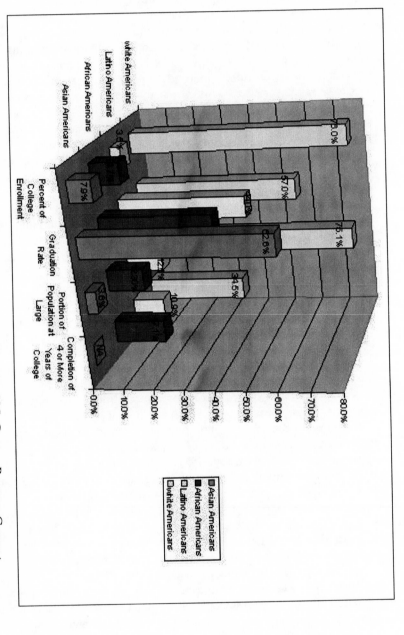

Figure 3.1. Race and ethnicity in college participation. (*Sources*: U.S. Census Bureau, Current Population Survey; Chronicle of Higher Education.)

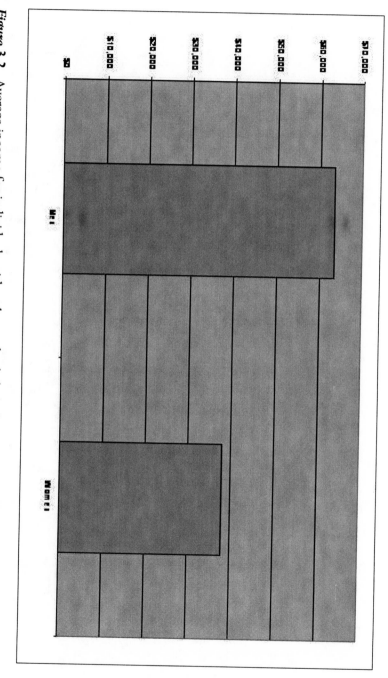

Figure 3.2. Average income for individuals with at least a bachelor's degree. (*Source:* U.S. Census Bureau, Current Population Survey.)

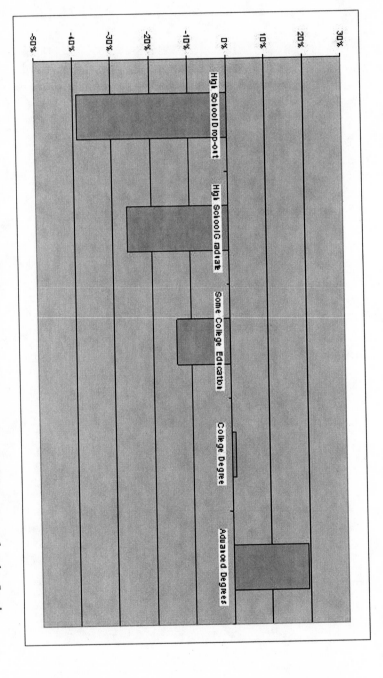

Figure 3.3. Change in median income for individuals (1970-2003). (*Source*: Pell Institute for the Study of Opportunity in Higher Education & U.S. Census Bureau.)

ic pressures of political economy that land-grant and conventional colleges and universities face. These institutional obligations, to commonwealth and fiduciary survival, are in tension with one another and have capillary effects throughout campus—curricula drift from generalist liberal arts education to studies only marginally distinct from vocational education, a move not entirely problematic if students were, in large, landing jobs commensurate with the debt load they are accumulating.

As mainstream higher education accelerates its drive toward costly job training, America's elite schools remain firmly ensconced in the traditions of liberal arts scholarship. This differential emphasis—pragmatic education for the masses and classical *belle lettres* for the future aristocrats—is axiomatic not just of the function of economic class in America, but also of all markers of social distinction. For those of us in composition studies and writing centers (WCs), the stratification of higher education becomes most real and local during recurrent crises over literacy and the sorts of students gaining access to our campuses. John Trimbur (1991) argues that, throughout U.S. history, these clashes have mitigated middle-class anxieties about its loss of privilege, redirecting fear to otherwise innocuous forms of difference and the ascendancy of the Other as an object of derision. The arbitrary cleaving of symbolic lines of class identity shifts literacy from the ends of a public obligation for democratic citizenship to private products of meritocracy. Nancy Grimm (1999) sounds a similar note of caution by calling attention to the ideology of individual liberalism that supports higher education. This way of thinking, Grimm believes, inevitably seeks out persons—students, teachers, and parents—for blame and accolades when failure or success happens, but never poses critical attention to the roles institutions and systems play in oppressing people. Both Grimm and Trimbur share an abiding concern for WCs and composition classrooms being spaces where the physics of oppression and opportunity are owned and acknowledged, and they would likely endorse a politics of creativity that foregrounds the implications of pedagogy for learning, resisting, and subverting structures and processes of domination in higher education.

Creativity in this context, as a means of pedagogy or as a product of learning, becomes a proxy for distinction in education and institutions that circulate it. In the midst of this volume's larger conversation about the objects and means of innovative writing center work, we need to own the historical and political imperatives of the mentoring, teaching, and learning that happen in WCs. More pointedly, I highlight the political economy that our efforts at innovative pedagogy must face and address. For WC practitioners, our work bridges and scaffolds others' access to academic discourse, and tutoring enables a modicum of security to hone voice and agency in an often amorphous and enigmatic academy. My concern is, without apology, self-serving: At each stage of my academic life, WCs have served those functions for me, so I am quite loyal to the "conventions" of our community. When our agenda and attention shifts from these interests and concerns to new audiences and methods attuned to creative expression, I worry about their implications for the historical mission of many WCs positioned to serve first-generation students or those who approach us with different abilities and forms of cultural capital. By creativity, do we mean broadening the genres of what we address? By creativity, do we mean using innovative pedagogy to foster student, tutor and teacher learning? By attending to creativity, do we stop fostering critical attention to institutional structures and dynamics that police access and agency in education? By turning conversation to creativity, do we foreground the individual as learner and interlocutor and slight the collective and social? As much as continual reflection on and innovation of our teaching, mentoring, and collaborating are crucial to those needs for empowerment and invention in WCs, our energies and vision must simultaneously look to their impact on the bodies and identities passing through and developing in tutorial spaces. Creative pedagogy that ignores the ubiquitous dynamics of social and cultural division risks blindness to re-inscription of bitter practices of racism, sexism and class bias in America. In the following sections, I explore those connections, particularly as they relate to the history and politics of negotiating WC practice, theories of discourse community, and the politics of identity.

> "Creative pedagogy that ignores the ubiquitous dynamics of social and cultural division risks blindness to re-inscription of bitter practices of racism, sexism and class bias in America."

THE BURDEN OF HISTORY

In the late 1960s, Stony Brook's WC came into existence as a response to student and curricular need.[1] It was staffed with English graduate students who split their time between one-to-one tutoring and administering the university's proficiency exam. Tutorials focused on students' work beyond the writing program because support for its courses was banned (administration thought tutorial support enabled instructors to shirk what it thought was their rightful obligation). During these years, the space, tellingly, was referred to as the "writing clinic." When Peter Elbow, and later Pat Belanoff, came in to direct the writing program, the clinic became a center, and the graduate students began administering a placement exam (instead of the former exit one) as well as tutoring students inside and beyond the writing program.[2] It shifted from the high-stakes gatekeeping of the competency-testing days to a reflective and culminating portfolio system, on which Elbow and Belanoff (2003; Belanoff & Dickson, 1991) have written extensively. A research grant enabled the provisional employment of a full-time director until permanent funding was secured, and these monies supported tutoring programs for historically "at-risk" students.[3] After this director left the position, subsequent Writing Program Administrators filled it as a course off-load for individuals from the pool of full-time, non-ladder faculty or as an extension for doctoral student funding. Over the WC's nearly 40-year history, the Stony Brook student population shifted from a predominately White population to a more diverse body reflective of New York City's outer boroughs and urban out-migration. Unlike the demographic changes that the City University of New York campuses experienced, this Long Island branch of the State University of New York, except under Elbow and Belanoff's years as WPAs, did not appear to consciously factor the changing student profile into its vision for campus-wide writing-across-the-curriculum (WAC), the writing program or the WC.

This partial history of Stony Brook University's Writing Center parallels Elizabeth Boquet's (1999) mapping of the emergence of contemporary expressions of tutorial support. Just as many colleges withered under the sheer diversity and uneasy fit of the students hitting college campuses in the late 1960s and early 1970s, Boquet argues (1999), WCs struggled with location and process as variables influencing work with students. As she notes:

> The theme of crisis intervention is repeated over and over in the scant histories written about writing centers during the 1970s, as writing centers were created largely to fix problems that university officials had difficulty even naming, things like increasing enrollment, larger minority populations, and declining (according to the public) literacy skills. Exactly how writing centers were to address these problems, however, is never quite clear. (p. 472)

These markers (increasing enrollment and diversity) of "open-admissions" access to education—symptoms of universities stretching for class, racial, and ethnic inclusiveness—did not dissipate as more conservative public education policies rose in the 1980s, but strategies for dealing with them have bogged down. Like the recurrent literacy crises that Trimbur (1991) analyzed, WCs also ebb toward anxiety, but those concerns allude to but rarely take on the actual bodies within the spaces. Directors and tutors alike find themselves fretting about where to intervene (in high schools, as fellows/assistants in writing intensive courses, at sites where students actually write) and how to reach "them" (directive vs. passive, banking vs. problem posing). After theorizing moved from pragmatics to complex dynamics, a good deal of current scholarship and conversation has gone back to the future, in a manner of speaking. On that movement away from intellectual questioning and academic experimentation, Boquet advises: "We must, instead, pay more attention to the things that don't always demand our attention, must remember that we only get answers to the questions we ask and that the asking determines the answers" (p. 479). Problem posing and questioning have always ranked high as WCs' best and most creative offerings to the students, tutors, administrators, and faculty that pass through our spaces, and we are well served when we use our pedagogy on ourselves.

The models to which WCs aspire are also monuments to innovation and collaboration in response to learning needs, and these structures represent attempts to deal or fail to contend with bodies at/in the center. As Lunsford (1991) writes, tutorial spaces can be understood as storehouses, garrets, and parlors, each having implications for perceptions of writers and writing instruction. The storehouse WC, like its analog in current-traditionalism, or what Joseph Williams (1998) calls the product model, envisions writers as consumers of knowledge and information and learning as exterior and positive. Tutors act as agents to transmit skills and to inoculate writers with techniques, making interaction linear and directive. For the garret approach and its companion expressivist mindset, writing involves solitary exploration of thoughts and process. Tutors prompt self-reflection that leads to comfort and proficiency, and session talk centers on drawing out knowledge and skills that are understood to be latent or interior to the writer. In the parlor approach, dialogue is central and ends are diffuse. The dynamic that Lunsford (1991) and Cooper (1995) imagines is rooted in dialogue and collaboration that brings the social back into tutorials. And with that interactive sensibility toward the writing process, the politics of agency and empowerment become increasingly crucial. The writer and tutor become a part of something that exceeds themselves as individuals, but the dialogue can also foster critical awareness of the logic and practices of institutions and their macro-purposes. That synergetic moment is the height of creativity and an expression that rarely draws enough attention or adulation.

Even though most colleges and universities (and even an increasing number of high schools) have WCs, their positioning and the models under which they operate struggle with who uses them and to what effect. As Boquet (1999) describes, the major push in the contemporary creation and direction of WCs has been to deal with the perceived explosion of "problem" writers on campuses. The frequency of error that those writers present is not terribly different from writers of prior generations, except that their identities are changing along with the types of issues they present (Bean, 2001; Connors & Lunsford, 1988; Fox, 1999). Embracing those "problem" writers, WCs got creative with teaching, providing collaborative and generative spaces, sites where interaction became a naturalized component of academic culture, rare experiences, oddly enough, at institutions where mass education dominated. The iterative and recursive work that has come to dominate WC practice functions best in true peer contexts where students and tutors are not separated by intellectual and cultural gulfs. The shared zones of experience such pedagogy presumes is complicated in WCs where sheer diversity—students from racially and ethically marginalized backgrounds, first-generation college students, non-native English speakers—translates into widely different sets of experiences that impact learning, mentoring, and teaching.

Diversity of identity in WCs, when not owned or mitigated, can impede collaboration, yet homogeneity of student populations can foster effective peer work. Although working through difference and challenging the familiar are clearly more satisfying than the alternatives, innovation, as many of the techniques that the essays in this collection offer, requires creative problem solving and dialogue. Who we tutor in WCs speaks volumes even when we do not create the space to acknowledge their presence: Everyone can see and feel difference, although it is often projected onto students' language as proxy. Marilyn Cooper (1995) puts the dynamic well: "Students and tutors who are outside mainstream culture are usually more aware of the way language coerces them, but all students and tutors know how institutions coerce them in writing classes" (p. 139). Nonmajority students know very well that multiculturalism embraces them to a degree; nevertheless a certain threshold Otherness becomes off-putting and awkward for many professors. Nonmajority students' very difference can provide flavor in expression, yet such styles of communication may also confound regard for conventions of academic discourse.

INTERSECTIONS BETWEEN DISCOURSE COMMUNITY AND IDENTITY POLITICS

For WCs, the social turn in composition studies has become the dominant means to mitigate marking "outsiders" as interlopers, but critical cultural studies also fosters creative questioning of institutional conventions. Regardless of whether their institutional populations are diverse or homogeneous, tutors coax students toward self-awareness and agency by awareness of rhetorical factors and audience affecting composition. This Freirian-inflected approach (2000) cultivates knowledge of a larger concept that unifies those expectations: discourse community, an umbrella term for the nexus of space, language use, and collectivity. Joseph Harris (1997) unpacks the idea quite well:

> We write not as isolated individuals but as members of communities whose beliefs, concerns, and practices both instigate and constrain, at least in part, the sorts of things we can say. Our aims and intentions in writing are thus not merely personal, idiosyncratic, but reflective of the communities to which we belong. (p. 98)

This explanation is elegant; the individual and social melt into one another and suggest that instruction is most appropriately directed to awareness of self, other, and audiences. For Harris, writing pedagogy is diffuse and awash in creativity, especially when instructors and tutors tap into students' innate expression and coach awareness of the social. By placing students in conversation with and making them aware of the communities of discourse to which they belong and to which they seek to join, they discover that these social creatures are dynamic and always changing.

In some quarters, "academic discourse" is a concept for the purported set of shared academic modes and style of communication, and students are led to believe learned facility with them assures educational access and success. But the academe, like any collective, is not a monolith of group-think and discursive practices. In hashing out research, insight, and interpretation, professors constantly contest and build on one another's venues and modes of expression. Academic books, journals, conferences, and informal posting sites are notorious discursive spaces where conventions about codes and ideas are championed and lampooned. Intellectual culture operates through the sharing and contesting of ideas, practices fully resonate with those that artists, writers, and other creative figures use with their peers. Instead, students and tutors alike need to understand that they belong to multiple communities all of which use language in contradictory and complementary ways. Against the pressure to learn one illusory code, Harris (1997) argues for students to be "encouraged towards a kind of polyphony—an awareness of and pleasure in the various competing discourses that make up their own" (p. 104). Envisioning a constellation of discursive possibilities counters the mindset that we subscribe to one community over another: Insider/outsider dynamics explode into thinking and practices rooted in improvisation, borrowing, experimenting, and playing with expression.

This tendency to pressure students to pick sides is misguided. Solitary and static notions of academic discourse community are false; rather, they are shape-shifting spaces of disciplinary discourses, which are themselves constantly pulsing and evolving sets of identities and experiences. By coming to college, students, especially those marked as outsiders, initiate change on the academy and themselves. Recurrent crises about students' language use testify to their presence and impact on academic discourse, and it actually depends on emergent and challenging discourses to shore up and grow their own meaning. As I argue elsewhere, tutors and students are well-served by "queering" that process—to help students appreciate the impact of their identities, experiences and expression on "mainstream" discourse. Harris (1997) envisions the potential of learning and teaching moments:

> The task facing our students, as Min-Zhan Lu has argued, is not to leave one community in order to enter another, but to reposition themselves in relation to several continuous and conflicting discourses. Similarly, our goals as teachers need not be to initiate our students into the values and practices of some new community, but to offer them the chance to reflect critically on those discourses—of home, school, work, the media and the like—to which they already belong. (p. 105)

Harris, Lu (1994), and I advocate critical reflection as a creative means to analyze the use of discourse to signify and police participation in communities and rhetorical occasions. When tutors reflect on and disclose their own experiences with negotiating place and voice in college life, they demystify that process, but they also must speak with awareness that their narratives provide one among an infinite number of possibilities, that other students have equally important experiences that make possible different realities. This critical talk—exploring the possibilities and limits of experiences and discourse, for self and audience—is the ultimate creative, productive environment.

Each semester when I begin training new tutors, I use a writing sample and have them read it with the assumption that the student did not have an agenda. I like using essays written in nonstandard code, be it from second language writers or native English speakers, because responses to textually coded difference are powerful. Inevitably, new tutors react to perceived surface error and make exhaustive editing notations. After a few moments, we debrief about their reactions and their reasoning. When reflection turns to codes, usually the first set of issues that new tutors mention, they talk about convention and the sample's distance from it. From that conversation, I introduce them to Elbow and Belanoff's (2003) ways of responding and to Gillespie and Lerner's (2003) discussion of prioritizing feedback on ideas and argumentations over mechanics and usage. My goals are to foster sessions where writers provide productive mirroring and feedback and to create spaces where risk-taking is prized and channeled toward improvement. But the best laid plans are often undermined by tutors' reaction to code, to markers of accent or dialect. Their hyperawareness of difference (even among tutors who are themselves people of color, second-language learners, or first-generation students) is curious, and tutors speak about it with a reluctance that signals their awareness of the complicated politics and implications of expressing identity difference through one's use of language. Comments get prefaced with a nervous, hushed,

"Well, you know, she's ESL [English as a second language]" or "He's from the city," and the unspoken message is that student is an outsider.

These reactions to difference signal the role of identity politics in the teaching and responding to writing, and it begs for talk to own, understand, and change. Yet those conversations rarely take place, and when they do, they are often unsatisfying. As Victor Villanueva (2003) says, "Part of the reason why this (racism continues to be among the most compelling problems we face) is so is because we're still unclear about what we're dealing with, so we must thereby be unclear about how to deal with it" (pp. 832-833). Typically, American conversations about racism as well as other forms of oppression are individualized, or better, are marginalized as the residue of isolated dysfunction. Specific folks are racist, sexist, or homophobic, and they do require concern, attention, and education. While not denying that racism manifests in individuals (and in fact, most benefit from its various manifestations and other forms of oppression), it is a set of discursive practices whose conditions of possibility are what we should attend to because those dynamics reveal its (and any other form of oppression's) systemic and institutional nature. Sadly, dealing with race and other social problems within composition studies and in the broader academy, as Villanueva notes, is often seen as appendages to or diversions from the real work of teaching writing. Fulkerson (2005) typifies this mindset suggesting that "socially committed teacher[s]" cannot provide a space for contrarian viewpoints and inevitably become indoctrinating (pp. 665-666). Curiously, the political gets evacuated from the teaching of rhetoric and expression, a move that seems profoundly incompatible and silencing of need to contend with social issues in the writing classroom. And Fulkerson's response performs precisely a move that Villanueva highlights in his writing.

Describing a conversation at an English department meeting called in response to a blackface incident at a Halloween party, Villanueva relates the disconnect between majority and minority students and faculty. Racism persists, even with a multicultural curricular emphasis because too little hearing and internalizing is happening, regardless of the amount of talking and space for dissident voices. Paraphrasing one student's thoughts, Villanueva reports, "She speaks about the difference between speaking and being heard, that if one is constantly speaking but is never heard, never truly heard, there is, in effect, silence, a silencing" (p. 837). Regardless of one's philosophical or pedagogical commitments, teaching writing should value enabling voice, not cutting it off, but the student's concerns are powerful and beg the question: When it comes to charged discussions, particularly of forms of oppression, how do we facilitate genuine cross-talk and mutual hearing? How do we create ethical spaces to explore disagreement and conflict? How do we resist the temptation to police dissident thought?

A recent thread on Wcenter, the online WC discussion group/list, provides a useful case study for those questions. After Villanueva gave a speech at a joint meeting of the International Writing Centers Association and National Conference on Peer Tutoring in Writing, the list experienced a flurry of postings. As I gathered from audience members, Villanueva spoke to the relative invisibility and silence of people of color in attendance and as a presence in the field, and he also addressed the institutional racism ubiquitous to both tutoring and academic life. These topics are consistent with his interests and writing that I have presented here, but the talk was greeted with stone quiet, prompting the list postings speculating about that reaction. Some respondents opined that the silence was a manifestation of racism itself, some suggested it was about people needing to intellectually digest Villanueva's argument, and others saw it as an occasion to spur collective action in the form of consciousness-raising, recruiting, and continued talk. Another vocal group reacted with recrimination and anger, to what they perceived as being guilty of racism by implication of their silence or to calls for attention to other, perhaps more foundational, forces of domination. The talk died out again, silenced, only to flare up again with similar currents of thought.

This thread on Wcenter was familiar to me because I had seen it before in other institutional contexts and activist settings. From a Colorado civil rights campaign to departmental in-fighting at other colleges where I have taught, ownership of oppression and responsibility for action become so hyper-local that productive conversations, listening, and coalition-building spontaneously combust. Turning the local into crucibles of withering atonement is in effect a powerful identity politics rooted in denying voice and space and fostering power and control. These dynamics are ironic because they invariably arise in connection with talks about dealing with diversity and oppression. In attacking the agents and practices of silencing and foregrounding race (or any form of identity), interaction can take on a dangerous sort of policing performativity. Debate requires speakers lay out their ethos as a condition of entry, and other self-appointed interlocutors judge its authenticity as an index of one's ability to narrativize experiences as participants in or objects of oppression. In this credentialing process, a person's confessional becomes both a means and ends of the conversation; the willingness and skill to self-flagellate for being oppressive determines the degree of voice in the conversation. Understandably, many people will withdraw from these dynamics out of a need for self-protection and political expediency, and an opportunity to make organic change will often be lost. These collective rituals, like the one on the listserv, do not serve productive ends and divide community; instead, we need to be aware such conflicts are best addressed by working toward local change and spreading awareness of the insidious and intractable nature of institutional and structural forms of oppression. Lacking a tenable menu of action options to deal with these dynamics, open conversations in risk-free spaces remain our best possibilities for mutual learning and discovery. However, talk will take us only so far; we must commit ourselves to outreach to populations lacking voice and presence in our profession, and that work requires an understanding of their needs and aspirations as stakeholders, which are often different than the majority or conventional organizational constituencies.

At Stony Brook, I had the privilege of having a diverse student body to reach out to and change the face of our WC, ensuring a space that rewards innovative voice and learning. When the capillary effects of oppression arise, we made them a focus of ongoing critical discussion. Against the backdrop of tutors' tendency to react to accent, my tutors, ironically enough, recently complained about second-language writers' inordinate concern for editing only for features of fluency, so I sought to get them to reflect on their own experiences as outsiders and attempts to become "unmarked." To me, this vertiginous attention to and ambivalence about "accent" was not just about pedagogy, but alluded to discomfort with cultural difference, most specifically with students from Asian backgrounds, but just as likely with students from other racial, ethnic and class cultures. The tutors were enacting othering, and they needed support to process and resolve it. From freewriting and sharing, the tutors, a number of whom are multilingual writers themselves, made connections between their own academic journeys and our students'. The tutors began to recognize that negotiation of academic place and self-presentation requires a degree of cultural capital, forms of experience and knowledge that enable one to integrate expectations with abilities. Self-reflection became a launching pad or bridge toward assisting their peers, and coached dialog helped them grow as well. Rather than have interaction focus on thinly veiled racialized suspicion or on equally silencing labeling, the tutors and students instead could engage in cultural bumping, moments of experiential overlap or liminality where mutual understanding and growth could begin to happen.

TALKING AND CHEWING GUM AT THE SAME TIME: MARRYING CREATIVITY AND SOCIAL JUSTICE IN WRITING CENTERS

In the midst of this rich collection of chapters on creativity in WCs, it is important to have an expansive notion of it; creativity is not just about particular types of figures or narrow means. Innovation, at its heart, is motivated by a desire to think about and perform differently issues and tasks that have otherwise become mundane, inefficient, or unresponsive. Teaching and learning, particularly about and with writing, is rife with recalcitrant objects and inept facilitators—students have a knack for resisting instructors' and tutors' advice for producing better work, and mentors, much to students' frustration, sometime use less effective methods to make learning happen. And WCs need not confine themselves purely to the work of complementing the instruction of academic writing and to the mission of scaffolding students whose access and place in educational institutions is not always secure. Becoming a venue for other forms of written expression certainly augments our core service and research, especially when such genres (and the theories and practices surrounding them) reinforce the collaborative problem solving and recursive processes for which WCs are celebrated.

But, in an academic world where resources are scarce, allocations invariably political, and outlets illusive for nonacademic writers, I wonder, risking to sound like a curmudgeon, what happens when we stray from our foundations. Can we, in other words, serve divergent interests equally well? When WCs become spaces for workshopping and mentoring poets, fiction writers, and playwrights, do students who need support for the common issues for composition and WAC get slighted? If a WC works with creative writers, in what ways does staff training or education for that mission compete with other needs? I also wonder whether the excitement with which folks approach the mentoring of other genres signals their real misgivings about conventional tutoring. Tutoring for creative writing becomes the privileged activity, and passion for academic writing wanes. We risk re-creating in composition studies and WCs the analog of stratification that happens in larger English studies—that is, the divide and privileging of literature scholarship and teaching over composition. We must be wary of making or positioning the teaching of academic writing as a tedious day job or an adjunct of creative writing. With students of color, first-generation college students, and working-class students as the disproportionate consumers of conventional tutoring, we must carefully consider the implications of moving away from them, yet we must also be wary of presuming those students could not benefit from such service (or themselves be effective mentors).

Lurking on the edge of a number of the pieces in this volume are creative responses to meet the needs of the very individuals historically slighted in American education. Wendy Goldberg and the Stanford Writing Center's poetry outreach to Palo Alto school kids represents an innovative connection between an extremely privileged institution and its surrounding community, a historically marginalized population. Both communities are replete with signifiers of class, race, and educational status, but for brief moments creative writing mitigates the gulf. Still the foundational divisions exist. At Lansing Community College, Jill Pennington's and Timothy Miank's "midnight madness" breaks new ground by offering responsive (and I might add, resilient) tutoring to students at an institution that grants access to postsecondary education, learning for a class of students that would not have happened without social movements to democratize education in America. Anne Geller's use of drawing as a staff education heuristic uses creative problem solving to promote and model risk-taking play in everyday conferences when conflict and resistance arise. For each of these cases, innovation is a tool to meet audiences and potential constituencies and to make change happen or, at minimum, create an environment for it to happen.

But to make change happen or to use creativity to mitigate our material realities, we must acknowledge the stakeholders and motives for taking action. Among the people whose interests are most central, obviously, are the students whom we teach and mentor and from whom we also learn. Coming to understand their needs is purely a matter of method, from informal conversations and structured interviews to focus groups and surveys. Based on the insight gathered, we can also explore, using similar techniques as well as those outlined in this volume, what our tutors and what we need as well as other institutional interests. The critical points here are that we must recognize who our interests are and actively dialogue and negotiate with them, and we must not assume their (or our) silence is affirmation, disinterest, or passivity. Just as expression and activity are productive, silence—or the withholding of opinion—is rich with meaning and the expression of power. In reviewing the essays in this collection, readers must consider the ways that technologies and theories of creativity grant voice or silence, because they do so not out of a motive (of malice or benevolence), but because their acts by definition foreground possibility and cut off others. We must wonder for ourselves and our local conditions about the implications of doing one thing and not another and whether they are without significant consequence or possess rich symbolic or material value.

CLOSING THOUGHTS: TOWARD CREATIVE SOCIAL JUSTICE IN THE WRITING CENTER

WCs and classrooms should not be places where social activism and change are the first order of the learning process, but those spaces do not exist as vacuums free from the influence of history and the physics of economic, social, cultural, and political dynamics. Markers of identity and their politics do not disappear or recede into the background in a supposedly neutral zone of teaching and learning. WCs and composition instruction already are awash in the signifiers circulating throughout society. And so we also need to be wary of the ways our pedagogy reifies wider institutional structures of oppression. I am reminded of Jean Anyon's (1992) and Lisa Delpit's (1995) work on the class- and race-coded practices of instruction.

Students encounter less restrictive and regimented ways of teaching as they rise in class position, and working-class African Americans often respond differently based on pedagogy rooted in their cultural experiences (Anyon, 1992; Delpit, 1995). The chapters in this volume invigorate the creativity that we bring to helping students learn and tutors mentor, and they must always be reflected on for their implications in the structuring dynamics at play in education. Still I worry: I hope that WCs and the teaching of writing do not assume themselves as the exclusive sites for change because too many of us are too marginal and too disempowered in larger structures of power on campuses. Doing so, we risk change without a safety net in institutional contexts where the system already does not know what to do or make of us.

Well-intentioned readers might wish for recipes or a shopping list of activities to create occasions and spaces for creativity and for those who occupy our margins. I oppose those sorts of requests because they are not pedagogically sound (especially for teachers and tutors): The best learning that is internalized and that results in substantial growth happens from inquiry, talk, and experiments. This volume offers numerous tangible and launching off ideas—to channel Beth Boquet for a moment, thoughts and experiences from which we might easily riff and improve. Anne Geller's chapter, in particular, makes a cogent point: We must take risks and make an environment where they are safe to take and reflect upon. Just as with innovation, failure needs to be rewarded and processed; people (administrators, directors, tutors, and students) must be allowed to fall on their faces and to learn from those experiences. We cannot bank their learning, and we must facilitate it by means that also invite challenge and security. Like artistic expression misfiring or not connecting with audiences, people will speak and act in problematic terms, so the biggest error we can commit is to police rather than process and problem-pose missteps. As a friend wistfully asked once, "Where do you go when people won't give you the chance to learn from your mistakes? What do you do when you don't know what you need to know?" If we look around our WCs and institutions and find glaring absences or particular silences, it is our burden to change that situation. We must "Make it work!" (to borrow from Tim Gunn, the inimitable mentor on Project Runway). Or as the famous ACT UP! posters screamed in the 1980s "Silence=Death, Action=Life."

In this chapter I have sought to beg the questions of social justice in the midst of a larger conversation about innovation in WCs. My discussion has sought to place discursive explosions about literacy crises in the United States in dialogue with the reality of educational stratification, the contemporary positioning of WCs and debates over composition pedagogy. As I advocate an attention to the social, I caution that unchecked, such approaches can get caught up in a self-defeating identity politics that ultimately does not serve our rightful agenda of fostering voice, expression, and

empowerment. I would encourage readers to return to the charts presented earlier in this chapter and consider them in relation to this thought from
John Trimbur (1991):

> In an era of diminished expectations, persistent economic anxiety, and
> a restricted political discourse, imagination and political courage are
> required if literacy is to be re-represented as an intellectual resource
> against injustice, a means to ensure democratic participation in public
> life. (p. 294)

As I write, fewer students have access to higher education, at a time when
only graduate education assures a long-term improvement in one's economic standing in this country. Public funding for grants and loans to pay
for college and university education are being cut as tuition increases continue to outpace inflation rates. Students who somehow manage to fund
their education and graduate, enter a job market laden with debt that positions them in the ranks of the working poor. Among that population, there
are increasing numbers who struggle for health care and who are losing
pension and retirement nest eggs. This class of people disproportionately
represents the growing numbers of men and women dying in Iraq, Africa,
and America from bullets, bombs, and viruses, and our ability and willingness to pose questions and demand answers inches toward being portrayed
as treason and threats to national security. I cannot imagine a more important time to teach people to think, speak, and write critically, often and
widely. Whether we are producing poetry, plays, paintings, sculpture, films,
expository essays or speeches, it seems incumbent to me that we do and say
something by whatever creative and socially aware means we can muster.

ACKNOWLEDGEMENTS

I want to thank Courtney Frederick, Virginia Draper, Anne Ellen Geller,
and Lori Salem for their revising assistance and encouragement.

NOTES

1. My representation of this history comes from Bruce Bashford and Dennis
   Clarke, two long-time Stony Brook University faculty. I have excluded my years
   as director since it's difficult to be exterior to and simultaneously create my own
   historical narrative. It can't help but seem self-serving.

2. As tutoring primarily focused on writing program students and as they became increasingly first-generation and second-language learners, the work lost its appeal for graduate students. They reported that as the center became more focused on grammar—it's unclear whether they, directors, students, or the program instigated this shift—tutorials prepared them less well for tenure-track jobs. At that time, the writing program also began its eventual separation from the English Department. Eventually, the graduate students' experience of teaching writing, whether within the WC or larger writing program, became less and less integrated with their actual professional mentoring. Put differently, a culture shift took place, and increasing numbers of graduate students saw the teaching of writing as a distraction from their academic development. That tension continues to the present.

3. Funding for the later directorship reverted to the Arts & Sciences College once the grant ended, and now the line is a ladder-track position that I held.

REFERENCES

Anyon, J. (1992). Social class and the hidden curriculum of work. In G. Columbo, R. Cullen, & B. Lisle (Eds.), *Rereading America: Cultural contexts for critical thinking and writing* (pp. 521-540). Boston: St. Martin's Press.

Bean, J. C. (2001). *Engaging ideas: The professor's guide to integrating writing, critical thinking, and active learning in the classroom.* San Francisco, CA: Jossey-Bass.

Belanoff, P., & Dickson, M. (Eds.). (1991). *Portfolios: Process and product.* Portsmouth, NH: Boynton/Cook.

Boquet, E. H. (1999). "Our little secret": A history of writing centers, pre- and post-open admissions. *College Composition and Communication, 50*(3), 463-482.

Connors, R. J., & Lunsford, A. A. (1988). Frequency of formal errors in current college writing, or Ma and Pa Kettle do research. *College Composition and Communication, 39*(4), 395-409.

Cooper, M. M. (1995). Really useful knowledge: A cultural studies agenda for writing centers. In C. Murphy & J. Law (Eds.), *Landmark essays on writing centers* (pp. 135-147). Davis, CA: Hermagoras Press.

Delpit, L. (1995). *Other people's children: Cultural conflict in the classroom.* New York: The New Press.

Denny, H. (2005). Queering the writing center. *Writing Center Journal, 25*(2), 39-62.

Elbow, P., & Belanoff, P. (2003). *Being a writer: A community of writers revisited.* New York: McGraw-Hill.

Fox, T. (1999). *Defending access: A critique of standards in higher education.* Portsmouth, NH: Boynton/Cook.

Freire, P. (2000). *Pedagogy of the oppressed.* New York: Continuum International.

Fulkerson, R. (2005). Composition at the turn of the twenty first century. *College Composition and Communication, 56*(4), 654-687.

Gillespie, P., & Lerner, N. (2003). *The Allyn and Bacon guide to peer tutoring* (2nd ed.). Boston: Allyn & Bacon.

Grimm, N. (1999). *Good intentions: Writing center work for postmodern times.* Portsmouth, NH: Heinemann.

Harris, J. (1997). *A teaching subject: Composition since 1966.* Upper Saddle River, NJ: Prentice-Hall.

hooks, b. (1989). *Talking black.* New York: Taylor & Francis.

hooks, b. (1994). *Teaching to transgress.* New York: Oxford University Press.

Lu, M.-Z. (1994). Professing multiculturalism: The politics of style in the contact zone. *College Composition and Communication, 45,* 305-321.

Lunsford, A. (1991). Collaboration, control, and the idea of a writing center. In C. Murphy & J. Law (Eds.), *Landmark essays on writing centers* (pp. 109-116). Davis, CA: Hermagoras Press.

Rodriguez, R. (1983). *Hunger of memory.* New York: Bantam Doubleday Dell.

Rose, M. (2005). *Lives on the boundary.* New York: Viking Penguin.

Trimbur, J. (1991). Literacy and the discourse of crisis. In R. Bullock, J. Trimbur, & C. Schuster (Eds.), *The politics of writing instruction: Post-secondary* (pp. 277-295). Portsmouth, NH: Heinemann.

Villanueva, V. (1993). *Bootstraps: From an American academic of color.* Urbana, IL: NCTE.

Villanueva, V. (2003). On the rhetoric and precedents of racism. In V. Villanueva (Ed.), *Cross-talk in comp theory: A reader* (2nd ed., pp. 829-845). Urbana, IL: NCTE.

Williams, J. D. (1998). *Preparing to teach writing* (2nd ed.). Mahwah, NJ: Erlbaum.

4

HIDEAWAYS AND HANGOUTS, PUBLIC SQUARES AND PERFORMANCE SITES

New Metaphors for Writing Center Design

Derek Owens

PRETTY PINK FLOWERPOTS

Whenever I get one of those "concerned commentaries" from a colleague—the passing hallway remark or e-mail memo informing me of the student who, after having paid a visit to the writing center (WC), still (gasp!) somehow managed to submit an essay containing "A LOT" of errors—I'm reminded of driving on the Cross Bronx Expressway in the 1980s. Back then, the highway was lined with decrepit, abandoned buildings in states of considerable disrepair. In an attempt to soften these tableaus of urban blight, the gap-toothed facades were covered with hundreds if not thousands of faux plywood windows. They had fake curtains painted on them, and a few even had the added flourish of a lamp or little pink flowerpot. In this way, drivers were prevented from having to look too closely at the poverty of the Bronx—a poverty created in no small part by the very presence of the Cross Bronx itself, built by Robert Moses, the ambitious visionary who designed much of New York City and Long Island in the mid-20th century. Moses' expressway displaced hundreds of thousands of people, destroying what had once been thriving ethnic neighborhoods and replacing them with a South Bronx landscape that has yet to fully recover. As a result, commuters were "spared a daily vision closer to bombed-out Dresden than their lovable Big Apple" (Swift, 1989).

I suspect that more than a few faculty and administrators view the WC (if not the entirety of first-year writing programs) as fulfilling a similar function: the rhetorical equivalent of a public housing project created to protect the sensibilities of passers-by, and where the blemishes of student prose are spackled over, their native dialects smoothed into the appropriate vernacular. Sometimes it can seem that so much of college writing is as empty as those abandoned tenement buildings, not for lack of student creativity but because of poorly designed assignments and low expectations. And despite the best intentions of WCs, inspired as so many are by expressivist and critical pedagogies, a good percentage of our daily labors remain preoccupied with prettifying student writing manufactured in response to those unimaginative and all too typical assignments. The result is often a homogenous prose that "works" for faculty and student, but is ultimately as forgettable as yesterday's lunch.

Our WCs, as many have remarked, operate in sites of ambiguity and contradiction. Our pedagogical orientations—so often inspired by the now canonical Northian idea of promoting better writers but not necessarily better writing—are often at odds with those of colleagues preoccupied with the latter. We sometimes lack the agency to challenge those views; WCs tend to be seen as services intended to respond to existing pedagogy and curricula, not as sites for instructional reform. Although WCs do of course play an increasingly major role in writing-across-the-curriculum (WAC) initiatives and faculty development, counselors probably spend even more time helping clients figure out strategies for responding to poorly designed writing assignments. WCs do what they can so as not to perpetuate the same old, same old of college writing instruction, but their effectiveness will always be determined in part by the surrounding curricula, the faculty's approach to writing instruction. As Lil Brannon (2005) asked, "should we uphold the language practices—the standards—that professors demand of students? If we don't, won't the students suffer? If we do, are we complicit in the perpetuation of racist and elitist practices?" ("Cultural Work of Writing Centers"). WCs occupy a liminal zone, operating somewhere between the "native" language practices of their clientele and the discursive demands of the academy. WCs try to acknowledge and respect the discourses of the disciplines without going so far as to interpret theirs as a gatekeeping role, where WC workers come to resemble stewards upholding the principles of some totalizing notion of "good academic prose." At the same time, WCs seek ways to legitimize, respect, and celebrate the student's own language practices, but without going so far as to romanticize

> "WCs occupy a liminal zone, operating somewhere between the "native" language practices of their clientele and the discursive demands of the academy."

"indigenous" dialects and discourses as somehow innately superior or more "authentic" than the writing forms faculty prefer and expect. Few sites in the campus landscape are as paradoxical and contested.

I am interested in how the architectural realities of WCs exemplify these contradictions, and how we might transform the local limitations of our centers to our advantage. In what ways are the struggles of WCs revealed in their structural and geographic realities? And what options exist for using these material conditions in furthering the mission of the WC as a force of creative, transformative change—whether the site exists in some overlooked, neglected corner of the campus, or sits center stage as a kind of showpiece, a testament to the university's commitment to service?

FROM CLOSET TO FAMILY ROOM

Perhaps most WCs can be located somewhere on a spectrum ranging from the invisible on one end to the highly visible on the other—a closet-to-centerpiece continuum. Our WC started out as a closet. Then we moved into a space closer to a family room—a more "livable," visible location, but still somewhat small and tucked away from the rest of the campus. Most recently however, we have been visited by a most unusual and rare windfall, a multimillion dollar gift from a donor that resulted in our WC expanding and relocating to the center of not one but two campuses. This essay charts that progression, documenting the different ways our WC mission has evolved as a result of this tremendous growth.

Most of our WCs probably began life on the far left side of this scale: the WC with its origin in a custodian's closet, under the stairs, or in the attic. In 1996, I was given the task of creating the first WC at St. John's University. I was given an 8 × 10 cubicle in the basement of St. John Hall with which to work my magic. It housed a desk, two chairs, and a salvaged loveseat circa 1953 emblazoned with broad brown and orange stripes. Plus a big, gaudy lamp on the desk, the kind my grandmother would have gladly positioned on top of her Hammond organ, next to her collection of Avon cologne bottles. And that was it. I was given the title Writing Center Coordinator (at the time senior faculty in my department, now retired, were uneasy with the unadulterated power a term like "director" might bestow on a junior faculty like myself), and to be honest, it wasn't a strenuous gig. How much coordinating, after all, can be done in a cube that will only hold three people? It was rather like being told to coordinate a basketball game in a bathroom; it simply can't be done, and nobody really expects you to do it anyway.

In 1997, we were able to come out of the closet as a supportive Dean intervened and managed to secure a new WC up on the second floor where there was considerably more student traffic than our original basement location. We became more popular, with student appointments typically booked several days in advance. We served on average 650 students a year, the majority of whom returned for on average three visits. Compared to the 20,000 students in our university, however, this was a drop in the bucket. The WC, although popular and active, was still inauspicious enough to be something of a secret to many university students and faculty. And that was partly intentional on my part; because our budget would not allow us to take on many more clients, we were not as aggressive as we could be in getting out the word for fear that we would have had to turn away even more walk-ins than we did (from mid-semester on, we can handle virtually no walk-ins).

The entrance to our WC was nothing flashy; just a small black sign jutting over a doorway tucked among classrooms in the oldest building on campus. The hallways are painted in institutional green, that lima bean hue used widely in hospitals and government buildings designed mid-century under the influence of modernist functionalism. The halls are not so much ugly as they are insistently nondescript, conduits absent of any aesthetic overtures, designed not for congregating or socializing but solely for bodily flow. The hallways are pedestrian avenues, the classrooms akin to so many exit stops, each with equally nondescript, overtly functionalist interiors. An educational building, in other words, with corridors and classrooms no different from those found in tens of thousands of American high schools and colleges where the interior spaces have been conceived as temporary holding tanks: Spartan, operative, and uninspiring. Students and faculty don't spend time in these places unless they have to; during the day

when classes are in session, the hall-ways are packed as students and staff are channeled, bovine-like, to and fro; later in the day and on week-ends, the rooms and hallways are often empty, lonely places.

Our WC sought to provide a counterbalance to the surrounding uniformity of the building. The site for our center was not that big, par-ticularly for a university our size. We had two rooms; the first contained desks for the secretary and associate director, a few computers, and four workstations.

This initial "receiving room" was where the lion's share of our day-to-day tutoring took place. The room, with its messy desks and busy bulletin boards and filing cabinets decorat-ed with 100 or so snapshots and illustrations, was noticeably different from other classrooms and offices on the floor; the combination of the visually hyperactive walls, the informal demeanor of the undergraduate and gradu-ate staff, and the inviting presence of Virginia Buccino, our secretary and unofficial WC "mom," all worked to help pull in the wandering student, and perhaps kept them coming back for return visits.

There is a second room that could be seen from the hallway, and here we took further liberties with the design. This was the room where tutors and their friends hung out while not working, where we had staff meet-ings and end-of-semester parties, and also held faculty workshops and presentations.

One wall sported a student collage that continued to get a little larger every week. The other featured a mural I painted one winter break when no one was around (a map of the universe, inspired by my 5-year-old son's drawings). A bathroom sat off of this room, decorated with a curious com-bination of glowing flamingos, malicious cartoon monkeys, and handbag ads.

We got away with decorating the walls in our own ad hoc, organic fash-ion partly because, although centrally located in the building, our WC was still somewhat removed from a lot of campus traffic flow and so a quasi-autonomous feel circulated here, especially in the lounge or "inner cham-ber" as some of the tutors called it. More importantly, the provost, deans, and vice presidents who on occasion made their way into the WC never voiced anything but support for our work and mission, nor raised any eye at the visually hyperactive surroundings (no small matter given the degree

to which our university, like so many U.S. institutions, has become increasingly concerned with the uniformity of its "brand image"). All day long, consultants and their friends, the WC groupies, used the space to argue, study, play Scrabble, and sometimes held meetings for student organizations. More than a few times, our students told me that the space was precisely the kind of relaxed, intellectual lounge area the campus needed more of. Almost 10 years ago, ours was a commuting university. Enormous strides have been made to build a freshman center, a large honors lounge, distribute laptops to all incoming students, and add new residence halls and sports facilities, all of which has radically changed the culture of the university and very much for the better. But one can never have too many of what Hakim Bey (1991) called "temporary autonomous zones," and our WC had in some small way tried to create a space that, in its best moments, vaguely approximated the feel of a salon, or coffeehouse, or community lounge.

> **"Our WC tried to create a space that approximated the feel of a salon, or coffeehouse, or community lounge."**

DREAMS OF BENIGN SORCERY: FROM FAMILY ROOM TO CENTER STAGE

In the early 1990s, the architect Will Alsop won a competition to design the National Writing Centre in Swansea, South Wales. This really wasn't a WC as we know it but a large complex intended to house a central library, exhibition galleries, a "Museum of the Word," ongoing displays, and "an international writers' centre carrying overnight accommodation [because] libraries are conducive to sleep and dreams" (Spens, 1993, p. 41). The complex was to contain a large bookstore, cafeteria, and activity spaces. "Here was an extraordinary example, in Britain, of a city council determined to stimulate a wide spectrum of literary culture, yet in a deep relationship not dependent upon adjacent academia." The structure was to have its roots in the local street geography, as pedestrians would be steered into the bookstore, museum, and exhibition spaces. There was to be a performance platform, a "story-telling bush" ("a structure to be crawled into"), and an expansive roof garden overlooking the city. One reviewer gushingly wrote that Alsop's proposed design was "a space to inspire new dreams, visions of many futures . . . just that degree of benign sorcery that the age demands" (p. 41).

If you haven't ever heard of this National Writing Centre, there's a good reason; it was never built. The museum got canned at the last minute, regulators and politicians spooked by the unusual architectural design. Fortunately for us, our plans for a new Writing Center met with greater success. With enthusiastic encouragement from the Provost and the President, and a Board of Trustees member who wanted to donate several million dollars to promote writing throughout the University, we submitted an ambitious proposal for the Institute for Writing Studies. This Institute would house a brand new First-Year Writing program, a new Writing Across the Curriculum program, and two new Writing Centers. Within less than a year of submitting the proposal, we had a new 8,500 square foot site built on the Queens campus, with another on the Staten Island campus. Although when finished we too lacked a story-telling bush that people could crawl into, we accomplished something more significant.

Early in the process we were asked to supply a conceptual sketch for the main site. After providing a somewhat amateurish and hastily concocted illustration, the architectural team of Perkins and Will identified the key elements of my design and reconfigured them into a plan that integrated expansive Writing Center tables, work stations, and lounges; a large conference room for Writing Across the Curriculum meetings; and multiple offices to house a newly hired First-Year Writing faculty. All of this was built over the course of one summer in the most visible place on campus: nearly half of the first floor of the University library, with ample windows overlooking the great lawn in the center of campus. A smaller site was placed on the Staten Island campus as well, also with considerable light and placed in a visible, high traffic location. Both sites have small but growing libraries; soon the Queens site will double as an art gallery as we begin exhibiting student artwork on the walls.

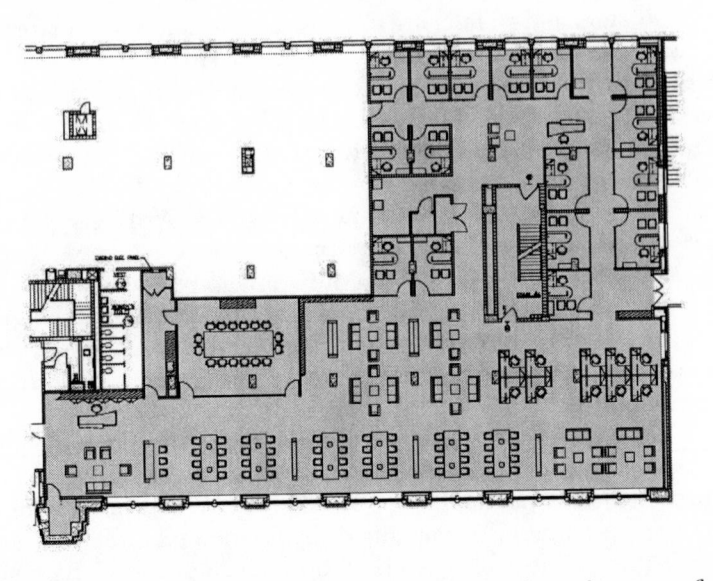

With the new site we were given the green light to hire new faculty: Harry Denny now directs both Writing Centers, with Tom Philipose and Chris Leary as Associate Directors on either campus. The impact of the new sites and faculty directors has been profound. For one thing, the number of students making appointments jumped from around 600 students a year to 6,500 sessions annually. Where we were once staffed at most a dozen consultants, we now have more than 50 tutors. Sessions are conducted face-to-face, via email, and also through IMP and Chat sessions, with webcams set up to enable students on one campus to work with consultants on the other.

Initially, I was interested in broadening the idea of the WC to take on a role akin to that a coffee house, a salon, what Ray Oldenburg (1999) called a "third place"—not a home or a workplace, but the type of public site that one seeks out in one's free time. A square, a commons, a gathering space for readings, speakers, presentations, performances, viewings, exhibits, and activities that, even if they do not directly translate into writing tasks, fuel the kind of creative atmosphere conducive to the thinking necessary for interesting writing. To create an island, an oasis, of a writing culture within the task-driven curriculum. But with the vision of my colleagues, the mission and focus of our WC has moved far beyond my limited and somewhat romanticized view of the WC as coffee house or a family room. Tom Philipose has made connections between the Writing Center and local community service and outreach organizations like

> **"We have an obligation to do what we can to create an island, an oasis, of a writing culture within the task-driven curriculum."**

Bread and Life. Chris Leary, along with doctoral fellows like Kerri Mulqueen, has begun partnerships with area high schools to train and mentor faculty and students who are now creating their own Writing Centers. And Harry Denny, whose background in Writing Center theory, research, and scholarship supercedes my own, has in just several semesters developed assessment projects, brought all scheduling and logs online, ini-

tiated videotaped focus groups, mentored more than a dozen consultants to present at conferences, and revitalized the consultant training process. In addition, our newly hired First-Year Writing faculty have helped transform the Writing Center space by scheduling open mics, film series, readings, and invited speakers.

What I've learned most throughout this entire process is how crucial it is to make sure that other talented faculty are not only encouraged to be part of the design process for new or developing WCs, but that visionary, more qualified colleagues are brought in to take over leadership roles when necessary.

MAKING THE MOST OF ONE'S LOCAL SPACE

Wherever our WCs locate themselves along the closet-to-centerpiece scale, how might we use our architectural, geographical conditions to further enhance if not broaden our mission? If one's WC is hidden, off-grid, behind the scenes, or stuck out in a corner of the campus, how might we use such below radar status to cultivate a more independent, organic, homegrown atmosphere designed by tutors and clients? For those whose centers are moving into a more high traffic, publicly visible locale, how might we use that added attention to our advantage?

In his book, *Getting Back into Place*, Edward Casey (1993) pointed out that the word "dwell" has two origins: it comes from the Old Norse *dvelja*, to linger, delay, tarry; but also from the old English *dwalde*: to go astray, wander, drift. How might we envision the Writing Center as both a site where people want to spend their free time as well as a magnet momentarily drawing students away from the busyness and task-oriented mindset inevitably fostered within much of the curriculum? A refuge, an intermediary space less formal than the classroom but more intellectually driven than the cafeteria—a locale shaped by our imaginations and not the corporatized models that are increasingly informing our institutional environments?

When I think of WCs, a handful of metaphors come to mind. The eclectic back yard grotto handcrafted by the eccentric neighbor living in the middle of the suburban neighborhood, which annoys the neighbors but is a delight to the children in the area. The basement family rec room circa 1975, with its beanbag chairs, sagging couches, dartboards, board games, and lava lamps. The visionary gardens of outsider artists. One metaphor, however, stands out above the rest: the wunderkammer, or cabinet of curiosities. These rooms of wonders came into popularity in the 17th century as collectors sought to symbolically replicate the universe within an enclosed space. Specimens of natural history, preserved anatomical oddities, rarified figures and finds, were displayed on walls and in drawers, suspended from ceilings and arrayed on tables. These collecting rooms gave way to elaborate cabinets and meticulously crafted boxes, and their appeal has continued into the 20th century, with Marcel Duchamp, the surrealists, and Joseph Cornell's shadow boxes.

A WC is, ideally, a cabinet of curiosities, a kind of box within the academy, a box within a box, wherein the preoccupations of students and faculty might find expression and insight through their engagement with writing and other media. To paraphrase an earlier quote: a place determined to stimulate a wide spectrum of literary, visual, and media culture, in a deep relationship with *but not wholly dependent on* adjacent academia.

REFERENCES

Bey, H. (1991). *T.A.Z.: The temporary autonomous zone, ontological anarchy, poetic terrorism.* Brooklyn, NY: Autonomedia.

Brannon, L., Mahala, D., & Owens, D. (2005, October). *The cultural work of writing centers: Contesting boundaries and the importance of local resistance.* Paper presented at the meeting of the International Writing Centers Association and National Conference on Peer Tutoring in Writing, Minneapolis, MN.

Casey, E. S. (1993). *Getting back into place: Toward a renewed understanding of the place-world.* Bloomington: Indiana University Press.

Oldenburg, R. (1999). *The great good place: Cafés, coffee shops, bookstores, bars, hair salons, and other hangouts at the heart of a community.* New York: Marlowe.

Spens, M. (1993). The National Writing Centre and city library. Visions for the future. *Architectural Design, 104,* 41-43.

Swift, R. (1989, December). Captives of design: Modern architecture. *New Internationalist, 202.* Retrieved November 7, 2005, from www.newint.org/issue202/keynote.htm.

5 ────────────────────

"LITERATIVITY"

Reconceptualizing Creative Literacy Learning

sj Miller

What is creativity, and how does it impact literacy learning? In this chapter, I explore the intersection of creativity and literacy, which I call *literativity* by contextualizing it within a thirdspace framework that allows us a unique view of how to make meaning of creative literacy practices. Next, I explore *literativity* and the learner and try to understand what motivates learning and how students and tutors might each benefit from *literativity*-based learning. Finally, I propose that as we adopt creative approaches to literacy and integrate them into our writing center work, we will attract a unique and self-motivated lot of learners who will take ownership over their writing.

CONCEPTUALIZING CREATIVITY

Creativity is a word many people use freely but struggle to define. This is likely attributable to its subjectivity and the lens of the individual who utters the words *creativity* or *creative*. Competing definitions tell us that the word *creative* generally implies uniqueness or something that is unusual (Cropley, 1999). In their research that synthesized 18 key studies on creative teachers, Bramwell, Kronish, Dagenais, Reilly, and Lilly (2005) found that creative teachers were those who esteemed learning, motivation, development, and relationships and who built such characteristics into their teaching. They also found that creative teachers possessed and demonstrated well-developed interpersonal interests and skills and incidentally guided students to be creative. As a whole, creative teachers were sustained in a reciprocal relationship with their environment in which they could both blossom and be shaped by their environment (Csikszentmihalyi, 1988). Such findings beget the question, do teachers, which broadly includes anyone instructing, including writing center directors and tutors, need to first be creative in order to approach literacy learning creatively?

In short, I would suggest, the answer is no. Because we are all learners, what we can do, if we do not consider ourselves to be naturally "creative," is look to other writing centers (WCs) and individuals who have taken risks by implementing alternative practices into their work. The individuals **"Like writing, becoming competent and confident in approaching one's work creatively takes practice."** included in this text are by no means the only people in the WC field experimenting with their work, but they provide approaches anyone can try. Like writing, becoming competent and confident in approaching one's work creatively takes practice.

As we are already using the word *creative* we should first look closely at the word *creative* itself. When I ponder the word *creative*, or think of someone or something that is creative, what comes to mind is approaching an idea, concept, or material through a lens that is a hybridization of past, current, and even future ideas, concepts, or materials. For instance, murals are often erected in spaces in cities as a way to stamp the importance of a person, event, or idea and are regarded as creative. Likewise, the individuals who put up murals tend to be viewed as creative individuals. But haven't we seen murals everywhere? Under bridges? Inner-city parks? In the malls? If murals are normalized what then constitutes the mark of their creativity? Creativity has a life span because what is considered as unique and unusual during a space and time may be replaced by something newer and more innovative. In other words, when something that is perceived as creative is codified it can be reified and once reified it may be co-opted by dominant culture for economic purposes and lose its creative prowess and be forced to morph and reinvent itself into something yet even more unusual or unique. I pose then, are murals becoming passé? Are we in the time of the "post-mural?" If so, what then is creative, the artwork, the individual, or their intersection?

Bakhtin (1986) can help us make sense of this question. Bakhtin suggested that what is original is not the creativity or the one who creates, rather it is the space in between the individual and the creation. We may find this intersection or hybrid in the coming together of the tutor and tutee and the WC and university. Bakhtin would argue that there are no original ideas rather that everything builds on what came prior and that the hybrid is what is original. Bakhtin would refer to our responses to events as an *answering*, which is essentially how we make meaning of our social and cultural worlds, and the way we author the texts of our lives. These texts can be creative because they are subjective experiences of the author, authoring responses to the world. Bakhtin suggested that languages and genres become available to individuals through the cultures in which individuals participate and become the means by which we interpret the world. When we mix those genres or voices, we create a heteroglossic mix. Our stories or creations then are an act of co-authoring a hybrid, which although not initially our own are created and bound by specific meaning to our social and cultural ties. Thus, our answering may shift from one moment to the next as utterances and answers intersect with other genres and as we engage in new and different contexts and experiences. The individual then who paints the mural may not be creative but how the individual is bound relationally and culturally and how he or she authors a text enters into a space between the act and the individual, which becomes a hybrid and can therefore be considered creative. Placing boundaries on what it means to be creative can help us understand then what isn't creative.

When we think about creativity, many things may flood our mind. We might think of a mural that was tagged down below the bridge in Pittsburgh's East Liberty, or we might think of the artwork hanging in the Andy Warhol museum, or we might think of the urban renewal project that grows vegetables for the homeless in the small lot next to Home Depot. Regardless of what comes to mind, creativity is highly subjective in the eye of the viewer or in the utterance. If we build on the idea that creativity is something that is unique and useful we can situate our understanding of its place in our lives.

LITERATIVITY AS THIRDSPACE

Creative approaches to teaching literacy have important implications for the learner. By combining literacy with creativity I offer a new term that conceptualizes their hybridization, *literativity*, which is the space in which literacy and creativity intersect. In order to conceptualize WCs as places where literativity flourishes, we might recognize centers in terms of Soja's (1996) research on thirdspace. Thirdspace is the amalgam of both the "real-and-imagined" journeys and the "thirding" of spatial awareness and imagination, an ideal place for creativity to flourish. According to Soja (1996), thirdspace is the

Knowable and unknowable, real and imagined lifeworld of experiences, emotions, events and political choices that is existentially shaped
by the generative and problematic interplay between centers and
peripheries, the abstract and concrete, the impassioned spaces of the
conceptual and the lived, marked out materially and metaphorically in
spatial praxis, the transformation of (spatial) knowledge into (spatial)
action in a field of unevenly developed (spatial) power. (Soja, 1996, p.
31)

If we think of WCs as thirdspaces in which literativity occurs, then we
open up the possibilities for students to access literacy in ways that can
motivate them to learn.

Rosenblatt's (1990) research on the transactional theory of reading and
writing has critical implications for the benefits of teaching literacy creatively. According to Rosenblatt, when an individual reads, the transaction
that occurs between the reader and the text contributes to "meaning." The
teacher or tutor can build on an "evocation" that arises from a literacy
transaction and help the learner reflect on whatever "meaning" was evoked.
The effort to clarify the evocation(s) can be built on creatively, which can
enhance individualized meaning-making. Essentially then, the learner and
the teacher/tutor are co-collaborators in the process of literativity because
what is evoked from one's experience is built upon as the teacher/tutor
recognizes the opportunity to enhance the learning of literacy. In summa-
ry then, literativity is the combination of Bakhtin's hybridization of ideas
that leads to creative utterances, Soja's thirdspace that allows for creativity to flourish, and Rosenblatt's transactional theory that can enhance individualized learning and meaning-making.

LITERATIVITY AND THE LEARNER

As we know, there is no one, sure-fire way to teach any content matter or
even at best, any one way we know that will tap into the interest of the
learner. Creativity then, is a subjective way to "hook" the learner and activate excitement about thinking and writing, and hence, literacy. Every individual brings a store of background knowledge and interests into the learning process and the teacher/tutor has the challenging task of trying to
understand what works for each pupil at a WC. This means, and this is a
great undertaking, taking the time to know the individual interests of the
learner so as to build on and generate transactions of contiguous and con-
tinuous teachable and learnable moments. The relationship between the
tutor and the tutee is then a shared effort whereby students can participate

in the creative co-construction of their worlds (Rejskind & Sydiaha, 2002; Sawyer, 2004). As students assume shared responsibility for their learning, they shift the power dynamics between teacher and learner. Such a shift can empower them to become proactive in their learning whether it be through **"Teachers who are open to creative responses from their learners can instill in them the confidence to take risks and open up new possibilities for literacy learning."** discourse, product, or outcome, and is more likely to lead to risk taking on assignments. Examples of such risks might include making a multimedia project as a response to a text, writing and performing a SLAM poem in response to a writing assignment, or even doing interpretive dance to demonstrate the angst of a character in a text. Teachers who are open to creative responses from their learners can instill in them the confidence to take risks and open up new possibilities for literacy learning in future spaces that they will inhabit.

As such, the relationship between tutor and tutee is interdependent. This relationship is bi-directional and nonbinary and has the capacity to further develop both the tutor's and tutee's creativity. Each individual in the relationship can benefit from and expand their repertoires of literativity, which can lead to increasing their understanding of their own creative processes.

LITERATIVITY IN MOTION

Each of the contributors to this book have approached WCs creatively and have each discovered ways to tap into their learners through unique and purposeful approaches to writing. When we consider how each of these creative approaches both stimulate and activate the writing process, they all share a bond that is generated in between the act and the actor. I turn to Scott L. Miller's (Chap. 2, this volume) discussion of play to illustrate the hybridity of creative approaches to writing. Miller declares that "the writing center is in fact a magnificent place for play in the institution, and that in fact we are remiss both if we don't foster such play and if we don't learn how to come to play's defense" (pp. 22-23). Miller tells us that his deepest fear is that someone will critique play in the writing center as non-viable and the WC will vaporize. Even as he points to key researchers in the field who, like him, make a call for play to be entwined in the writing process, he raises the concern that because there is a dearth of research on play, others may be reticent to approach teaching writing through play. Miller writes:

> Play . . . can militate against the high seriousness, the *religious* serious-
> ness, of academic labor; play can offer counter-hegemonic potential for
> destabilizing power structures, knocking over stuffed-shirt (and power-
> laden) subjectivities, and pointing out the parodically ascertained truth
> (small-T) to all. (p. 26)

I believe that the deeper rationale for the fear that emerges out of those
who deviate from traditional practices of teaching writing is that the product will result in something that lacks normalcy and thereby has no exact
means for assessment. Our field is often critiqued for not doing work that
supports a quantitative agenda because it cannot produce concrete numbers that can be compiled, crunched, and correlated. When we cannot
measure or assess something, it cannot be considered viable by agreed upon
standards in our field. Isn't one of the obstacles to change, however, the
times when we have no agreed on way to measure or assess the outcome?
Do we as a field or even as a country have a tendency to dismiss that which
we cannot assess? Do we refrain from creative approaches to WC work
because of the inherent difficulty to measure creativity? How can creativity be assessed when it changes every time it is activated through WC
work? The concept of play illustrates these concerns because it is difficult
to measure. Miller counters this difficulty with, "clearly we can and do play
as we work and work as we play" (p. 28).

Play takes on the experience of the player(s) and is an act that is fluid,
constantly changing and shifting, as the experience of those playing shift.
The act of play and the play that is acted is what is generated in that hybrid
space, or that space that Bakhtin would say is creative. Play is therefore, as
I suggest, always creative because one can never play the same way over
and over for there is always a change of time, place, people, and events. Play
then is literativity actualized by the players who co-create the space in
which they play. But because play is fluid and subjective to the players,
assessing it as play without agreed upon standards of what play is leaves it
in a hybrid disjunction. Although we cannot measure play, we can have fun
while we learn and continue to forge ahead.

BENEFITS OF LITERATIVITY
IN A WRITING CENTER ENVIRONMENT

Studies about constructivism have shown that when students have ownership over their learning they are more likely to not only enjoy it more but
are likely more willing to go the extra mile to make the work worthwhile
(Bomer & Bomer, 1999; Lewinson, Flint, & Van Sluys, 2002; Shannon,

1989). There are several benefits to the student who can work on writing through a literativity approach. First, a student who can better conceptualize working on writing through a learning style that best suits the process is likely to internalize the event and draw from it at a later time. Next, a student is likely to have a high level of interest in the writing process and the outcome. Furthermore, there may be an increased opportunity for small writing groups to form and for community building to occur either within or outside of the WC. This process of socialization, therefore, generates interest in possibly extending writing to other aspects of one's life. There may also be a general buzz of excitement about creative approaches to writing and as a result, more learners may seek the support of WC tutors. There may be increased confidence in writing, which may lead to greater productivity. Learners may gain the tools to take ownership over their writing and be able to more effectively problem solve how to work through complex moves in their writing. Finally, learners may begin to think of writing as something pleasurable and fun and which may continue into a life-long love affair of writing.

THE FUTURE OF LITERATIVITY AND WRITING CENTERS

We pause now to reflect on how writing will continue to change well into the future. There is no doubt that with the advent of technology and the increased access to media in all of its forms, that writing may be supplanted with yet different forms of writing from what we now know and understand to be writing. Although some of us may grieve its loss, others may celebrate the birthing of its change. Change opens us up to the possibilities for places wherein creativity can blossom beyond what we now know it to be and its relationship to writing can grow interdependently. No matter how writing emerges and morphs in time, we must be open to the possibilities of its craft and the one who crafts. When a writer crafts words into ideas, he or she is dipping into a reservoir of cumulative knowledge and the history of his or her human experience. For the writer, his or her past experiences serve as templates and material from which to draw on and construct into new verbal signs. New meanings in a postmodern era can evolve out of new ways of restructuring past experiences as they interact with new experiences. These meanings and ideas if framed into and by a genre of creativity in thirdspace can lead to new understandings of creativity and their meanings. If we add onto Bazerman's (1997) research on genre studies, which suggests that genre in literary study can frame social relations and social action, creativity as a genre might evolve into a viable component of teaching across all disciplines and content areas.

Several questions come to mind about the future of literativity. I ask, how can we encourage literativity approaches to WCs if creativity has yet to become normalized in research studies and is yet to be germane in our understanding of what it means to tap into learners' needs? A first step toward a call for such a genre is to ask ourselves how we can push educators to be more creative in their teaching approaches to literacy. The next question to ask is how we can support the educator who takes such risks prior to the normalizing of literativity. Third, we need research on the benefits to those who are being taught through literativity practices. Fourth, we need to find out what other hybrid spaces there are and how they differ by discipline. It is my belief that creativity should become normalized and an inherent component of education because it adds to the multitude of pedagogical approaches that have the potential to reach a constantly expanding landscape of students who are influenced by an ephemeral matrix of stimuli.

Creativity is a way to help students walk the tightrope between participating in dominant culture while also allowing them to experience the world through their own eyes. As we open ourselves up to new and more innovative approaches to literacy teaching, we inevitably expand what it means to be creative and what creativity can come to mean in hybrid spaces. Most importantly, is that creativity is interdependent on the relationship and the transaction between the tutor and the tutee. Ultimately, teachers and tutors must strive to nurture and continue to develop the correlational aspects of the effectiveness of teaching creatively alongside one another. As we continue to open up dialogue about how we teach and ways to teach with other faculty and WC directors, we can ultimately expand our approaches to teaching literacy creatively. Collectively, our imaginations can elucidate and generate creative approaches to teaching in WCs and activate and excite our students to write in whatever way that best suits their needs. Literativity can liberate and open doors to new possibilities that over time may lead us to subvert traditional paradigms that were once used to keep people silenced and marginalized.

REFERENCES

Bakhtin, M. M. (1986). *Speech genres and other late essays.* Austin: University of Texas Press.
Bazerman, C. (1997). The life of genre, the life in the classroom. In W. Bishop & H. Ostrom (Eds.), *Genre and writing* (pp. 19-26). Portsmouth, NH: Heinemann.
Bomer, R., & Bomer, K. (1999). *Reading and writing for social action.* Portsmouth, NH: Heinemann.

Bramwell, G., Kronish, N., Dagenais, J., Reilly, R., & Lilly, F. (2005, March). *Creative teachers: A synthesis.* Paper presented at American Educational Research Association, Montreal, Canada.

Cropley, A. J. (1999). Definitions of creativity. In M. A. Runco & S. R. Pritzker (Eds.), *Encyclopedia of creativity* (Vol. 1, pp. 511-524). San Diego: Academic Press.

Csikszentmihalyi, M. (1988). Society, culture, and person: A systems view of creativity. In R. J. Sternberg (Ed.), *The nature of creativity* (pp. 325-339). New York: Cambridge University Press.

Lewinson, M., Flint, A. S., & Van Sluys, K. (2002). Taking on critical literacy: The journey of newcomers and novices. *Language Arts, 79*(5), 382-392.

Rejskind, G., & Sydiaha, D. (2002, May). Creative teachers, creative students? In G. Rejskind (Chair), *Creative teachers: Portraits, products, and challenges.* Symposium conducted at the meeting of the Canadian Association of Educational Psychologists, Toronto, ON.

Rosenblatt, L. (1990). *The transactional theory of reading and writing* (Tech rep. No. 416). Illinois.

Sawyer, R. K. (2004). Creative teaching: Collaborative discussion as disciplined improvisation. *Educational Researcher, 33*(2), 12-20.

Shannon, P. (1989). *Text, lies and videotape: Stories about life, literacy and learning.* Portsmouth, NH: Heinemann.

Soja, E. W. (1996). *Thirdspace: Journeys to Los Angeles and other real-and-imagined places.* Malden: Blackwell.

PART II

Creativity and Tutoring Writing

6

A PLAY ABOUT PLAY

Tutor Training for the Bored and Serious, in Three Acts

Lisa Zimmerelli

CAST OF CHARACTERS: 12 undergraduate students and 1 instructor

PLACE AND TIME: The Writing Center, 2001 fall semester,
The University of Maryland, College Park

ACT 1: ANOTHER YEAR, ANOTHER TUTOR TRAINING COURSE

A hot, late August afternoon at the University of Maryland. Students sit pensively in seats—already arranged in a circle—in a basement classroom. A new writing center (WC) assistant director (she's a graduate student; this is her teaching assistantship, [TA]) walks determinedly down the hall toward her charge—12 writing tutor interns. She hears murmuring—hushed whispers—and slows her step.

Intern 1: I heard this class is pretty intense—lots of reading, lots of tutoring. Do you think we'll have to tutor right away?

Intern 2: Well, I got an "A" in English 101 at least, but I have no idea how I did it.

Intern 3: I got a "B." Barely. English 101 was basically my life last semester. Honestly, I'm surprised I'm here—my teacher said something about "having gone through it, I should be able to help other students." I enjoy writing, but I'm worried that I'm not a good enough writer to be a writing tutor.

Intern 4: Hey—do you think we have to know grammar? Like really *know* grammar? 'Cause I don't.

The WC assistant director enters the room, takes a deep breath, and smiles broadly.

Instructor: Hello! Welcome to the University of Maryland's Writing Center Tutor Training course. My name is Lisa Zimmerelli.

When I taught my first tutor training course, I was struck by the immediate engagement of the students. They were there because they were truly interested in becoming tutors; they were there because they were invigorated by writing and wanted to share their energy with other students. But they were also rather nervous and intense. I was partly to blame. The syllabus was demanding, with readings in both composition and WC theory each week, grammar and mechanics exercises and exams, and both reading reflection and tutor reflection papers. I allowed them time to share their tutoring experiences each week, but the majority of the class was devoted to their comprehension and analysis of the readings. I wanted to ensure that my tutor interns understood that they were joining a complex, diverse set of writing professionals. Part of this was my perception that our WC was underappreciated within the English Department—I wanted to prove that this was a full-fledged, theory-driven, "serious" course. My students, at least, got the message. They tutored with fervor, as though summoning WC theory god/desses alive from the pages of *The Writing Center Journal* and *The Writing Lab Newsletter*. I was proud. I had helped create WC proselytes—tutors devoted to the pursuit of better writing. But when I listened, really listened, to what was going on, I overheard two types of tutoring sessions: either interns were completely hands-off and noncommittal, or they offered advice that, although well-meaning, sounded dogmatic and rigid.

The writing center is abuzz with eager students and their early semester papers. A line is forming at the front desk and the smell of burnt coffee permeates the air. The tutor training instructor surreptitiously walks among the cubicles.

Intern 1: I don't know. What do you think? Well, you see this isn't my paper—it's up to you to decide if this paragraph should be rearranged. No, I really couldn't say; again, this is your paper, not mine.

Intern 2: This is a better place to put your thesis. But you should switch your claims around, so that you end with your strongest argument. There. See how much better that works?

Some of my interns were fervently following Jeff Brooks' (1991) *basic* minimalist tutoring: "1. Sit beside the student . . . 2. Try to get the student to be physically closer to her paper than you are . . . 3. If you are right-handed, sit on the student's right; this will make it more difficult for you to write on the paper . . . 4. Have the student read the paper aloud to you" (p. 2). However, these interns were not progressing to Brooks' articulation of *advanced* minimalist tutoring; they were not developing the necessary strategies that lead to a student's active involvement with the paper. My other interns easily fit Muriel Harris' (1992) characterization of new tutors: "anxious to prove their credentials [tutors] can—unless reminded—try too hard to cast aside their 'studentness' and play the all-knowing professional" (p. 284). This set of interns felt compelled to do anything and everything in their power to ensure that the student walked away with a better paper; the emphasis was on product, not process.

Furthermore, my interns' class participation mirrored their tutoring styles: Some students quietly listened and dutifully took notes; other students dominated the class discussion with their tales of tutoring sessions gone good or bad. I was in a quandary. I wanted to respect the individual learning and tutoring styles of my interns, but I also wanted all of them to examine reflectively a range of tutoring practices.

ACT 2: PUTTING THE "PEER" BACK IN THE PEER TUTOR TRAINING CLASSROOM

The instructor sits at her desk, drumming her fingers and sipping on burnt coffee.

Instructor: (internal monologue) Hmmm. What is missing in my tutor training class? They seem "stuck," scared, even, to step outside of their comfort zone. Comfort . . . comfort . . . why are they uncomfortable? What would make them more comfortable? I mean the class is going well: They're doing the readings; they're showing up for their tutoring appointments; they're participating in class. But they don't smile much. They seem worried, constantly worried, about "doing it right."

A light bulb flashes over the instructor's head.

Instructor: Hmmm. Maybe the reason they're so obsessed with "doing it right" in the tutoring session is because I'm so obsessed about "doing it right" in my tutor training classroom. I have set up a teacher–student hierarchy that they are replicating in their tutoring sessions. I need to break that down and lighten up the classroom. Next class, we'll play some "get to know you" games.

It was when I realized that my class environment set the tone for their individual tutoring environments that I began to see the possibilities of the tutor training classroom as a model for the tutoring session. My class was missing a sense of "peerness" and was rather preoccupied with a need for competence and proficiency. In turn, the interns' tutoring sessions were missing the collaboration that is at the heart of peer tutoring.

At first, I thought I needed just to "lighten up" the atmosphere. I had used games as icebreakers in classes before and decided to fit in one "get-to-know-you" game every few weeks. I asked fellow composition teachers for icebreaker game ideas; I searched the Internet for party games; and I came up with some games on my own. As I collected games on my desk, in my e-mail, and in my mailbox, I recognized a common thread: community building. The purpose of the games was to build trust and commitment among the players. It was clear to me that what I had initially sought out as a "break" from the "work" of my tutor training course could, in fact, be critical to my students' development as effective writing tutors.

The idea of "serious play" is not new to researchers and scholars in education. Collaborators Joan and Erik Erikson's (E. Erikson, 1974, 1987; J. Erikson, 1998) theory of identity progression rests on the premise that a person must continually resolve emotional conflicts in order to fully develop as an adult. Fun and play, according to the Eriksons, is an important piece in that progression. Rieber, Smith, and Noah (1998) defined play as "that special kind of intense learning experience in which both adults and children voluntarily devote enormous amounts of time, energy and commitment and at the same time derive great enjoyment from experience" (p. 29). According to Rieber et al., when adults play they strive toward a goal with intense effort despite false starts and frustrations. Play thus allows learners to engage in creative higher-order thinking in a completely engrossing way. Because play strikes a balance between anxiety and challenge,

"Play allows learners to engage in creative, higher-order thinking in a completely engrossing way. Play, consequently, parallels—furthers even— the goals of education."

learners are willing to take more risks and become more vulnerable. Play, consequently, parallels—furthers even—the goals of education, for games "promote situations where a person is motivated to learn, is engaged in the learning act, is willing to go to great lengths to ensure that learning will occur, and at the same time finds the learning process (not just learning outcomes) to be satisfying and rewarding" (p. 31).

I already knew that fun and laughter is disarming. But my research into fun and educational development proved that games help break down psychological barriers and link peer to tutor to teacher. As researchers Beasley and Crerar (2005) articulate, games are structured activities that "make social situations easier and provide a focal point for people from different generations or backgrounds" (p. 6). As teachers, we tend to see the classroom as an academic setting; however, the social component of our classroom clearly informs what kind of and how much learning can take place. Furthermore, whether she or he wants to be or not, the teacher is an integral part of the classroom's social mélange. At the very least, the teacher is discoursally representational to the students; at the most, he or she privileges particular modes of learning and communication in the classroom. When games are the focal point, they move the epicenter of knowledge from the teacher to the group. As collaborative ventures, games require the engagement of all participants. In this way, they not only change the social dynamic of the tutor training classroom, but they also parallel the acts of tutoring and of writing. Like tutoring, if a student is not engaged in the game, then it is up to the other student, the tutor, to encourage the student and solicit a response. Like writing, games are just as much about the process as they are about the product.

With renewed purpose, I attempted to connect meaningfully the games with WC theory and practice. I ensured that each game required conversation, fostered collaboration, allowed for a multiplicity of response, and theoretically could be linked to tutoring and/or writing. I listened for my interns' tutoring fears and inhibitions and looked to play as a teaching tool to help them become stronger learners, collaborators, writers, and tutors.

ACT 3: LET THE GAMES BEGIN!

SCENE 1: Pass the Hat

A breezy late September fall day. Interns gather in the classroom, take off their jackets, and sit in seats already arranged in a circle. They notice directions on the board: "Shhhh! No talking! Please sit down and jot down any tutoring questions or concerns that arose for you this week." On the table below the board are index cards and a University of Maryland baseball cap. The instructor arrives, sits down, and also begins to write. A few minutes later, she addresses the class.

Instructor: As I've listened to you in class and in tutoring sessions, I've noticed that together we have a wide variety of tutoring styles and strengths. Undoubtedly, you also overhear each other and therefore have lots of questions as to effective and ineffective tutoring methods. Please look over your questions and select one that you would like to have the class answer.

The instructor passes out one index card to each student.

Instructor: Please write one of your questions on the index card and then put the card in the University of Maryland cap on the table. You don't need to sign the index card—your question can be completely anonymous.

The students fill out the cards and place them in the hat. The instructor takes the hat and passes it to a student

Instructor: Okay, this is how "Pass the Hat" works. You will take one question out of the hat, read the question, then answer it. In turn, everyone in the circle will also answer the question. Only after everyone has answered all of the questions will there be discussion, and discussion will be limited to 5 minutes per question. Remember, there is no wrong or right answer!

"Pass the Hat" is a fairly simple game and a nice introduction to the idea of gaming in the classroom. It encourages students to discuss more openly, and with less reservation, their questions about and approaches to tutoring. As students share what they have learned from their tutoring sessions, they begin to recognize their collective wisdom and experience. This game, therefore, is both knowledge building and community-building. Students develop community because *each* shares his or her perspective on each tutor's question. "Pass the Hat" allows a degree of anonymity for the question-asker, but engages the entire class in the answer; consequently, students who may be hesitant to voice their opinions in class have the opportunity to participate equally.

The teacher's role can be limited to monitoring time and moving the class to the next question after a set period of discussion. Although I put a question in the hat, I did not answer any of the interns' questions. If we had played this game toward the end of the semester, it may have been more appropriate for me to do so. To address each question, the class must be small (I typically met with 10 to 15 students for a 3-hour seminar each week, so time was not a factor). If time is limited, students can answer each question, then move on to the next question, saving all discussion for the end.

"Pass the Hat" has many possible variations. One alternative is for the teacher to ask a question and then have tutors write their responses and put them in the hat. In turn, each person will pull an answer out of the hat, read it, and respond. The instructor can therefore control the specificity of what tutors write. Other questions might be: "What was your favorite reading this week and why?" or "Have you ever had a teacher comment that you misinterpreted?" Another option is to assign each student a week to bring in a question. The game is thus spread out over several weeks, with only 10 or 15 minutes devoted to one question each week.

SCENE 2: In the Dark

The next week in class. The instructor arrives early and arranges five sensory stations around the periphery of the room; they are labeled touch, smell, taste, sound, and sight. The touch table is covered with a variety of fabrics and shapes; the smell table contains items with strong odors, such as herbs, coffee beans, soil, perfume, and cedar; the taste table has five bowls with mint chocolate chip ice cream, salt and pepper potato chips, nasturtium, and cauliflower; and the sound table holds various party noise makers, a cowbell, and sandpaper and wood. The sight table, however, has a pile of sample, problematic, papers. She covers each table with a sheet. The interns enter the tutor training classroom and immediately are tipped off that they'll be playing another game.

Instructor: Please pair up with another student. You will be working together at each sensory station. The hitch is that one person will be blindfolded.

The instructor passes out the blindfolds.

Instructor: Put the blindfolds on. Okay, the blindfolded person has to rely on his or her partner to 1, get to the sensory stations, and 2, guess what is at each sensory station. There are three major rules. First, the blindfolded tutor can only use the sense represented at the station. Second, the sighted partner can only answer questions; that is, the blindfolded person has to ask questions to arrive at the identity of the object. Third, you must arrive at the sight station last. At the sight station, you will find a pile of student papers that have a variety of concerns. There, the tutor may take off his or her blindfold, but still must rely on questions to try to resolve the writing issue evident in the paper. Don't worry about reading through the entire paper—just pick a paragraph or two.

"In the Dark" is a nice foil to "Pass the Hat." The latter helps students build community and share equally valid perspectives on tutoring issues. The emphasis in "Pass the Hat," however, is on answering. "In the Dark" is an effective game to follow "Pass the Hat" because it is focused on questioning, and it serves as a metaphor for tutoring. Sometimes tutors are in the dark when they read papers, and asking appropriate questions and trusting the writer is critical for a successful tutoring session.

This game is most helpful if the instructor allows time for follow-up discussion. Ask the students who the blindfolded person represents: the tutor or the writer? The students should share the tactics they used to arrive at the final station. They then can be encouraged to explore how they might apply those strategies to tutoring.

SCENE 3: PERSON/FACT MATCH

Mid-October in the WC. Decorations of witches, pumpkins, and leaves adorn the waiting area. The expressions on a few of the tutor interns are pretty scary too.

Student 1: If I get another ESL [English as a second language] student, I will scream. They are so much harder to tutor than regular students.

Student 2: At least they're usually into the tutoring session. My last student couldn't care less. He just sat there text-messaging his friends. I only spent 15 minutes with him because it wasn't worth my time if he didn't care.

Student 3: Well, I've had three of Professor Cranky's students. He is such a jerk. You should see some of the comments he puts on students' papers. He totally shouldn't be allowed to teach here.

When I overheard my students talking about their tutoring sessions, I initially was quite excited—they were essentially playing "Pass the Hat," just in an informal setting with no boundaries. However, quite a few of the comments I heard were intensely critical of both students and instructors. They had built community among themselves, but had not extended that community to include all writers. In their eyes, there were "good" instructors and "bad" instructors, "good" students and "bad" students, and "good" papers and "bad" papers.

I chose the next game, "Person/Fact Match," to challenge my students to question their assumptions about writing, students, and instructors, and to reinforce the importance of questions in getting to know a person and his or her approach to writing and to the paper at hand.

A few days later in the tutor training classroom.

Instructor: Please get out a small slip of paper and write down one incident from your life or fact about you that probably no one else knows. Then, pass the slips in to me. Now, get another piece of paper out and write down the numbers 1 through 13.

The instructor numbers the slips of paper.

Instructor: I am going to read each statement aloud. Please write down to whom you think each incident or fact belongs. After I've read each person's slip and you've written down your guesses, I'll identify the slips one by one. I'll ask those who guessed correctly to raise their hands and explain why they chose Tutor "A" for this particular incident. Then, I'll ask everyone else to share why they associated someone different with this incident or fact.

"Person/Fact Match" is an excellent game for building community and understanding the complexities and differences among the community members. The tutors love learning new idiosyncrasies and facts about their peers. This game generates a substantial amount of conversation, and often tutors will ask each other to elaborate on the incident or fact they shared. This game is also good for opening the door to a necessary discussion regarding assumptions about writers based on stereotypes. Tutors will tend to use rhetoric like "You look like the type," "You seem like a fan of," "You're a pretty [shy] [athletic] [well-read] person—I assumed it'd be you." You may want to point out this rhetoric at the end of the game and ask them to elaborate on how they can apply the game to tutoring.

An alternative is to limit comments to school or writing (e.g., "Write one fact about how you write"; or "What was the hardest paper you ever wrote?"). Tutors can thus discuss their writing processes and writing auto-biographies. Indeed, interns often have just as many assumptions about how a student should write as assumptions about the student.

SCENE 4: Scavenger Hunt

Two weeks before Thanksgiving break. The WC is swamped, as students are frantically juggling mid-term exams and papers. The interns are feeling the pressure, too—a few have e-mailed the instructor complaining that they feel overwhelmed and that the students seem to want "uber tutors" who can answer every question and concern. This is the buzz as the instructor enters the class.

Student 1: Can you believe that a student actually got mad at me when I told her I had never written a paper in APA [American Psychological Association] style before? I helped her use the handbook, but it was new to me, too.

Student 2: I had a student who basically needed help interpreting the instructor's comments. The instructor said that the student had "comma splices" and "awkward sentence structure." I'm still not even sure what a comma splice is. I'm embarrassed to admit it, but sometimes I get those same comments on my papers!

Student 3: Don't we have a handout on that? Hey—you know what I would love a handout on? Thesis development.

Student 1: We have a handout on that.

Student 2: We do? I've never seen it . . .

Instructor: This week, I'm giving you homework. I would like you to explore the vast array of resources that we have in the WC.

The instructor hands out a scavenger hunt worksheet. (See below for an example.)

Instructor: You have 7 days to complete this scavenger hunt—we will share the answers in class next week, collate them, and post them on the WC bulletin board so that everyone in the WC can benefit.

The "Writing Center Scavenger Hunt" is a fun way for students to familiarize themselves with the WC's resources. When thinking of questions, try to broaden the concept of "resources" beyond handouts and handbooks; questions can include queries about your WC policies and history. The ultimate benefit, however, is that tutors begin to see each other as a resource. Their knowledge base is extended to include both the materials and the people of the WC. Furthermore, because interns have to engage everyone in the WC, from the director to the graduate tutors to the office manager, they extend their community base as well.

If the scavenger hunt is particularly long or difficult, you may want to pair interns together. Give them about 1 week to complete the scavenger hunt. Then, post or e-mail the answers to everyone in the WC, demonstrating that your tutors have just created yet another resource!

WRITING CENTER SCAVENGER HUNT

Directions: Please answer all of the questions below by next week. For the questions in quotation marks, you will need to find one person for whom the statement is true. For the other questions, you may have to hunt around the writing center!

1. "I can explain punctuation really well." _____

2. "I am proficient in writing lab reports." _____

3. Name three OWLs that can help a student with organization and structure.

   _____, _____, _____

4. "I understand what it's like to learn English as a second language."

   _____

5. What are three sources you could use in looking up APA citation guidelines?

   _____, _____, _____

6. When was our writing center started? _____

7. Where are the cover letter handouts located? _____

8. By what week in the semester should your schedule be finalized?

   _____

9. What is the sequence of papers in English 101? _____,

   _____, _____, _____

10. "I have presented at a writing center conference."

    _____

    Title of Presentation:

    _____

11. "I have tutored in another writing center." _____

    Where? _____

SCENE 5: Identify the Writing Center Theorist

The week after Thanksgiving break. A few interns are killing some time before class in the writing center waiting area, chatting about their final paper—a synthesis of their tutoring philosophy with the theories they have read in class. They are clearly anxious about the paper. The instructor is seated at the front desk, sorting through feedback forms.

Student 1: I think I'll use Mickey Harris to talk about my frustrations with faculty perceptions of the WC.

Student 2: Don't you mean North and "The Idea of A Writing Center?"

Student 1: Oh, right. Man, I'm going to have to re-read everything just to write this stupid paper.

Student 3: Nah—just skim the first and last paragraphs, and you'll get the gist.

The instructor logs onto her email and writes the following message to her class:

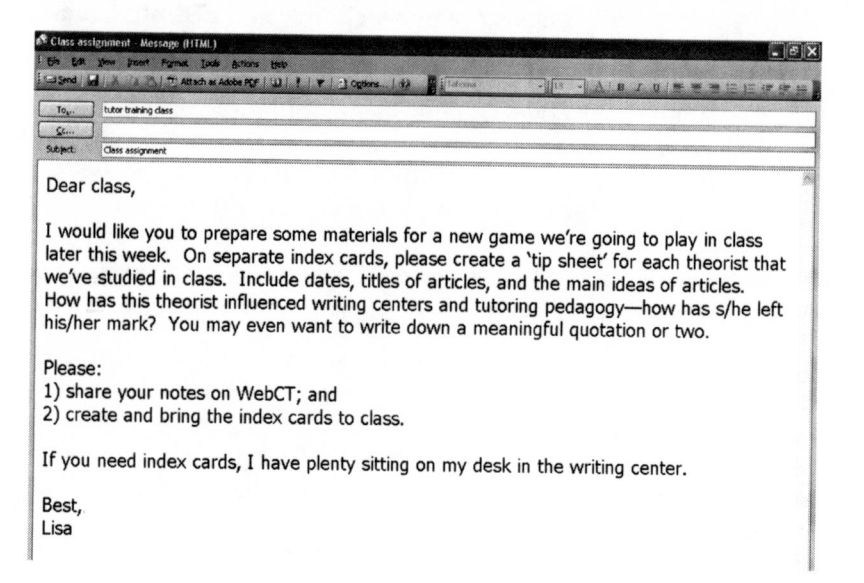

Dear class,

I would like you to prepare some materials for a new game we're going to play in class later this week. On separate index cards, please create a 'tip sheet' for each theorist that we've studied in class. Include dates, titles of articles, and the main ideas of articles. How has this theorist influenced writing centers and tutoring pedagogy—how has s/he left his/her mark? You may even want to write down a meaningful quotation or two.

Please:
1) share your notes on WebCT; and
2) create and bring the index cards to class.

If you need index cards, I have plenty sitting on my desk in the writing center.

Best,
Lisa

A few days later, preparing for class, the instructor fills her IWCA bag with the following items:

- *Separate labels with the names of the theorists, printed on bright paper.*
- *Tape*

- *Costume materials: wigs, glasses, hats, pipes, costume jewelry, fake mustaches, etc.*

Instructor: I understand that the final paper is demanding, as it asks you both to articulate your philosophy of tutoring and to synthesize that philosophy with the theories that we've read in class. In other words, what I am asking of you for this final paper is that you enter a conversation with other people in the writing center field.

Well, we're going to practice that conversation today! I will affix the name of a theorist on every intern's back. You will then get up, mingle, and ask each other "yes and no" questions to try to arrive at the identity of the theorist on your back. You can use your index cards for help in both generating questions and answers.

Now, please don't just run down the list of names; you must ask each person at least four questions before you guess the name on your back. A few examples of questions are: "Was I involved in the early days of writing center theory?"; "Does my research focus on ESL students?"; "Have I been integral in tutor training?."

When you've figured out who you are, please have a seat and jot down the questions and answers that helped you arrive at your identity. Then come up to the table, pick through the costume materials I have here, and create a costume that you believe represents the "new" you.

After everyone has deduced who they are and is in costume, the instructor asks each to get up and introduce him or herself as the theorist in the first person.

"Identify the Writing Center Theorist" serves as a nice review for WC theory. The index cards that the tutors create can be used later as they study, and if they post their notes online, they can share and create knowledge together. If you do have an online component, I suggest allowing ample time for discussion so that tutors can debate about the theories and their contribution to WCs.

An alternative to this game is for tutors to role-play theorists. A week before class, ask each tutor to pick a theorist that they particularly identify with. Let them know that they will be "embodying" this theorist, and ask them to practice representing him or her. In class, put two tutors in the middle or front of the class, with one tutor role-playing as the student and the other role-playing as the tutor. The tutor should then tutor in the style best represented by the theorist they've selected. The class must then guess whose theory the tutor is utilizing in the tutoring session.

SCENE 6: Tutoring is Like . . .[1]

It's the final tutor training class. The instructor piles markers, magazines, scissors, posterboard, glue, glitter, and other miscellaneous art supplies on a table in the middle of the class.

Instructor: Congratulations! You've successfully made it through a very demanding course. For our final class, I would like you to explore what the act of tutoring symbolizes or means to you. In other words, I would like for you to come up with a metaphor for tutoring. I have brought an array of magazines for you to flip through to help generate ideas, or you may already know what "tutoring is like." Each one of you should grab a posterboard and visually represent your tutoring metaphor. Be creative! You certainly can use a combination of pictures and text if you'd like.

Asking tutors to create a metaphor for tutoring is a wonderful way to conclude the semester or training program. Tutors tend to select a fascinating array of metaphors, from flight attendant to pastry chef to jazz player. Using metaphors helps tutors to reflect on their beliefs, assumptions, and apprehensions of tutoring. It is important to provide enough time for tutors to share and discuss their tutoring metaphors, as classmates often help them extend the metaphor even further. An alternative, and one that works better earlier in the semester, is to ask tutors to think of a metaphor that characterizes writing and the roles tutors and writers play in the process.

> **"Asking tutors to create a metaphor for tutoring is a wonderful way to help them reflect on their beliefs, assumptions, and apprehensions about tutoring."**

Games can often be prewriting activities for written assignments. "Pass the Hat" and "In the Dark" can help prepare tutors to write a paper on tutoring "best practices" or a paper detailing the theory and praxis of conversation in tutoring sessions. "Person/Fact Match" will help tutors begin to open up regarding the difficult issue of gender/race/class/sexuality in the WC. Having talked and shared informally from their personal experiences, they may be more apt not to address such a topic from a "me versus them" binary. "Identify the Writing Center Theorist" requires tutors to review and synthesize the various theories they have read in class. This is nice preparation for any writing center formal or reflection/response paper. Finally, tutors can explore their tutoring metaphors through both text and image, and a paper serves as a nice complement to "Tutoring is like . . . ."[2]

In WC circles, we often talk about developing rapport between the writer and tutor, and we use strategies that hopefully make the writer comfortable and receptive to advice. Equally important is developing tutor-to-tutor rapport. For me, these games helped to synthesize what John Trimbur (1987) identifies as the two main impulses in tutor training: the model that "regards the peer tutor as an apprentice and often designs training courses as an introduction to teaching writing" and the model that "emphasizes the peer component" and "casts peer tutors as co-learners" (p. 292). If, as Trimbur asserts, "tutoring is a balancing act that asks tutors to juggle roles, to shift identity, to know when to act like an expert and when to act like a co-learner" (p. 292), then tutor training should provide tutors with the tools to negotiate how and when to juggle these roles. WC teachers are really good at providing tutors with content to help tutors act like experts; more difficult, I think, is teaching them how to act like co-learners. When tutors play games together, they learn together, collaborating as they play, analyzing as they laugh, and reflecting as they share.

> **"When tutors play games together, they learn together, collaborating as they play, analyzing as they laugh, and reflecting as they share."**

The last day of exams before holiday break and the WC is closed. The instructor hangs the tutoring metaphor posters around the center, hoping they'll inspire tutors and students alike in the spring semester.

NOTES

1. Thanks to Wendy Hayden, University of Maryland, for suggesting this visual activity.
2. For a "Creating a Metaphor for Tutoring" assignment sheet, please see Ryan and Zimmerelli (2006).

REFERENCES

Beasley, N., & Crerar, A. (2005). *Motivations for adults playing games*. Retrieved December 1, 2005, from http://isaga05.gatech.edu/pap/p026/ISAGA05_beasley.doc.

Brooks, J. (1991). Minimalist tutoring: Making the student do all the work. *Writing Lab Newsletter, 15*, 1-4.

Erikson, E. (1974). *Dimensions of a new identity: The 1973 Jefferson lectures in the humanities.* New York: W. W. Norton.

Erikson, E., & Erikson, J. M. (1987). *The life cycle completed.* New York: Norton.

Erikson, J.M. (1998). The importance of play in adulthood. An interview with Joan M. Erikson. Interview by Daniel Benveniste. *Psychoanalytical Study Child, 53,* 51-64.

Harris, M. (1992). Collaboration is not collaboration is not collaboration: Writing center tutorials vs. peer-response groups. In R. W. Barnett & J. S. Blumner (Eds.), *The Allyn and Bacon guide to writing center theory and practice* (pp. 272-287). Boston: Allyn & Bacon.

Rieber, L. P., Smith, L., & Noah, D. (1998). The value of serious play. *Educational Technology, 38,* 29-37.

Ryan, L., & Zimmerelli, L. (2006). *The Bedford guide for writing tutors* (4th ed.). Boston: Bedford/St. Martin's.

Trimbur, J. (1987). Peer tutoring: A contradiction in terms? In R. W. Barnett & J. S. Blumner (Eds.), *The Allyn and Bacon guide to writing center theory and practice* (pp. 288-295). Boston: Allyn & Bacon.

7

PUTTING THE "PLAY" BACK INTO ROLE-PLAYING

Tutor Training Through Interactive Performance

Sandee K. McGlaun

PROLOGUE

At the age of 6, I attended a production of the musical *Gypsy* presented at the 2-year college where my father taught as an assistant professor of chemistry. I imagine the scene in reality was less lavish than I recall it, but at the time I was enthralled by the whole affair: plush fold-down seats, a live orchestra, the colorful bright lights that came up on the stage. And then, a small group of children appeared on stage, portraying child acts auditioning for Uncle Herbie's traveling show: a girl with a flute, a boy with a drum, still another girl wearing tap shoes and a frilly dress. I recognized the girl with the flute as the daughter of another professor. She was only a few years older than I was. If she could be in a play, why couldn't I? At intermission, I tugged on my father's coat sleeve. "Daddy, *I* want to be in a real play with real costumes!"

A hard-knock life in the fickle theater was not what my father had in mind for his only daughter, so to his great relief, I ultimately chose another vocation for full-time employment: I studied creative writing, and then composition, and later became a writing center (WC) director. But I have remained a part-time stage actor for 25 years, and my theatrical background has given me an affinity for using skits and role-playing games to teach students about writing processes and tutoring practices. I have learned that for these exercises to work most effectively, it is imperative to bring out the "play" in the role-playing—a task that I, despite my own extensive experience as a stage player, have at times found challenging. Recalling my childhood desire to be in a "real play with real costumes" has proven instructive. Providing tutors with guidance on the rudiments of basic character development and theatrical delivery and integrating simple theatrical artifacts such as costumes and props into role-playing activities can open up new creative channels for tutors as they are learning their craft. Such "play" enables growth and development even as it relieves new tutors of some of their anxieties and creates an inviting atmosphere for all students who make use of writing center services.

ACT I: THE NECESSARY EXPOSITION

According to Catherine Garvey's seminal study on play, first published in 1977 and re-issued by Harvard University Press in 1990, "[p]lay is most frequent in a period of dramatically expanding knowledge of self, the physical and social world, and systems of communication; thus we might expect that play is intricately related to these areas of growth" (p. 1). Although Garvey's study focused specifically on childhood play, I think few would argue that the college experience, for most students, is marked by dramatic shifts in self-knowledge and a growing awareness of the complexities of the world they inhabit; students hired to work as tutors in a university WC may experience a particularly profound shift in their relationship to speaking, writing, and interpersonal "systems of communication" (p. 1). And yet, in a collegiate WC setting, where selective play might well enable growth in these areas, play is not so frequent; in fact, one popular textbook on tutoring devotes its first chapter to emphasizing the writing center as a "professional" space (Ryan, 2002), a descriptor that may well be seen as antithetical to play. Although issues of confidentiality and the consequences of making inappropriate evaluative comments must certainly be addressed with new tutors, allowing for some play in the writing center is beneficial, perhaps even necessary. As Scott L. Miller notes in Chapter 2 (this volume), the calls for "play" in the writing center are getting louder; Elizabeth Boquet (2002) specifically adopted the metaphor of "noise" for productive and playful writing center work. Putting the metaphor into (ahem) play is perhaps the challenge. Garvey (1977/1990) linked the "structures of play to the productive power of language" (p. 1), and her research indicates that "play has been linked with creativity, problem-solving, [and] language learning," among other "cognitive and social phenomena" (p. 5). Tutors and the writers who come to be tutored, then, could well benefit from the introduction of guided play into tutor training, especially if that play is productive, a conduit for learning, what Hans Ostrom (1997) called *plerk*: a fusion of "work and play" that is "more than the sum of the two parts" (p. 77).

ACT II: (WRITING CENTER) DIRECTING 101

For a theater buff such as myself, the most obvious mechanism for integrating "plerk" into the WC is role-playing. The value of this practice for tutor training seems to be taken for granted in tutoring textbooks, whose authors often include instructions for such exercises without any further context for or analysis of the merits of those exercises (see Meyer & Smith, 1987; Ryan, 2002). The general acceptance of the practice may result in part from the fact that tutors—perhaps, as Boquet (2002) noted, in unconscious homage to the "lockstep repetition of much of our advice to [them] ('Begin by asking the student what he or she would like to work on')"—tend to follow unwritten scripts of sorts anyway (p. 71). Boquet lamented the ways in which these self-imposed scripts circumscribe our work, potentially trapping us and the writers who visit us "in a feedback loop that becomes less and less about limitless possibility and more and more about modulation and control" (p. 71). Adhering too closely to the roles we are expected (or expect others) to play may restrict learning. "Where is the fun?" she asked (p. 71).

I found myself asking the same question when I decided to incorporate role-playing in my own tutor training workshops and classes during my first year as a WC director at a small state university in the north Georgia mountains. Like the textbooks, I, too, assumed the value inherent in such exercises, but when I asked students to role-play in class or staff meetings, I was typically disappointed in the results. The role-plays felt artificial: In scripted role-plays, the tutors tended to read their parts in halting or colorless voices; if improvised, the tutors seemed self-conscious and uncomfortable. They often had difficulty staying "in the scene" and instead looked frequently at their classmates and me to approve of their choices. At the time, I puzzled briefly over this state of affairs, but with so much else yet to learn, I did not dwell on it for long.

Then, my tutors came to me with a problem. As part of their training, we had read Jeff Brooks' (1991) "Minimalist Tutoring: Making the Student Do All the Work" and had discussed, at length, the differences between collaborative tutoring practices that promoted deep learning and the ongoing development of the writer and her process,[1] and product-oriented, "fix-it shop" practices that not only interfered with learning but violated our academic integrity policy in the form of collusion. We noted that tutors who focused on improving a single paper and therefore made decisions or corrections for the writer would not only be defeating our collaborative mission; they would also be in violation of Article One of our campus integrity policy, which stated that "No student shall receive or give assistance not authorized by the instructor in the preparation of any essay, laboratory report, examination, or other assignment included in an academic course."

Armed with this newfound knowledge, the WC tutors became concerned about some students in the honors program who were working as "subject" tutors sans any formal tutorial training. Several members of the WC staff who were also part of the honors program witnessed some of the subject tutors correcting mistakes for other students and feeding them ideas during honors program tutorial sessions. Their collusion was clearly unintentional; these were good students, hard workers who were simply uninformed. The WC tutors wanted to address the problem, so we decided to create a workshop on effective collaborative tutoring strategies and present it to the honors program tutors, as well as to the Corps of Cadets Academic Non-Commanding Officers (NCO), who were charged with coordinating subject tutoring and general academic assistance for first-semester cadets.

I recognized this project as an opportunity to extend and enhance the WC tutors' training, so I elected to let them develop much of the material for the workshop. During an initial brainstorming session, we determined that the most effective way to present the material would be in the form of role-playing skits, because skits would enable us to entertain as well as enlighten. Ultimately, we decided to create and present three role-playing skits, which we fondly came to refer to as the good, the bad, and the ugly. The good skit would demonstrate effective collaborative tutoring practices, and it would actually come last in the presentation, as a model send off; the skit demonstrating bad, collusive strategies would come first, to spark recognition. In the middle, framed with some discussion, we would "mix it up" and present the "ugly" skit, and ask the audience members to interrupt our performance to name which practices were collusive and which were collaborative.

I assigned the tutors the task of drafting the skits, working in pairs. They drafted and revised, and together we polished and honed the language (see Appendix A for copies of the skit scripts). The final scripts were witty and smart: the "bad" skit, "The Domino Theory (of Tutoring)" punned on its title, featuring a discussion of a history paper on the Domino Theory as related to the Vietnam War, as well as a series of collusive practices that piled up one on top of the other; the "ugly" skit, in which the writer decided to argue that "the greatest invention of the twentieth century" was the paper clip, made several tongue-in-cheek references to the dreaded "Red Pen O' Doom"; and the "good" skit neatly demonstrated how to tutor a student in the importance of backing up claims with evidence and correct comma usage all in one 6-minute session. I assigned each tutor a role to play in one of the three skits, and I enjoined them to rehearse their parts in anticipation of our presentation to the honors program tutors and the Academic NCOs.

The resulting presentation taught me a valuable lesson about why the role-plays I was employing in training had not measured up to my expectations. A natural performer and (admittedly) a bit of a ham, I had not thought to "direct" the tutors in terms of expression and staging in the workshop skits; I anticipated that they would differentiate characters and find appropriate vocal emphasis on their own. I thought they understood that we had chosen skits—and that I had elected to do role-plays in class—precisely because it would enable us to "play," or perhaps more accurately, "plerk" (Ostrom, 1997): Writing and performing the skits would allow them to have fun and be creative at the same time that they were interrogating and modeling effective tutoring strategies; likewise, our workshop audience would "plerk" as they learned and laughed simultaneously. But although this first presentation of the workshop went well on the whole—the tutors were prepared and most professional—none of us was particularly playful, and the participants' evaluations[2] signaled that although they had found the session informative, they had not found it entertaining. We had worked, but we had not effectively played, either in the sense of having fun or of being theatrically engaging. Only then did I realize that the tutors weren't getting the "play" in the role-plays. They were too anxious and self-conscious to relax into the playful aspects of the exercises. And because it was precisely the linking of the "structures of play to the productive power of language" that facilitated learning (Garvey, 1990, p. 1), if they didn't get the play, they didn't get much out of the exercises.

A similar problem is explored in many acting textbooks. An actor who is too self-conscious and cannot forget about the self-as-actor cannot fully realize a character, cannot effectively "play." Thus, many such texts emphasize the importance of physical action, of concentrating on "doing" rather than "being" or "feeling." "The question never is, 'How would I feel if I were a character in these circumstances?' The question always is, 'What would I do?'" (McGaw & Clark, 1987, p. 45). By focusing on doing and other external characterization techniques—movement, gestures, manipulating props and costumes—the actor may lose self-consciousness and experience the power of believing that the acting moment is real. In tutor training as in acting, the more real a role-play becomes to the role-player, the more real and engaging it will be to the audience—and the tutor is more likely to learn from that which feels akin to a "real" experience.

To bring out the "play" in the role-playing skits, I knew that I would need to rehearse a few new roles myself: acting coach and costume designer. These tasks became especially important when our workshop was accepted for presentation at the 2003 Southeastern Writing Centers Association Conference. Although we had always considered the workshop interactive, in light of the audience participation it involved, I now began thinking of it also as a *performance*. First, the tutors and I re-envisioned each of the characters in the skits as *characters*, with distinct personalities, and we discussed how to realize these characters specifically through external techniques such as gesture, props, and dress. The writer in the "bad" collusion sketch was costumed in a heavy, buttoned-up coat and a baseball cap pulled low over the eyes to signal lack of interest in and resistance to the tutorial. This resistance was emphasized by the actions of crossing the arms, sitting back in the chair, even drifting off to sleep every so often. The writer in the "ugly" skit, who was supposed to be confused, twirled her hair and alternately studied the pattern in her arty floral scarf and gazed distractedly around the room. The writer in the "good" skit strode in confidently, made direct eye contact with the tutor, and wore jeans and a T-shirt (our attempt to represent "Everystudent").

The simple costumes visually cued the audience to a sense of playfulness that had been missing from our earlier presentation. Because the "tutors" in the skits needed to be representative, almost archetypal, we dressed the "bad" tutor devilishly, complete with a headband of flashing red "devil" horns. The "good" tutor, conversely, was dressed angelically, her "goodness" emphasized by a feather boa "halo" headband.[3]

The costumes clearly signaled our intent to entertain as well as enlighten and gave the audience permission to laugh, although the biggest laughs came from a prop. For the tutor of the "ugly" session, we fashioned a two-foot long "Red Pen O' Doom" from a red-painted mailing tube and a funnel. During the performance, the tutor and tutee wrangled over the giant pen, pushing and pulling it back and forth in an exaggerated battle of wills and (if I do say so myself) a marvel of comic timing.

The conference audience loved our interactive performance. Their positive feedback gave us the courage to revise the workshop for a general student audience, with the goal of presenting a campuswide version at our home university the following fall. We reasoned that if honors program tutors were unaware of how to help others without colluding (even if unintentionally), there was a reasonably good chance that students who "helped" their friends and roommates were colluding as well. The tutors, in fact, regularly saw evidence of collusion in their own dorms and in marked-up papers that student writers brought to the WC. In keeping with our mission, we felt we needed to do more to promote collaborative tutoring practices across campus. We tweaked the skits and the handouts so that they referenced "friends" instead of "tutors," and scheduled our first presentation of "Collaboration vs. Collusion: What Every Student Needs to Know." We publicized the workshop as a follow-up to the Academic Integrity Council's annual "Panel Discussion on Plagiarism," which introduced students to three kinds of plagiarism: intentional borrowing from print or internet sources, unintentional borrowings resulting from careless citation practices, and collusion. Students always had questions about collusion at the end of the plagiarism panel; our interactive performance could offer answers. And because many instructors required their students to attend the Panel on Plagiarism, we felt reasonably certain they would encourage attendance at our presentation as well.

The tutors have since presented "Collaboration vs. Collusion" at least once a year to a packed auditorium of mostly first-year students. They rave about how much fun they have preparing and performing together each year, and the experience of memorizing lines and rehearsing characters really helps them internalize knowledge of effective tutoring strategies. A second benefit of these repeat campus performances reflects this collection's thesis: If students outside of the writing center get to "play" with us and perceive the WC as a fun place to be, they are more likely to seek out our services.

> **"If students outside of the writing center get to "play" with us and perceive the WC as a fun place to be, they are more likely to seek out our services."**

Because the WC staff changes each year as experienced tutors graduate and new ones come in, interactive performance continues to play a role (pun intended) in tutor training; however, that role, in relation to "Collaboration vs. Collusion," has made a necessary shift from featured to supporting. Because the tutors typically perform the workshop in October, it cannot contribute to setting a friendly tone at the beginning of the semester, and it comes too late to help allay new tutors' anxiety about their new jobs. Recognizing this, I transferred the lessons of the interactive performance experience to the role-plays I conduct in pre-semester tutor training and in tutor training class, partly to balance the necessary emphasis on professional behavior with a little play, and partly to help relieve new tutors' anxiety about their first tutorials.

ACT III: THE PLAY'S
THE TUTOR TRAINING THING

A number of tutoring textbooks deal with writer's anxiety (Meyer & Smith, 1987; Rafoth, 2000; Ryan, 2002), but a less explored subject is the anxiety that *tutors* feel when they are first learning and practicing their craft. I believe this anxiety is at the root of tutors' self-consciousness in role-playing exercises, so for one of our pre-semester tutor training workshops, I adapted some of the lessons I had learned from "Collaboration vs. Collusion" to the in-class role-plays.

After covering operating procedures, talking about our tutoring philosophy, and going over some basic tutoring strategies, such as asking "how" and "why" questions and letting the writer hold the pen, we turned, as I had always done in previous training sessions, to role-playing tutoring scenarios. But this time, I had come prepared to turn the role-plays into interactive performances. Drawing an exercise outlined in Leigh Ryan's (2002) *A Bedford Guide for Writing Tutors*, I designed an exercise that would engage the new tutors in what I hoped would be genuine plerk. First, I created six characters (one for each of six new tutors): Conrad Complainer, Donna Demanding, Flora Flake, Frederick Freshman, Robert Rebel, and Stella Studious. I was concerned about inadvertently stereotyping students, so I based the portraits largely on behaviors rather than on categories such as "English as a second language writer" or "nontraditional student," and I made a point of creating gender equity. For each of the six characters, I composed a written character portrait (see Appendix B) that included the character name, a description of the costume pieces I was supplying and their significance, a list of characteristic gestures, a list of props with a description of their significance, a description of the situation that brought the character to the WC, and an opening line with which to begin the improvisation.

During the role-playing part of the training workshop, I distributed the character portraits, with instructions that each tutor would take turns playing the writer, as specified in their individual character descriptions; and the tutor, as themselves. I explained that the rest of the staff and I would watch each mock tutorial unfold for 5 to 10 minutes, and then discuss what had worked well in the session, and what alternative choices, if any, the tutor might have made to better help the student writer. Then, after each tutor had had a chance to read over his or her character card, I gave each a sealed grocery bag, which I had prepared the night before. Each bag contained a nametag with the character's name, the specified costume pieces, and a few props. Before each role-play, the "writer" stepped out into the hall to assume his or her new identity and re-entered the WC in costume.

Some of the costume pieces, such as Stella Studious' wool blazer and Frederick Freshman's Widespread Panic T-shirt (because he loved the band and because he was feeling "widespread panic"), were simply pulled from my own closet, but several of the costumes were designed (literally) especially for the exercise: I created character-specific T-shirts from copyright-free clip-art printed out onto iron-on paper and ironed on to extra-large tees. In this way, I provided Donna Demanding with a T-shirt that read "What part of NOW don't you understand?" to accompany her large watch, which she consulted frequently and ostentatiously, and Conrad Complainer with a T-shirt that featured a man bent under the weight of knowledge in the form of a very large book. Poor Conrad also carried a heavy anthology in his hand. Robert Rebel (inspired by the writer in the "bad" tutoring skit described earlier) was supplied with an oversized sweatshirt to retreat into, as well as headphones and a hat to pull low over his eyes, while Flora Flake (inspired by the writer in the "ugly" tutoring skit) was outfitted with a "funky hat and arty scarf," also taken from my own closet. Props were also suited to character and situation: Stella Studious brought a tidy book-bag filled with a notebook, grammar handbook, pocket dictionary, highlighter, pen, pencil, and project folder, her assignment tucked neatly inside; Robert Rebel, whose key identifying characteristic was that he "would really rather be somewhere else" brought along a "crumpled paper that has been graded and returned," and nothing else.

Despite the fact that none of the tutors outside of one had any previous serious theatrical experience—and none of them had any formal tutoring experience—all of them rose to the occasion with great enthusiasm. Robert sulked convincingly, Stella spoke confidently, and Donna interrupted rudely. I knew from my own acting experiences that external characterization techniques are key to the loss of self-consciousness in stage performance,[4] but I was surprised at the degree to which this was true for the tutors in their role-plays, as well. In *Building a Character* famed actor, director, and teacher Constantin Stanislavski (1936/2003) recounted an incident in his own training when he and his fellow students were instructed to select a costume from wardrobe and perform a "masquerade" for their instructor Tortsov. Dressed in a mildewy, faded morning coat and made up with greasepaint smears that mottled and erased his features, the persona of Stanislavski's own inner Critic emerges, a bold, brash character who rudely challenges the elder Tortsov in ways the "real" student Stanislavski would never dream of doing. In analyzing Stanislavski's successful performance, Tortsov remarked, "What makes him so bold? The mask and costume behind which he hides. In his own person he would never dare to speak as he does in the character of this other personality for whose words he does not feel himself responsible" (p. 28). The tutors' writer-character costumes served as disguises of sorts; by physicalizing the characters, the costumes gave them permission to behave differently, largely freeing them from their self-consciousness and giving them space to (literally) play.

What was most impressive, however, were their performances in these role-plays as "tutors." As previously noted, when I had asked tutors to role-play in the past, sans props and costumes and silly names, I often got half-hearted performances on both sides; those playing writers seemed uncomfortable, and although those playing tutors typically approached the activity with a great (perhaps too great) seriousness of purpose, they remained uncomfortably self-conscious as well. Although one might think that costumes and props would only add a layer of artificiality and thus increase discomfort, they had the opposite effect, for the reasons Tortsov named above. The writer-character performances invariably elicited giggles, which dispelled tension and took some of the focus off the "performance" of the tutors-as-tutors. With the loss of self-consciousness, they were more able to experience the mock tutorial as "real"; consequently, their first (mock) tutorials were at once more real and more fun than they expected. I saw some of the most effective "first (mock) tutorials" I had ever witnessed, and the tutors and I came out of the training confident about their ability to learn and grow as tutors and persuaded that tutoring is, indeed, fun.

EPILOGUE

For my performance as ovarian cancer patient Dr. Vivian Bearing in a campus production of *Wit*, I buzz-cut my normally chin-length hair down to a half-inch nub. I cut my hair in stages to soften the blow, and although I now wish I had had the courage to go all the way and shave my head bald, I nonetheless felt my understanding of the character's fear and pain grow with each successive trim. I am not recommending that WC directors do anything so dramatic as shave their heads, nor even that we make a major theatrical production out of every role-playing exercise we bring into our tutor training classrooms and workshops. But playing with theatrical artifacts such as costumes and props has enabled my staff to put the play back into role-playing in our WC, which in turn has lessened new tutors' anxiety and helped them to internalize effective tutoring strategies; playing with interactive performance has also enabled us to reach out to other tutors on campus and address crucial writing issues with students in an engaging and entertaining way. Overall, it has made our writing center a more inviting place to be. As Sharon Pugh, Jean Wolph Hicks, and Marcia Davis (1997), authors of *Metaphorical Ways of Knowing* suggest, we need not sacrifice the "values of experimentation, originality, and playfulness" for those of "precision, structure, and clarity" (p. vii). Instead, we can work—and play—to create WC spaces in which all of these values are cultivated.

> **"Interactive performance has enabled us to reach out to other tutors on campus and address crucial writing issues with students in an engaging and entertaining way."**

APPENDIX A
"Collaboration vs. Collusion" Skit Scripts

These are the most recent versions of the skits, revised for presentation to the campus at large. The "Friend" in each skit is the "Tutor." When we presented the interactive performance, we framed the skits with some discussion of the concepts of collaboration and collusion. During the performance, we played Skit 1 through first, then re-played it, having asked the audience to stop us whenever they saw examples of collusion. We did the same with Skit 2, in that case asking the audience to stop us when they saw examples of either collusion or collaboration. Typically we closed with Skit 3.

Note: I frequently have more female than male tutors working in my writing center, so several of the skits were constructed around female characters initially—thus the feminine pronouns in Skit 2. Any of the skits can be altered to suit the casting pool, however. We once performed a version of Skit 2 featuring a male student as the "flaky" writer. We eliminated the scarf and added some business with the pen—scratching behind the ear with it, and so on. It worked well.

Skit 1: The Domino Theory (of Tutoring)
(the "bad")

(Friend sits at a table with two chairs, wearing a headband with flashing red devil horns. Writer enters from stage left, wearing a thick down parka and a baseball cap pulled low over the eyes.)

Writer: Hey _____, you're a good writer. Can you proofread my paper? It's for Dr. Jane Doe. She's the hardest professor here. She's so boring and mean!

Friend: Yeah, she is the worst professor here.

(Writer slings book bag onto floor and roots around for the paper. Hands it to Friend, then sits down and leans back in chair. Crosses arms. Still wears coat and hat, maybe even headphones.)

Friend: *(Reads paper silently.)* Oh, uh, what's your assignment exactly?

Writer: *(Without much interest.)* Something about the reasons for the U.S. getting involved in the Vietnam War.

Friend: Oh, okay. I had that class! (*Reads again and makes a note on the paper.*) I would just add some more evidence here, explaining what the domino theory is.

Writer: I don't even know what that is.

Friend: It's when politicians believed that if Vietnam fell to Communism, then it would open the gateway for Communism from China to spread to the rest of Southeast Asia.

Writer: (*Takes pen from Friend and writes word for word on paper. Reads aloud as s/he writes.*) "Then it would open . . . gateway . . ."? Can you say that again?

Friend: Sure! Politicians believed that if Vietnam fell to Communism— (*Writer looks up with a puzzled expression*). Oh, C-O-M-M-U-N-I-S-M—then all of Southeast Asia would fall, too.

Writer: (*Searches through notebook.*) Oh, should I write about the, uh, containment theory with that?

Friend: Nah, I wouldn't in this paper.

Writer: Okay. Um, I really don't understand commas. How do I fix that? (*Hands pen back to Friend, pushes paper over, and sits back in chair, as before.*)

Friend: (*Writes on Writer's paper.*) Well, you don't need one here. Let's see . . . this one's good. This one is unnecessary. (*Continues writing on paper, making corrections. Writer, meanwhile, is either drifting off into a snooze or rocking out to music on headphones.*)

Friend: Okay!

Writer: (*Opens eyes but makes no move to reclaim the paper.*) So after you fix everything, what grade do you think I will get?

Friend: Oh, I would definitely give you an A. This paper is great.

Writer: Sweet!

Skit 2: The Paper Clip Predicament
(the "ugly")

(*Friend sits at a table with two chairs. The Red Pen O' Doom is concealed behind or underneath the table. Writer enters from stage left. She is easily distracted and not a little flaky. She frequently twirls her hair around her finger and stares off into space.*)

Writer: Hi, _____. I have this big paper I'm writing about the greatest inventions of the twentieth century, and I already had my brother proofread it. Could you just look at it and tell me what else I did wrong, and fix it?

Friend: Well, I can't really proofread it *for* you, but we can look at it together, and talk about how to improve it.

Writer: Okay, whatever.

Friend: (*Scans paper, then whips out the Red Pen O' Doom. Starts making marks. Finally catches self and stops. Pushes pen toward Writer.*) You need to reword your thesis.

Writer: (*Taking pen reluctantly.*) What do you mean?

Friend: Well, I don't understand your argument. Could you more clearly define exactly what you want to convey about the significance of paper clips within this paper?

Writer: (*Shaking head and handing pen back to Friend.*) I don't understand. How do I do that?

Friend: (*Taking pen, but not writing with it.*) Well, you could say something like, "The paper clip is the most useful invention of the 20th century because (*gestures absently with pen*) it can hold things together, it is magnetic (*Writer now enthusiastically grabs Red Pen O' Doom from Friend and starts writing on her paper*), it can be made into a chain necklace, and it is very shiny." (*Writer copies down everything Friend said, verbatim. Friend looks uneasy.*)

Writer: Yeah, that sounds good. I'll put that.

Friend: Well, um . . . that was just an example thesis. You need to decide on one for yourself that you write. What are *you* trying to argue with this paper?

Writer: (*Struggles a moment, then speaks slowly as she crosses out some words and rearranges the sentence composed by Friend.*) I guess I am trying to say . . . being very shiny, being able to be made into a chain necklace, being magnetic, and holding things together all make the paper clip the most useful invention of the 20th century. (*Gives Friend a quizzical look.*)

Friend: Um . . . it sounds . . . well, it sounds like you've just reworded everything I said.

Writer: Is that bad?

Friend: Well, it's better if you write it in your very own words. What I gave you was just a suggestion. Do you really want to argue that paper clips are useful because they are shiny? I was just . . . you know—

Writer: Yeah, but I liked that. It's funny. Whatever. I'll work on that later. Anyway, I was wondering about how to reorder these paragraphs and ideas? What do you think? What should go where?

Friend: You can start by putting this information before *this* information (*Friend takes pen and starts to organize paper for the Writer*). And you could move this paragraph here, and then. . . . (*Makes a few more notes before actively and noticeably catching herself and stopping. Pushes pen back toward the Writer.*) What arrangement do *you* think would best suit what you're trying to say? What order do you think would flow the best and make the paper stronger, overall?

Writer: (*Getting the picture and taking pen.*) Oh . . . well, I guess if I move this paragraph here . . . (*Makes a note*). What about elaborating this idea? I think it would make my quote here fit in better . . . (*Begins to work on her own, randomly making comments aloud to herself. Then, still holding pen—*) Well, thanks for all your help!

Friend: You're welcome! See you later.

Skit 3: Don't Hesitate to Collaborate
("the good")

(*The Friend sits at a table with two chairs, wearing a feather boa halo. The Writer enters from stage left, carrying a notebook.*)

Writer: Hi, _____, you're a good writer. Can you proofread my paper?

Friend: I can't proofread it *for* you. But I'll be happy to read your paper and respond to it. We can work on your paper together.

Writer: (*Sits down.*) Okay, I need help. This paper is for the toughest professor on campus. He's so mean.

Friend: A lot of professors are challenging, but you can learn a lot that way.

Writer: Yeah, I guess.

Friend: Can I see your assignment?

Writer: Here's my assignment sheet. (*Pulls paper from notebook and hands it to Friend, who peruses it.*)

Friend: It looks like your assignment is to do a character analysis.

Writer: Yeah, I decided to discuss Hamlet.

Friend: Okay, there are a couple of ways we can do this. One of us can read your paper aloud, or I can just read it silently.

Writer: Would you mind reading it silently? (*Hands paper to Friend.*)

Friend: No, that's fine. (*Takes and reads paper silently for a few moments.*) Could you explain to me why exactly you feel that Hamlet hesitates?

Writer: Have you read the play?

Friend: Yes, but why don't you tell me what you think. What would be good evidence to support your assertion that Hamlet hesitates?

Writer: Okay. I think that Hamlet shows hesitation when he holds back and doesn't stab Claudius when Claudius is praying. I could use that example.

Friend: Great. Be sure to back up all your claims with evidence, like you just did. Ask yourself if you have evidence to prove your argument. Can you find any other places where you might want to add examples?

Writer: I say that Hamlet uses a lot of strategies to try to prove the king's guilt. I could follow that claim with the example of when Hamlet brought the play to the palace to watch the king's reaction.

Friend: That sounds like another good example.

Writer: Okay. (*Makes a note, then frowns at the paper.*) Could you help me with commas? I don't understand them. Every time I have a conjunction, I put a comma before it, but I don't think that's right.

Friend: I can't fix it for you, but I can show you a great comma strategy. If you're debating whether or not to put a comma before a conjunction, then just cover the conjunction with your finger. Read what comes before and what comes after. If both phrases are independent clauses, meaning that they each contain a subject and a verb and would make sense if you read either of them alone, then place a comma before the conjunction. Otherwise, you may not need one. Let's look at a couple of examples.

Writer: Okay.

Friend: (*Flips over sheet of paper to write an example.*) Let's come up with an example not in your paper. If your sentence says, "I went on a walk with my dog and stopped by the post office," should you put a comma in this sentence?

Writer: Okay . . . I cover the "and" and read what comes before it. (*Reading.*) "I went on a walk with my dog." Okay, that makes sense by itself.

Friend: Good.

Writer: Now I read what comes after the "and." (*Reading.*) "Stopped by the post office." Okay, that doesn't make sense. It can't stand alone, so that means I don't need a comma there.

Friend: Great! You can apply that strategy anywhere in your paper.

Writer: Thanks so much for your help!

Friend: You're welcome!

APPENDIX B
Sample Character Portrait Cards
for Interactive Performance Role-Plays

Conrad Complainer

Costume: T-shirt featuring picture of a man bearing a heavy book burden

Characteristic Gestures: Lots of loud sighs. Laying head down on desk. You are overwhelmed, and show it with great drama.

Props: Assignment sheet: comparison of *Romeo and Juliet* with *A Midsummer Night's Dream*. Heavy textbook: *The Norton Shakespeare*. Heavy three-ring binder notebook. Everything seems heavy to you these days. Sooooo heavy. . . .

Situation: You are not a whiner—but you do have a lot of complaints. The class is too hard, the assignment is too difficult, the plays are impossible to read, the professor is mean, the book too heavy. . . . The tutor has a hard time getting you to talk about the writing assignment, because you keep talking about everything else. You need to unload on someone, and you treat the tutor more as a therapist than as a writing helper.

Opening Line: "I am so tired of lugging this book around. Good grief. And I can't believe this assignment!"

Stella Studious

Costume: Sharp blazer and studious glasses.

Characteristic Gestures: Whatever studious means to you . . . see props!

Props: You have a notebook, paper, project folder, pen, highlighter, pencil, your textbook, a dictionary, and a style guide. You neatly lay all of these items out on the table, in a precise arrangement, when you first arrive. You are Prepared with a capital P.

Situation: You are a good, solid student, so of course you came to the writing center! You are so eager that you do all the talking. Tutors love you, because you mostly think aloud and all they have to do is nod. But sometimes they might give good feedback if you'd slow down just a little . . .

Opening Lines: You don't say much until you have everything lined up and laid out. Then you don't stop—but it's all good stuff. "I have this assignment on great inventions, and I think I am going to write about sticky notes!"

ACKNOWLEDGMENTS

I offer a special thank you to the peer tutors who were the original co-authors and performers of the skits for the honors program tutors and Academic NCOs, and who made a poster presentation about their experiences at the 2002 IWCA conference in Savannah, Georgia: Sarah Ballew (the devious mind behind the "Red Pen O' Doom"), Carly Farrell, Eva Isselstein (who was instrumental in designing the original workshop structure), Jennifer (Koch) McCall, and Amanda Wood. I also wish to thank the cast of the interactive performance at our subsequent conference presentation entitled "Workshopping for Change: Collaboration vs. Collusion," given at SWCA 2003 in Charlotte, North Carolina: Sarah Ballew, Eva Isselstein, Anna Terry, and Amanda Wood. Thanks, too, to all the subsequent tutors who performed the skits on campus with enthusiasm and finesse.

Thanks also go to the editors of this volume, Kevin Dvorak and Shanti Bruce, for their insightful and generous feedback on drafts and the suggestion to claim the name "interactive performance" for my work, as well as to my WC colleague Scott Miller, who got me thinking about "play" in the first place.

NOTES

1. We are, of course, indebted not only to Jeff Brooks, but also to Stephen North (1984) and "The Idea of a Writing Center" for this philosophical and pedagogical stance, as are so many other WCs.
2. The half-page evaluations contained three questions:
   1. Please indicate your perception of the usefulness of the material presented in the workshop for you as a tutor: *very useful, useful, somewhat useful, not useful, neutral.* Please offer a brief statement explaining your choice.
   2. Please indicate your perception of the effectiveness of the presentation: very effective, *effective, somewhat effective, not effective, neutral.* Please offer a brief statement explaining your choice.
   3. What other writing-related topics would you like to see addressed in future WC workshops?
3. I am aware of the potential religious connotations of these costume choices; we chose the symbols for their iconic power to symbolize "evil" and "good," respectively, even in a secular setting.
4. I have played, among other roles, a fairy queen (Shakespeare's *A Midsummer Night's Dream*), an end-stage cancer patient (Margaret Edson's *Wit*), and more

recently, an 8-months pregnant woman with a vicious temperament (Tennessee Williams' *Cat on a Hot Tin Roof*). In each of these cases, external elements led to key character choices: Titania's filmy cape, given to me early in the rehearsal process, made me re-imagine my arms and hands as graceful wings capable of powerful emotional expression. As Vivian Bearing in *Wit*, the intravenous pole I was attached to for much of the show became my constant shadow, almost another character, one that caused Vivian frustration early in the play but later literally, physically supported me. And a weighted pregnancy pad changes one's entire center of gravity (as, of course, does pregnancy), as I discovered in *Cat on a Hot Tin Roof*, a particularly instructive experience. My character's nemesis, "Maggie the Cat," was played by a friend of mine, and in early rehearsals we had a hard time summoning up the venom for our "cat-fight" scenes without getting tickled; once I was in full costume—"pregnant" and sway-backed, capped in an ugly wig, and clad in a plaid maternity "tent" dress with an absurdly sweet sailor collar—I no longer looked or felt like myself, and "Mae's" envy of and hatred for the beautiful, manipulative "Maggie" made absolute sense. Many actors I have spoken with report similar experiences.

REFERENCES

Boquet, E. H. (2002). *Noise from the writing center.* Logan: Utah State University Press.

Brooks, J. (1991). Minimalist tutoring: Making the student do all the work. *Writing Lab Newsletter, 15*, 1-4.

Garvey, C. (1990). *Play* (enlarged ed.). Cambridge, MA: Harvard University Press. (Original work published 1977)

Meyer, E., & Smith, L. Z. (1987). *The practical tutor.* New York: Oxford University Press.

McGaw, C., & Clark, L. D. (1987). *Acting is believing: A basic method.* New York: Holt, Rinehart, & Winston.

North, S. (1984). The idea of a writing center. *College English, 46*(5), 433-446.

Ostrom, H. (1997). Grammar "J" as in jazzing around: The roles play plays in style. In W. Bishop (Ed.), *Elements of alternate style* (pp. 75-87). Portsmouth, NH: Boynton/Cook.

Pugh, S. L., Hicks, J. W., & Davis, M. (1997). *Metaphorical ways of knowing.* Urbana, IL: NCTE.

Rafoth, B. (Ed.). (2000). *A tutor's guide: Helping writers one to one.* Portsmouth, NH: Boynton/Cook.

Ryan, L. (2002). *The Bedford guide for writing tutors* (3rd ed.). Boston: Bedford/St. Martin's.

Stanislavski, C. (2003). *Building a character* (E. R. Hapgood, Trans.). New York: Routledge. (Original work published 1936)

8

INCORPORATING PLAY AND TOYS INTO THE WRITING CENTER

Chad Verbais

Psychologically, what are the reasons we play? Often, we play for escape—from the task at hand or a future task. And although this behavior can be dangerous, when used sparingly it can help us find a renewed sense of reason to continue. As an example, imagine sitting at a computer typing a long paper while receiving and sending several instant messages to a friend. Does this behavior interfere with the task at hand? Yes. However, does it help you focus once your conversation is over? Yes—especially if you were just given some information you had been waiting for. Just as important, however, did the brief bit of play renew you enough to continue? Chances are, it did.

* * *

When I was 8 years old, my parents bought me a desk so I could do homework in my room instead of at the kitchen table. This new arrangement worked well, especially considering that the kitchen in my house was usually a busy (and loud) place. However, being locked in my room with the distraction of a small clock radio, an army of action figures, sporting equipment and balls of all sorts, and several cases of Hot Wheels Cars proved to be a strain on my homework productivity. After the first week went by, and I started to get in trouble at school for not completing my assignments, I realized that I needed to lay off the fun and get serious about my studies. (Actually, if memory serves, my parents were the ones to quickly remind me that I should "buckle down" or else.)

Yet, the fun of playing glared at me from the top of my dusty shelves where figures and cars were sitting ready for action. I quickly reasoned that the toys needed to be played with, and wanted to be played with, especially because I was spending so much time in my room. However, I knew that if I did not complete my homework, the next day in school would be brutal. These two realizations brought me to the only logical conclusion—do both.

I decided that I would reward myself with some playtime after I had completed a certain percentage of my homework. The idea was that after I had completed a set of math problems, for instance, I would spend a few minutes zooming cars down a plastic racetrack before going on to the next set of problems. After a few hours, I was surprised at how much fun I could have learning and playing at the same time. Not only was I learning the assigned material, but I was also relaxing and having fun while doing so—homework did not seem like work anymore.

This learning style (of rewarding myself with a brief bit of play after a task) followed me through high school and college, and continues in some ways today. In college, I would often take a quick study break and play a computer game or practice golf mechanics by putting into a cup on the floor of my room. Now, I take breaks by quickly surfing the web between tasks or kicking/throwing a ball with my kids . . . ok, and sometimes I still play computer games. However, it was not until I came across a book during graduate school by Otto Weininger (1979), *Play and Education*, did it occur to me that play is actually an important part of the educational process. As Weininger stated, "if through dramatic play children learn something about expressing needs in a way both satisfactory to them and acceptable to society, they are learning something just as important to them as a cognitive skill, such as reading, and no doubt this learning will contribute to reading acquisition" (p. 40). This statement helped me realize something that I, perhaps, already knew—that in play it is easy to set up scenarios that have yet to occur so that when they do occur one has a certain degree of familiarity with the situation. It is through this familiarity that the person playing can anticipate reactions to situations and then provide educated responses to certain stimuli. Yet, more importantly, at least for me, is the idea that imagination is inspired through play—when we play we are in a fantasy world that often times is not bound to familiar dimensions of existence; rather, in play the rules are abolished in favor of whimsy and chance.

Prior to working in a writing center (WC) I did not think about using play in a professional setting—it seemed like something that was best utilized in a private setting. However, after finding Weininger's text again and reading a few other articles dealing with play and education, I began to notice how play, and especially spontaneous fun, was absent from our WC and from composition classes in general. This seemed troublesome because I knew how much anxiety students usually carried into a writing session, and it seemed like fun/play could help energize the atmosphere. Besides, the one word constantly mentioned in the articles I read was *creativity*, which naturally evolves from play. And because WC practitioners are constantly stressing creativity to students, it seemed logical that play could be incorporated into WC practice.

The more I thought about it, the more logical it seemed that the WC was a natural place to attempt to incorporate play in writing, especially considering our old name, *The Writing Lab*, and all the "experimental" ideas associated with a lab. However, the challenge would be to strike a balance so that all interested parties would still find the center inviting. So, by reading different articles and books about play and play theory, as well as discussing these thoughts with staff members and discovering that they too were interested in making the WC a fun and more inviting place where creativity flowed freely, we decided that at our center play was not only needed but also wanted as a component of the writing process.

> **"At our center, play was not only needed, but also wanted as a component of the writing process."**

THEORY

The theory of play might seem like an elementary topic to some. After all, as children we all play, and even as adults most of us play. However, what are the effects of play on the learning process?

L.S. Vygotsky (1978) stated that "play creates a zone of proximal development of the child. In play a child always behaves beyond his average age, above his daily behavior; in play it is as though he were a head taller than himself" (p. 102). This could explain why play in education can help us understand methods and concepts beyond our current learning ability. If we assume we are older, then the knowledge of that age should be easier to comprehend. However, to take the thought a step further, if we use play in education the degree to which we understand a concept could be increased due to the fantasy of being older, and thus wiser. Ideally, we would pretend to incorporate the knowledge into our new, and older, play-self but then find ways to incorporate that knowledge into our everyday thought processes. The same holds true for writing—if we challenge ourselves by playing with advanced concepts and/or expand our vocabulary by learning sophisticated words and playing with the varied complexities of sentence and paragraph structure then play, in that sense, will help make us more knowledgeable scholars.

Nina Lieberman (1977) stated in her book *Playfulness: Its Relationship to Imagination and Creativity* that "being able to accept fantasy assimilation in the young child expands his cognitive horizon and will stimulate original products" (p. 132). This idea lends itself to the thought that playfulness can stimulate creativity. Such creativity can obviously create interest in not only the project at hand, but future projects as well. Play, in this sense, is a precursor for creativity and understanding. In a WC, play can help students be creative and expand their thoughts. By allowing a student time to play, creative forces could likely be engaged and result in a more original text.

Furthermore, Michael J. Ellis (1973) wrote in his book *Why People Play* that "in the school play is justified from the viewpoint that its byproducts will be useful later. In recreation play is justified because it is accompanied by immediate benefits" (p. 120). It is easy to see how in recreation play is often considered part of our athletic training or simply staying in shape. However, in school the educator must carefully consider play before interjecting it in a classroom setting. Play that is used to fill gaps in the day will not be as productive from a learning standpoint for the student as compared to play used to reinforce or introduce a lesson. Play, when used appropriately, can help the student see connections that were not apparent before. In the WC, play can be used to visually demonstrate how a verb works, for instance, perhaps by zooming a car with a pencil attached to the roof. Play can also be used in the WC to, among other things, help students see connections or make outlines by grouping various toys together.

Most importantly, however, at least for my initial dive into this idea, was how Howard Gardner (1983) expanded on Jean Piaget's views to detail several intelligences that shape how an individual learns. According to Gardner, a tactile or kinesthetic learning characteristic is "the capacity to work skillfully with objects, both those that involve fine motor movements of one's fingers and hands and those that exploit gross motor movements of the body" (p. 206). Using toys in a WC environment can, in many ways, introduce a tactile learner to various writing concepts. A tactile learner can touch and manipulate toys that might represent parts of speech, or play with a toy such as a stress ball, which might help stimulate creativity during the session. Tactile learners can also play with magnetic poetry to physically move around words, just as they could play with hypertext on a computer screen. The idea of physical play can appeal to tactile learners who may be accustomed to the typical, and for them handicapping, visual presentation of writing instruction. The activity of play can then open up new doors of possibility for the creative writing forces within the mind of a tactile learner.

Psychologically, however, what are the reasons we play? Often, we play for escape—from the task at hand or a future task. And although this behavior can be dangerous, when used sparingly it can help us find a renewed sense of reason to continue. As an example, imagine sitting at a computer typing a long paper while receiving and sending several instant messages to a friend. Does this behavior interfere with the task at hand? Yes. However, does it help you focus once your conversation is over? Yes— especially if you were just given some information you had been waiting for. Just as important, however, did the brief bit of play renew you enough to continue? Chances are, it did.

In her article, "The Power of Play," Hara Estroff Marano (1999), talks with a leading proponent of play theory, Brian Sutton-Smith, who stated,

> the connections in the brain fade away unless used. We know that early stimulation of children leads to higher cognitive scores. Playful stimulation probably hits all kinds of synaptic possibilities. It is all make-believe and all over the map. The potentiality of the synapses and the potentiality of playfulness are a beautiful marriage. (p. 69)

Such an idea speaks volumes to WC practitioners who regularly play with words and ideas. This play, according to Sutton-Smith, is helping to expand our mind and make us even more creative. We need play, in a way, to connect patterns in our mind so that we can utilize the complex ideas that are born from such neural connections.

Play can renew. Play can inform. Above all, play can help an individual move forward and use some of the knowledge and comfort gained from such an activity while facing future challenges and improving on past performances. It seems only natural then that with a task such as writing, which requires a substantial amount of practice to become good, play is interjected with success.

WHY ARE WE CREATIVE IN THE CENTER?

Writing is such a personal activity, especially when you consider that most people sit alone with a pencil and paper, or monitor and keyboard, expounding thoughts. It is only natural then that such a personal activity creates a certain amount of stress when you invite someone to share it. When students ask for help with their personal writing, this feeling of stress can be compounded because of a fear of failing to meet the writing assignment criteria, being unclear in how they convey their thoughts, or simply because of previous bad experiences with feedback concerning their writing.

To alleviate student fears and anxieties, it is important to create an atmosphere conducive to relaxation and, in some ways, fun. Some centers try to create such an atmosphere by plastering the walls with artwork, inspirational posters, or insightful quotes; yet, others will populate the space with oversized chairs or comfortable couches, while some go as far as creating different moods with light from windows or overhead bulbs. Partitions are erected, offices are built, and white noise is used all in an effort to make the student feel safe, unembarrassed, and free to discuss thoughts and writing without fear.

And while the feeling of safety is often apparent in a WC, fun is still almost always missing. People usually come to the WC in a highly stressed state, which can be exacerbated by a hostile environment. Introducing an element of fun into the center can help relax people and take their minds off the problem at hand. When we introduced fun in our center, the idea was to not only help people see that coming into the WC could be fun, but also to help them see that the writing process could be fun as well.

> **"To alleviate student fears and anxieties, it is important to create an atmosphere conducive to relaxation and fun."**

Like many WCs, we constantly fight a battle between what is in line with our mission and what the faculty, staff, and students think should be included in our services. Individuals often viewed our WC as a place where they could have their work proofread and, even worse, edited. Because these expectations were not decreasing as much as we would have liked, and based on our discussions on play and education, we decided to interject some fun into our sessions to see how individuals would respond. The idea was that we would help the students relax and look at their own writing from a different perspective. Our hope was that the students would like the new approach and attempt to utilize these techniques during future writing sessions on their own.

We also noticed that even though the students were coming to the center with questions, they were not really engaged in the writing task. Many simply wanted to get an "A" on the paper and needed advice on how to do that, whereas others were required to have someone else give feedback on their work before turning it in. In both cases, the student was nervous that the "red pen of death" would rear its ugly head and shatter all hopes of making confident and independent changes that could result in a better paper and more knowledgeable writer. In other words, students were apprehensive about coming into the center for help. We wanted to change that feeling and make the whole experience fun and rewarding.

METHOD OF CREATIVITY

I suppose it would be fair to say that I was alone with this idea when I first implemented it. The whole concept really started one summer when our WC was not as busy with students and not as congested with tutors—actually, I am the only one on staff during most summers, but the students seem to be very understanding. I began by throwing a football to selected incoming students, or a beach ball, or asking one to putt into a cup before we sat down. In each case, the activity was a natural icebreaker, and the students seemed to relax considerably. After a few sessions, I even began asking several questions about their paper as we were performing the activity. The success was wonderful in that the students really began opening up about their writing and were obviously having fun while doing so.

I recall one particular session when a student and I started putting into a cup while talking about her paper. She wanted help with the organization of the text and to make sure it "flowed" properly (a common request in our WC). And although she was getting lucky and making a few putts from long range, while I was misjudging what had to be a hidden slope in the floor, we kept talking about her paper and the organization of her ideas. I was stressing clarity when she sank what was about a 25-foot putt and exclaimed, "just like that—get right to the point, eh?!" It was a bit humbling, especially because this was my "home" course, but the lesson seemed to sink in. After we talked more about organization and I helped her with some transition points, she told me that our session was her best writing experience ever.

Based on that experience, and others that went much the same, I wanted to get the entire staff involved in this new process. However, because our staff is comprised primarily of veteran consultants, and I wanted them to be comfortable with such an idea before forcing it on them, our efforts started small. I did not want them to look at this activity as something that wasted time; rather, I wanted the staff to embrace it as a new method of working with students. Therefore, we tried to get to know the writer and lighten the situation with additional small talk. Of course, we have always started out each session with a compliment, but students still clutched their pencils and waited for the negativity once we started discussing their writing. So, when we decided to try to lighten the situation by finding various topics outside of class and their writing to talk about when the student first sat down, such as sports or campus activities, we anticipated students opening up a bit. However, students were still very nervous when it came to discussing their actual writing, and after discussing it with several consultants, the time we spent at the beginning of the session making small-talk was considered wasted at the end of the session.

After remembering my own learning process, and again reading some articles on play theory, I decided that something else needed to be done so that more time could be spent on helping the student. So, in an attempt to combat this nervousness and provide a fun distraction, objects—toys— were placed in the writing center. We did this hoping that we could use them to tap into a student's tactile and kinesthetic learning intelligence. I brought a few toys from home, but after detailing our idea we were fortunate enough to receive a small budget allowance from our department for a variety of other items including small cars, figures, stress balls, toy gliders, super balls, facial disguises, and the like. The items were placed in the center of the table so that students would have to either move them or place their materials on top of the items—either way the students would see the toys. The idea was that students would pick up the item during the session and use it as a break of sorts from the task at hand. However, what happened was even more interesting.

Students began picking up the toys during the sessions and playing with them in their hands without any prompting by myself or the other consultants. Many students were obviously using the item(s) to relieve stress and/or as a distraction when they were nervous or stumped about how to proceed with a thought. The toys were becoming an integral part of many sessions. It seemed that my learning style was more widely used than I originally thought.

During one session, I remember a student continuously picking up a water tube and rolling it in her hand as we talked. I could tell she was apprehensive about her writing, and the activity she was engaged in seemed to help relax her. At one point she said, "this thing (the water tube) is awesome. It really helps relax me and focus my thinking." Later, during another session with a student that day, I used a few toy cars and plastic figures to illustrate the parts of a sentence and show a few different organizational patterns. At the end, the student told me that it was the first time writing actually made sense to him.

Other consultants began reporting similar results, and everyone seemed to enjoy the toys in the center, especially the young children of students who sometimes accompanied parents to sessions. Admittedly, most of the toys were male-centered (balls, figures, cars, etc.); yet, the female consultants and female students never seemed to have a problem using them, and I never heard a complaint concerning a gender bias with toy selection. In the future, however, we may try to utilize a more diverse selection of toys in an attempt to include everyone, especially those silent individuals who might never voice a negative opinion, in our fun.

BENEFITS

The benefits of adding toys and fun into the WC environment can be tremendous. College students, who are still for the most part transitioning from the care-free days of high school to the stress-filled days of adulthood, are especially going to see that an environment filled with toys is more fun than a stuffy lab setting. Toys almost always evoke childhood memories of carefree days and hours of fun.

Consultants often state that the toys are the most fun part of the WC and that they might play with them more than students do. However, they too recognize the importance of taking a break from the sometimes-mundane task of writing. When you consider how often students multitask in front of a computer, with instant messaging and e-mailing for instance, it is no wonder that a toy placed on the table beside them offers the same sort of escape and relaxation. Consultants also realize how toys, and more importantly play, can add another trick to their toolbox of teaching techniques. The use of toys and play is simply another method that can be used to reach students who do not want to engage or who have trouble putting thoughts into words.

Yet, the real benefit can be seen during each session when students appear more relaxed and are having fun interacting with a consultant. I can remember one session in particular when I was working with a student who was holding the stress ball and squeezing it while asking questions. I asked her about her behavior, and she said that she never really used such objects before, but it was really nice to have it as a distraction and as something to reduce the stress she was feeling from discussing her writing (which she thought was poor). Another time, a student was zooming a car into his hand over and over while reading his paper aloud to me during a session. When I asked him about the car, he said he didn't really know why he was playing with it, but that it was sort of like a habit he had of beating pencils on his desk at home when he is thinking about something. Clearly, the toys were being used to relieve stress, stimulate creativity, and keep interest in the topic at hand.

The consultants seem to always find new ways to use the toys in their writing center work. Of course, many times the consultants use toys in the same ways students do—to relieve stress (especially when working with students who might be pressuring them to do more editing than consulting) and keep interest in the topic at hand when they are working on one of their own papers during down time in the center. Often, however, consultants will comment on how the toys serve as a nice reminder that the WC is a place where fun should be present in the learning process. During sessions I have witnessed consultants using the toys as visual tools for discussing the parts of a sentence, how to outline a paper, brainstorming, and even discussing reliable and unreliable sources. During one session, I sat at a table near a consultant and was amazed at how the consultant was using different small cars and a few figures to visually outline the composition of a paper for a student. The outline was fairly complex, but the consultant was able to give a great visual of the paper in an almost comical fashion while the student obviously understood what was being discussed.

> **"Toys serve as a nice reminder that the writing center is a place where fun should be present in the learning process."**

Overall, this new technique is connecting well with students. Our numbers have continued to climb, and I have numerous students who have not yet taken advantage of our services ask about the toys during class presentations I periodically give around campus. It definitely appears that our new strategy is helping students see the writing center in a more positive and welcoming light.

DRAWBACKS

As with any endeavor, there are certain limitations and drawbacks. Obviously, not every student is going to like using toys in a session, especially if they are tired, cranky, and really just want some answers to specific concerns. Likewise, not every student is going to like the idea of trying to make the session fun and informal. Some students may actually thrive in an environment that is formal where they perceive the consultants as all-knowing instead of as guides through the writing process. Also, many students accustomed to coming to the WC for a session might be shocked at first at the apparent lack of formality displayed when using toys. Some students come to expect a certain atmosphere, and when it is changed they can backlash to a degree. However, after the initial adjustment period, in our experience, most have come to appreciate the new technique.

Also, as shocking as it sounds, some students might simply not like toys. Perhaps there was a childhood accident, or the fact that they have tried to escape childhood for so long and are now being brought back into it, that offends them. For whatever reason, toys might not be the best to use when helping certain students. With that in mind, I think it is worth stating that one should always judge the audience before doing anything. The use of toys is not something that older, nontraditional, students seem to appreciate. These students typically are in a rush and have only a few specific questions, so formality is usually the best course of action here. It goes almost without saying, but it pays to know your audience before attempting any new technique.

It should also be assumed that consultant reactions will likely mirror student reactions in some ways. Many returning consultants, especially those who are older, have become accustomed to the traditional ways of working with students. They are used to sitting at a desk and verbally discussing a text while looking at specific examples in a paper while the student participates in a semi-active state. For these consultants, new, and what might be perceived as odd, ways of approaching a tutoring session are often scoffed at and never fully embraced. It is vital then that you sell the idea to the consultant before you expect them to participate. Yet even after a hard sell, the consultant might never fully integrate the technique into his or her repertoire of strategies. The consultant might use a toy once or twice, but never give the technique an opportunity to really grab hold, or say that he or she will use the technique but remain the one person who does not use the new strategies in sessions. And I'm sure anyone who works with students for several hours at a time can attest that sometimes he or she just wants to get through the session and might forgo using additional techniques in the interest of time saved. These things are important to remember if you expect everyone to be on the same page concerning technique usage.

CONCLUSION

It should be apparent that play and fun is not for everyone when they come into the writing center. Simply put, some people have already reached a boiling point of stress and nothing will calm them down; however, for a majority of individuals play and fun can be just what is needed to further their educational threshold.

Of course, you can take the idea of play in the WC beyond toys. Playing with language is something everyone should do and research suggests that to some degree we have all experimented and played with language in our formative years. Why then do we give up such a novel and transformative task such as play in our daily lives? Is it the pressure to conform to society's expectations, or is it that we find such endeavors childish and below our current way of thinking? Whatever the excuse, play is definitely a wonderful source of creativity and something that should not be overlooked.

Plato once stated "you can discover more about a person in an hour of play than in a year of conversation." As writing center professionals, it should be important to get to know the writer you are working with so you can help pull out his or her inner voice. Play is a wonderful way to get to know the writer on a deeper level and takes only a few minutes of time in each session. As WC populations continue to grow and change, a familiarity with play might become essential to our work in reaching students in the future. More importantly, however, it is a method we can experiment with right now—and have fun while trying.

REFERENCES

Ellis, M. J. (1973). *Why people play.* Englewood Cliffs, NJ: Prentice-Hall.

Gardner, H. (1983). *Frames of mind.* New York: Basic Books.

Lieberman, N. (1977). *Playfulness: Its relationship to imagination and creativity.* New York: Academic Press.

Marano, H. E. (1999). The power of play—psychological benefits of play. *Psychology Today, 32*(4), 36-40, 68-69.

Vygotsky, L.S. (1978). *Mind in society: The development of higher psychological processes.* Cambridge, MA: MIT Press.

Weininger, O. (1979). *Play and education: The basic tool for early childhood learning.* Springfield, IL: Charles C. Thomas.

9

TUTORING CREATIVE WRITERS

Working One-to-One on Prose and Poetry

Hans Ostrom

It happened again. My department was beginning the last phase of a search for a new tenure-line colleague in creative writing. We had invited several candidates to campus, and we had decided that, for the formal presentation, the candidates would read from their fiction. A day after the first candidate's presentation, a colleague said to me, "I don't know what to say about yesterday's reading. I know how to evaluate a scholarly presentation, but I don't know how to evaluate a short story."

I have heard similar comments my whole career. Earlier in my career, I tended to over-react to them. I would pounce on what I regarded, and still regard, as their absurdity. For here, in my opinion, is the situation implied by such a comment: *Individuals who are trained professionally to study literature are claiming to be unable to evaluate literature.* This situation does not make any sense, especially because even individuals who are not trained professionally to study literature can, may, and do have opinions about—if not full strategies for evaluating—poems and stories. They hear or read a poem or a story (maybe the story is part of a stand-up comedy routine), and then they say what they think of it. "That was funny," they say, or they say, "I don't get it." My colleague—with a PhD in literature—could not summon even this much to say about the story he had heard a candidate read.

I no longer overreact to such comments because (a) I'm older than I was and can't afford to expend the energy and (b) I fully realize that the situation is more complicated than the apparently blatant absurdity suggests.

CREATIVE WRITING AS
"OTHER"

For a variety of reasons, creative writing in high schools, colleges, and universities is viewed as an "Other." My colleague has been part of this culture for a long time; no wonder, then, that he reflexively regards creative writing as Other, as something about which he has nothing to say. In disciplinary terms, creative writing is viewed, ironically, as not-Literature. Many moons ago in an article on undergraduate creative writing, I connected this situation to a xenophobic Dickens character, Podsnap, who goes around saying things are "not-English!"—and are therefore unacceptable (Ostrom, 1989). People in English studies may argue incessantly about issues connected to literature, composition, or rhetoric. They do love to quibble. And they may even demean or undervalue the teaching of composition, so that teachers of college-level prose-writing—or workers in writing centers (WC)—may rightly feel alienated at times. But most people in English studies do not regard these standard parts of English studies—literature, composition, and rhetoric—as entirely Other, as freakish, as things about which they simply cannot form an evaluative judgment.

Alongside or perhaps out of this view of creative writing as Other have sprung additional reflexive responses to creative writing. For instance, creative-writing classes are thought to be "too easy" or "not rigorous." Creative writing is viewed as a kind of "therapy" or at least as indulgent. It may also be viewed as "too personal," so that responding to someone's poem or story is associated with responding to the person him or herself.

WHAT TO DO
WITH CREATIVE WRITING

Unfortunately, such attitudes about and reflexive responses to creative writing often occur not just in English departments but also in WCs. By necessity, most of the training in WCs concerns "papers": Writing that students produce in composition classes and in courses across the curriculum. So when students bring creative writing to a center to seek help, WC tutors may not know what to "do" with such writing. Consequently, I provide a list of ways in which WC workers can respond usefully to creative writing that students bring to the WC. Such workers are variously known as tutors, consultants, instructors, advisors, and so on. For the sake of simplicity and consistency, I refer to them—to you—as *tutors*. If you work in a WC but your title is not "tutor," just automatically translate "tutor" to the title you prefer.

The creative writing that students may bring to a WC might be personal essays, creative nonfiction, parts of screenplays or plays, poetry, short stories, or parts of novels. Most of the time, however, a student will bring in a draft of a poem or a short story, so for the sake of streamlining the discussion here, I direct my list toward helping students with poems and stories; however, tutors may easily adapt the ways of responding I list to other kinds of writing.

Before I get to the list of suggestions, I address two more items. First, because I am presuming to be in a position to offer advice about WCs and creative writing, I should try to generate some street credibility. I have written and published poetry and fiction for more than two decades; of course, this fact says more about my age than my poetry or my fiction. Nonetheless, I believe I can legitimately claim to know much about how hard it is to write a successful poem or story but also about how pleasurable it is to write poetry and fiction. Also, I have taught the writing of poetry and the writing of fiction at the college-level for about 23 years. (I also regularly teach courses in literature and composition.) So to a large extent, my job has involved responding to poems and stories students have written. I have read and responded to thousands of poems and stories by undergraduates. Often, my responses come in the form of a conversation—a tutorial, if you will—in my office or the campus coffee shop; such circumstances are similar to a WC tutorial.

You may be glad to hear that I have also worked in a WC. I worked in and helped direct a WC at a large state university, and I started up a WC at a liberal-arts college, where I remain in close contact with the director and with many students who work there. I am also one of numerous persons in English studies who have tried to change the way creative writing is viewed in our profession; in the reference section, look, if you want to, at works developed by Wendy Bishop and me, as well as important ones produced by other people in this area of inquiry.

Second, I need to identify the major premise underlying my approach to helping students with creative writing. It is that creative writing is *writing*. The premise is not only awfully obvious, but it is also a tautology, but in my defense, I direct you to the anecdote with which I began. That is, there are all sorts of literary experts in our midst who claim to be unable to respond to creative writing; they can make this claim with a straight face only because they are proceeding from the premise that creative writing is somehow not writing; if creative writing were, in fact, writing, then, as literary experts, they would not seriously claim to be unable to say anything about creative writing. I invite you, then, to begin from the assumption that, like an essay, a poem or a short story is composed of words, phrases, and clauses, and as an essay is almost always composed of paragraphs, so poems and stories are almost always composed of parts or sections—such as stanzas or scenes.

In other words, my overarching suggestion is that you treat the creative writing that students bring to you pretty much as you would treat drafts of essays they bring to you. True, the genres are different, and my list takes that difference into account. Nonetheless, you should, in general, proceed as you usually do. Your first move should be to demystify creative writing, even if parts of it remain appropriately mysterious. Don't change any of the fundamental training you have received in WC work; don't change your professional behavior.

Someone has brought you a piece of writing with which he or she would like help. Therefore, as with the work you do on drafts of essays, keep the focus on the writing—the draft. Under no circumstances let the adjective "creative" throw you off balance. What do you usually do when someone brings a draft of an essay? Perhaps your WC asks visitors first to fill out a form so that you may gather information about the piece of writing, what class (if any) the writing is connected to, what stage the draft is in, and so forth. If this is the case, then have the person fill out the form. If the form doesn't seem to accommodate creative writing, then perhaps your WC might consider altering the form or developing parallel ones for different genres, including—but not limited to—creative writing.

If you usually begin a WC conversation or tutorial a certain way, then, when you are dealing with creative writing, begin it the same way. As you work with the person, see her or him as a writer and a student, not as a "poet" or an "artist," per se. Why? Because if you start treating her or him as a poet or an artist, you will be tempted to change your WC behavior, and then you and your visitor may lose the benefits of your training and experience.

No doubt your training and experience have led you to treat the papers you see as writing by students, not as writing by professionals. Papers by students can be very good, but they are almost never as good as essays by professionals—and why would they be? Similarly, we should not measure poems and stories by students against poems and stories by William Shakespeare, Langston Hughes, Eudora Welty, Gary Soto, or Maxine Hong Kingston. That would be illogical and unproductive.

Now it's time to list some specific ways—there are 10—of responding to poems and stories students bring to the WC. Although they are in no particular order, and although all of them, of course, cannot be used in a single tutorial, the first one is not a bad way to begin most tutorials in creative writing.

STRATEGIES FOR RESPONDING TO POEMS AND STORIES IN WRITING CENTER TUTORIALS

1. Ask yourself and the writer the following question: *What type of work is this?* Another version would be this: *What type of work does this piece of writing aspire to be?*

   - "Type" might mean "subject." Is this a **love** poem? A **thing** poem? Is this a poem about an important **place**? Is this a poem about **a person who has died**? Is this a story about **hunting** or **fishing** or **cooking** or **eating**? Is it a love story? Is it a story about **family conflict**? Is this a **"road"** story?

   - "Type" might also refer to **form** or **category**. Is this a coming-of-age story? A horror, gothic, mystery, or science fiction story? Is it a loss-of-innocence story? Is the poem a sonnet? A haiku? A dramatic or an interior monologue? Is it a narrative poem? Is it in the form of a song? Is it a very short poem? Is it a long poem?

   - "Type" might also refer to **who "speaks" in the poem or story**. Is this a first-person lyric poem? Is it a poem in which the persona seems effaced—all description and very little "voice"? Is it a poem with several distinct voices? Is the story told by a first-person or a third-person narrator? Is the narrator reliable? Is the story mostly narrative, mostly dialogue, or a mix of both? What kind of "voices" can you "hear" in this poem or story?

Here is the point: If you and/or your visitor can identify what type of work this is or implicitly aspires to be, then the work no longer exists in isolation, and it now can be discussed in context. The work exists in the midst of some conventions that come with sonnets, coming-of-age-stories, interior monologues, science fiction, or stories that depend almost exclusively on dialogue. The writer may choose to work within or against the conventions, or both. In any case, you and the writer may now discuss how to revise the work in the context of what type of work it is. Often, I have found that even relatively experienced, rather accomplished undergraduate writers are so close to their work that they do not, at first, realize what type of poem or story they are writing. Once they or I identify the type of work they have undertaken, they can usually see the draft more clearly, just as we all often see objects better against a good backdrop or in comparison with other similar objects.

If you and your visitor disagree about what type of work this is, that disagreement can be productive, too. You might say, "I read this as a nostalgic poem," to which the author might say, "Oh, no, I think of it as a poem that carefully observes a place—that was what my teacher wanted." Then you can point to words or phrases that seem "nostalgic," and the writer can point to words or phrases that convey vivid but more or less "objective" description. A good discussion can come out of two different readings; so can a good revision.

This work of identification also sets aside the question of how good the poem or story is, but, paradoxically, it often leads to making the poem or story better, regardless of how good it is. Such delay is not only useful but also probably necessary. Identifying what kind of work we are experiencing is a way of being a better, more responsive audience. For instance, if a friend of yours has invited you to join him or her for a light, easy-going evening at the theatre, and you get in your theatre-seat only to realize that the play is *Hamlet*, then you need to readjust your expectations—as well as your estimation of your friend, perhaps. If you were looking for laughs that evening, then *Hamlet* is not a "good" play.

Finally, the work of identification is also in line with what most writing centers teach with regard to tutorials—namely, that tutors should work from "global" matters to "local" matters with a piece of writing, or from "macro" to "micro." That is, the discussion of an essay-draft should not begin with comments about misspellings or typographical errors, which are definitely in the "local" and "micro" categories. Identifying what type of work a piece of creative writing is falls squarely into the "global" and "macro" categories.

2. Ask your visitor whether the work was assigned or suggested by someone else, such as a teacher. If it was, then perhaps an actual written-out assignment exists, or at least your visitor can recapitulate the assignment. In either case, you, as a tutor, now have something to go on, something against which to see the draft. You can help the writer revise *toward* goals explicitly or implicitly given by someone else. If the work was not assigned or suggested, then you may ask what goals or aims the writer him or herself had. Just helping the writer articulate such aims or goals is of enormous use because sometimes writers don't realize what they were after, exactly, until they tell someone.

> "Helping the writer articulate goals is of enormous use because sometimes writers don't realize what they were after, exactly, until they tell someone."

3. Tell the writer what you think is good, compelling, and/or inter-esting about the piece. Is the subject or topic interesting? How about a certain image, scene, section of dialogue? Do you like the title? Do you like the way a poem or a story starts? What's the best line of the poem, in your view? Why? What part of the short story really drew you in, made you want to read on? Why? Writers need to know what they have done well as much as they need to know what isn't working, but often readers reflex-ively begin by saying what they think is "wrong" with a piece. Telling a writer what works is not a matter of being polite; it's really useful. There's nothing wrong, however, with being polite, too.

4. In whatever way seems most productive to you, work with the author to identify conventions or expectations that attach themselves to the kind of work the author has undertaken. For example, because I have read so many short stories in the real-istic mode, I know that to begin a story with the line "He woke up" or with an alarm clock going off has been done so many times that it is rarely a satisfactory way to begin a short story. Originally, this may not have been a bad way to begin a story. It does, after all, get the narrative going; something happens. So I—or you—can tell a student that beginning quickly *is* a good idea but that readers of short fiction probably expect something different, less predictable, than "He woke up" or "Brrrrrinnnng —Bob's alarm clock went off." With regard to how stories end, the "and it was all a dream" ending is the counterpart to "He woke up." Similarly, a student new to writing lyric poetry may not know that readers often expect short, free-verse poems nowadays to include a lot of imagery—much specific, concrete detail. So I—or you—can simply suggest that the writer try a second draft in which there is more detail: specific things to "see" or "smell."

You and the writer may also discuss what internal expecta-tions the work sets up. For instance, in a short story about two people having trouble in a romantic relationship, the expecta-tion of a "break-up" or a "reconciliation" might emerge as we're reading along. So I—or you—can say, "You know, I wouldn't be surprised if most readers will want to know whether these two characters are going to stay together." The writer might say, "Well, I want the story to leave that in doubt." And you can say, "That's fine; then the ending of your story will have an unset-tling effect on most readers—but that might not be a bad thing." Or a student might bring in a free-verse poem broken into three three-line stanzas, one two-line stanza, and a four-line stanza. I—or you—can say something like, "You know, this poem seems to 'want' to be all in three-line stanzas. You might try it that way. There's this poet William Stafford who wrote a lot of free-verse that he nonetheless organized in stanzas with the same number of lines."

5. Ask writers what stage they consider the work to be in. Do they consider it to be a first draft? A darned good draft with some work left to do? A finished piece? Try not to argue writers out of their position on this, even if you think a "finished" piece is actually an extremely rough draft. Instead, use the information to guide you in your suggestions. For instance, if a writer indicates the work is an early rough draft, then all sorts of revision options will materialize. If, on the other hand, a writer seems quite attached to the idea that the work is almost finished, you nonetheless have something to suggest. For example, let's say the work is a poem, spoken in first person by someone not unlike the writer, and concerned with describing a homeless person, a bus driver, or a professor. You get the sense that the writer thinks the poem is "done" and that the writer is, for the moment, unmovable on that subject. You can say, "Okay, well, in that case I have a suggestion. What if you tried another poem, a kind of companion poem that's spoken not by an observer but by the homeless person, the bus driver, or the professor? I'd really be interested in seeing that poem—hearing that bus driver speak." You haven't wasted your time trying to argue with a temporarily stubborn or defensive writer, but you've still done your job by suggesting, in effect, a way to revise the poem—by writing another poem. Just helping new writers to realize that there are numerous ways to write the same kind of poem is of enormous service to them.

6. Image, scene, action. Whether it's a poem or a story, there is almost always something for you to say about what the work makes you see in your mind. It is almost always helpful to a writer when a reader points to a specific part of a poem and says, "The imagery here is a little unclear to me. Is there a way to sharpen it?" Or when a reader says, "In this scene in the story—on page 3—are Mike and Sylvia still in the restaurant when they're arguing, or have they gone outside? The action's a little unclear to me there."

7. Sound. Although in literal terms, poems and stories on the page are mute, they create in our minds the effect of sound. You or the writer might simply read the poem, or part of it, out loud. You or the writer might read a section of dialogue in a story out loud. Or you both might read aloud and have the one not reading jot down notes about what he or she hears that's really good or that seems to need work. Point to sentences that seem knotty, or to lines of a poem where the rhythm gets derailed, or to a line of dialogue that seems out of key with the rest of the dialogue. Often just the process of outloud reading suggests, uncannily, obvious revisions in a way that silent reading does not.

8. Be alert to "the explanation" and to "but it really happened that way." It is fairly common for newer writers to respond to criticism by trying to explain the poem or story and/or by asserting that "it" (what is described or narrated in the work) "really happened that way." When writers explain an image or a scene, a line or an episode, to you, one way to respond is to say, "You know, I get what you were going for now, but I think you need to revise the [story; poem] so that it conveys more clearly what you just explained. Without your explanation, I don't know that most readers will get what's going on." If writers respond to a critique by insisting that, in effect, the creative writing is based on a real-life experience, you may raise the question of genre. You can say that one way to handle this material is autobiographically—by writing down "what really happened." You can also point that when writers choose poetry, fiction, or drama, they are actually free to change "what really happened," to shape it. You can then point to poems, stories, novels, plays, or movies you know that are based on "true stories" but that deliberately change "what really happened" by inventing scenes, characters, or episodes. You may also point out that one way to free oneself from the burden of the facts is to begin changing the facts almost arbitrarily. Set the story or the poem in a different place; change a character's gender or age; if there were really five children in the family, reduce the number to three; if that famous argument happened in a bar, make it happen in a church. And so forth. Stress how liberating what's known as "poetic license" is for creative writers.

9. Keep in mind the option of "radical revision." You certainly do not want routinely to suggest to writers that they tear up what they have written and start all over again. Ultimately, writers

themselves may reach that conclusion, but a WC tutorial should be focused on keeping the writer productive; such blunt advice can be counterproductive. However, after you are sure that you and the writer have arrived at a good understanding and that the writer is ready to hear about a variety of revision options, you may bring up the idea of radical revision. Actually, even if a poem or story is very good, radical revision remains an option. Instead of, or in addition to, writing a poem on the topic, the writer might write a story—or vice versa. The writer might treat a serious subject comically or a comic subject seriously. The writer might move from free verse to a traditional form, such as a sonnet or a villanelle, he or she might go in the other direction. The author might experiment with radical changes of point of view, setting, plot arrangement, voice, beginning, ending. The author might make a long story short or a short one long. Keep radical revision in mind, but make sure the writer with whom you are working is ready to consider such an option.

10. Pleasure. Remember that writing poetry and fiction, like all art, is essentially play. It is play not in the sense of goofing off but in the sense of improvisation, exploration, and trial and error. Writers play with words in the way painters play with paint, sculptors with clay, and musicians with notes and tempos. Therefore, it is often good for tutors to invite writers to think about what has been pleasurable about writing this poem or that story. It is also often good for tutors to be self-reflective about what they enjoyed about a poem or a story, as opposed to or in addition to judging the whole piece. That is, it is all right for a tutor and writer to forget for a moment whether the piece is an overall success or failure and to focus on whatever is pleasurable about the piece. It is also helpful to writers when tutors help them think about what parts of the writing and revision processes are pleasurable. Writing is hard work, but it is more than hard work; it is pleasurable work, which is also known as play.

> **"Writing is hard work, but it is more than hard work; it is pleasurable work, which is also known as play."**

Here, then, have been 10 ways to respond to creative writing. I close by mentioning just two more ideas. First, try to assemble a small library of books concerning creative writing in your WC or add to what is already there. Books on creative writing can be helpful. A few titles are listed in the

References section. Try to gather some good anthologies of literature, too. Second, tutors in the WC should write poems and stories themselves and conduct a workshop on them. This will turn tutors into creative writers and allow them to see the process from the other side. It is an instructive, pleasurable process, but also a demystifying, humbling one.

REFERENCES

Addonizio, K., & Lux, D. (1997). *The poet's companion: A guide to the pleasures of writing poetry.* New York: W. W. Norton.

Bishop, W. (1990). *Released into language: Options for teaching creative writing.* Urbana, IL: NCTE.

Bishop, W. (2000). *Thirteen ways of looking for a poem: A guide to writing poetry.* New York: Longman, 2000. [Contains numerous specific writing-prompts and ideas for invention, development, and revision.]

Bishop, W. (2004). *Acts of revision: A guide for writers.* Portsmouth, NH: Heinemann.

Bishop, W., & Ostrom, H. (Eds.). (1994). *Colors of a different horse: Rethinking creative writing theory and pedagogy.* Urbana, IL: NCTE.

Bizarro, P. (2003). *Responding to student poems: Applications of critical theory.* Urbana, IL: NCTE.

Hugo, R. (1983). *The triggering town: Lectures and essays on poetry and writing.* New York: W.W. Norton.

Ostrom, H. (1989). Undergraduate creative writing: The unexamined subject. *Writing on the Edge, 1*(1), 55-65.

Ostrom, H., Bishop, W., & Haake, K. (2000). *Metro: Journeys in creative writing.* New York: Addison Wesley Longman. [Contains numerous specific writing-prompts and ideas for invention, development, and revision.]

Padgett, R. (2000). *The teachers and writers handbook of poetic forms* (2nd ed.). New York: Teachers and Writers Collective.

Painter, P., & Bernays, A. (1990). *What if?: Writing exercises for fiction writers.* New York: HarperCollins.

Tobin, L. (2004). *Reading student writing: Confessions, meditations, and rants.* Portsmouth, NH: Boynton/Cook.

10

DRAWING THE (PLAY)SPACES OF CONFERENCES

Anne Ellen Geller

Sometimes I sit in my office and I listen. My office door is almost always open simply because my small space gets too hot when the door is closed. That open door entices an endless stream of visitors, but it also allows me to eavesdrop on the conferences my staff holds just down the hall in the writing center (WC). Sometimes I hear laughter. Sometimes I hear frustration. Sometimes I hear negotiation. But I'm always in search of fuller versions of the conferences I overhear, and every now and then, I'll wander into the hallway as a conference ends and a student writer leaves, and I'll smile at the consultant who just finished a conference. Or I'll raise an eyebrow, or I'll make what my staff calls my "yikes" grimace. Those aren't faces of surveillance, however. They're faces of understanding, of questioning, of invitation. They say, come in, if you want, and talk about that conference because I might be able to offer some insight. Or I say "That might be a good conference to describe in our meeting," hinting that all of us, as a staff, might be able to offer insight.

No one on my current staff worked in the old Clark Writing Center. It was down a creaky staircase, in the basement of the English house. No one remembers the way the old space had three separate areas for conferences. In the current WC there are usually two consultants working at a time, and their spaces are divided by bookcases in the center of the WC's single room. Sound travels over those bookcases, however, and the consultants eavesdrop on one another, listening to the choices made in conferences, listening for the way those choices play out. The consultants, too, are always in search of fuller versions of the conferences they overhear. I find them in the kitchen, or on the front porch of our building, comparing their impressions of writers, sharing their strategies, and seeking affirmation for the way they worked with the writers they saw.

The question for me is how we value this eavesdropping, how we encourage it, and how we bring the support, collaborative staff learning, and problem solving it promotes into our more official work together. What creative practices in the public space of staff meetings might encourage the consultants to notice moments of possible play in the more hidden, private spaces of conferences? Most important, how can I, as a director, help the consultants know to be meta-aware of those moments as they occur in conferences, willing and able to recognize for student writers that they are about to work their way through something difficult, in the text or beyond it?

WITNESSING THE WORLDMAKING
OF WRITING CENTER CONFERENCES

In *Getting to Know City Kids: Understanding Their Thinking, Imagining, and Socializing*, Sally Middlebrooks (1998) introduces six urban children involved in what she terms *worldmaking*. Middlebrooks studies "the three-dimensional structures children build and then inhabit," "away from adult eyes," "at the edges of the world" (p. 4), and she claims it is in these spaces that children "make sense of themselves, others, and the world" (p. 16). These are also places where children's play is slightly hidden even as adults know play is happening. A teepee in Brenda's housing development bedroom, for example, or the "'little house'" Isaac creates with blankets draped over his bottom bunk bed, or Rex's "'Eskimo thing'" made of "a sheet or coverlet over two chairs" (pp. 4-7) are all bounded "private universes," spaces where the children have reduced their everyday worlds to a "smaller, more manageable size" (p. 4). "Guided by the children," Middlebrooks says she is going "behind the scenes to unveil something of the breadth and depth of their curiosity, industry and imagination" (p. 18). As adults, and as teachers, Middlebrooks argues, we don't usually look inquisitively into kids' three-dimensional playspaces. If we did, we might be surprised at what we'd find, and we might be surprised by what we could learn. Instead, we usually say children are just playing in their imaginary structures, and we ignore them, thinking they don't want to, or don't need to, share their hidden play.

What struck me about Middlebrooks' research the first time I saw it and why I have never forgotten it, is the way she asked her young participants to share their spaces with her. She asked them to draw, and then she asked them to use the drawings to tell her about their playspaces. Their representations were creative acts. But what is more important to Middlebrooks is the way in which the representations the children drew for her allow her entry into the imaginative lives they play out in these spaces. Seeing the places with the children as guides, she can ground herself–and them–in what happens in those spaces. It is in the talk about the pictures that more arises. As Middlebrooks notes: "Often as children talked about their drawings, they realized that important pieces of their story were missing" (p. 34). They added those pieces to their drawings, "saying more and drawing more" (p. 34), realizing that details they had forgotten or discounted were, in fact, important enough to acknowledge. Middlebrooks could listen to their thinking as they did this, asking herself, and them, why they added what they did.

Although the connections between urban preadolescents creating and building imaginary spaces for childhood play in their neighborhoods and WC tutors creating and building real spaces for intellectual play in their conferences might not seem obvious, it has always struck me that Sally Middlebrooks—a longtime educator in urban environmental programs—and I—a WC director and mentor to graduate WC consultants—are both interested in the worldmaking that takes place hidden from us. We want to know how children and WC tutors make worlds and "make sense of themselves" in those worlds. We know something playful and something serious is happening in those hidden spaces, and we think it is important to let what happens there be both private *and* shared. Is it too much of a stretch to think of conferences as playspaces and to imagine that tutors are worldmaking in their conferences? I don't think so.

Most WC directors do try to enter WC conferences and learn about the worldmaking happening there without being a part of the conferences themselves. Some WC directors silently sit in on their tutors' conferences, and, later, to varying degrees, evaluate the practices they see or offer feedback. Other WC directors ask tutors to sit in on one another's conferences, talk about decisions made, and reflect on similarities and differences in their tutoring. Tutors tape conferences, sometimes transcribe them, and share their tapes or transcripts with the rest of the tutoring staff and their director (see, e.g., Gilewicz & Thonus, 2003). These are all good attempts to see the work that stays mostly hidden in each conference.

I think we should acknowledge as directors that we want (and need) to know what's happening in conferences. But it's dangerous for staff creativity, as I explain later, to believe that closely monitoring tutors to see if they make certain cookie-cutter moves in every conference—does the student ask first what the assignment is, does the tutor make certain not to write on the paper, does the tutor ask only open-ended questions—and tightly evaluating their conferences, is the best way to ensure some consistency of good practice or encourage creativity. What we want is for tutors to pay attention to every conference and to realize that every conference has moments of teaching and learning that are important for them and for student writers. To encourage tutors to pay attention to those moments, directors must pay attention to those moments, and yet we find ourselves in a paradoxical supervisory position because we're seldom present for those moments as they happen.

DRAWING CONFERENCE CREATIVITY

I can imagine the first time I took colored pencils, markers, and white paper to a writing center meeting. It might have been a dark, mid-winter Massachusetts afternoon. Perhaps it was the semester we met weekly at 4 pm when the sky would darken as we talked. Or maybe it was raining and I felt we needed to do something different. Or maybe I just opened a messy desk drawer and was reminded that I had a supply of colored pencils and markers. What I do remember is that I began drawing with my first Clark University WC staff—John, a biologist, Rita and Aparna, economists, and Tamer, who studied literacy and science education. This was an intellectually creative staff, and I think they would argue they had little or no talent or inclination for visual art. Yet those earliest images were rich in what they taught us.[1]

Of those early drawings, one is my favorite: a line sketch capturing the moment when a student writer tells Aparna what she wants to work on in a conference. "Everything," the student says. Aparna's response is captured in a thought bubble of ampersands, asterisks, exclamation, and question marks. It is a drawing that appears and reappears in some form across many semesters of drawings. It is a conference moment difficult for any tutor to avoid.

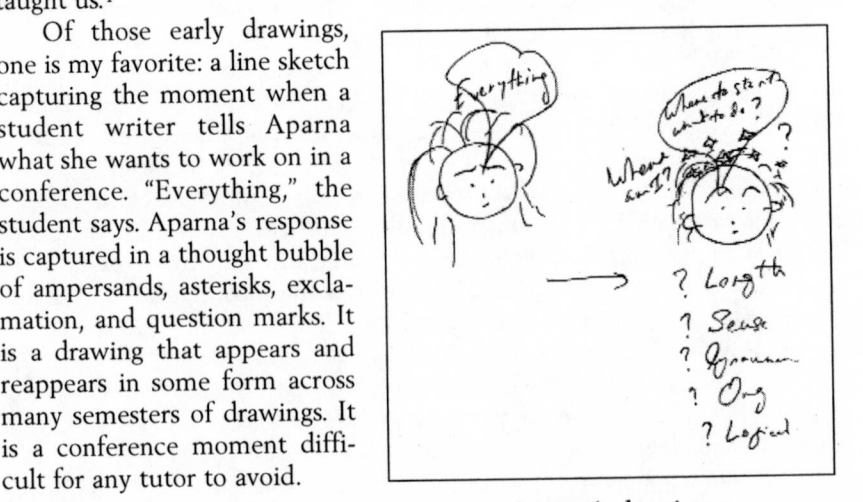

Aparna's drawing.

This chapter is in this collection because drawing is art, and art is creative. But art—the physical act of drawing—is only one aspect of the creativity I want to point to in the staff education practices I describe here.[2] Drawing can certainly help all of us represent our thinking and our experiences differently than we might with words. As Sandra Weber and Claudia Mitchell (1996), who have been studying the drawings created by teacher education candidates, note:

> Drawings offer a different kind of glimpse into human sensemaking than written or spoken texts do, because they can express that which is not easily put into words: the ineffable, the elusive, the non-yet-thought-through, the subconscious. Much of what we have seen or known, thought or imagined, remembered or repressed, slips unbidden into our drawings, revealing unexplored ambiguities, contradictions and connections. That which we have forgotten, which we might censor from our speech and writing, often escapes into our drawings. (p. 304)[3]

For me, the creative and reflective talk that surrounds the drawings is the most important part of this exercise. Weber and Mitchell find this, too. Their students draw a teacher, and write about the drawings, "reflecting on how they had represented 'teacher'" (p. 306). In "the next class meeting, individual students shared their drawings with the group and discussed what their drawings meant to them" (Weber & Mitchell, 1996, p. 306). At the end of the semester, after their experiences student teaching in schools, their students redrew pictures of teachers and "the drawing/journaling/discussing experience enabled students to articulate previously unexamined ambivalences and tensions around their identity and work as teachers" (Weber & Mitchell, 1996, p. 306). Weber and Mitchell argue that

> inviting teachers to draw, and then to share their drawings, or to write and talk about them, provides an excellent forum for critical reflection, bringing to light the nuances and ambivalences in people's views of teachers, as well as the historical, social, cultural and personal stereotypes that can inform our professional knowledge. (p. 312)

Hearing, or, in this case, seeing, which moments the consultants remember as significant also tells me a great deal about my staff. The moments that are significant for them are usually those when they didn't know what to do, or those when they were surprised to realize they did know what to do, or those they retrospectively come to see were those when they had more than one option of what to do. What my staff chooses, then, is also significant for what work I choose to do with them. I know developmentally where my staff is by what they struggle to figure out in their conferences, and what they struggle to figure out is sometimes as subtle as a feeling or a doubt or a fear.

I have a hunch that the early prompts I offered were more like "Draw a picture of a conference you had this past week," and it wasn't that the images responding to that prompt did not focus on moments, it was that the prompt didn't offer room for the abstraction I have seen in more recent images, abstraction that captures some of the richer, more fluid moments of conference negotiation and some of the more intangible, affective feelings of one-to-one conferencing.[4] So the prompt I now offer in staff meetings as I dole out pencils, markers, and paper is usually "Capture a moment that you're left thinking about from a conference you had this past week and represent it visually."

As I drafted this chapter, I found myself forgetting what these meetings feel like, and I needed to remind myself of *why* we do this drawing exercise in staff meetings. I remembered that the why, the circumstances that may lead me to suggest drawing as the day's activity, vary. In the past, there have been semesters when my staff as a whole has had an overwhelming aura of timidity. Drawing drew out quieter staff members. At other times, the staff has been overwhelmingly funny. Drawing grounded us. Jokes were still constant, but we didn't get off track in our conversations when we had written or visual texts as the foundation of our talk.

I have a scrappy staff this semester. I don't note this as a negative, but I have been attentive to how aware they need to be of their confrontational tendencies. More than any recent group of consultants, this staff seems to engage with students' aggressive requests and play out their own aggressive responses to those requests. We've been reflecting on that all semester, and I've been trying to help this staff learn to slow down their reactions and consider more possibilities for their interactions with writers. But to understand when and why and how these in-conference confrontations boil up, I need—and the rest of the staff needs—to "go behind the scenes" (Middlebrooks, 1998, p. 18) of the conferences in which they occurred.

When any of us take on creative staff education exercises, we must ask ourselves how the exercise meets our staff's needs and how it relates to the rest of the work we do together and the work we do in conferences. What's the exercise? How do I do it?—are the first questions we might ask. But more important to us should be questions like: Why is this creative exercise valuable for where my staff and I are right now in our thinking? How—and what—will this exercise help us all learn from one another right now? What could we take from this creative exercise back into our work with student writers?

So, in a meeting a few weeks ago, we did as we always do. I asked my staff to draw a moment from a conference they held the past week, and we all spent about 10 minutes drawing. Then, we agreed someone would show a picture and explain what it represented. Whoever had a picture that connected in some way would follow, and we would continue that way. What we've usually done in meetings when we've drawn is share every drawing, and then open the discussion to the whole group. Which picture would you like to talk about? What themes do you hear and see across pictures? Which of these intrigues you and makes you want to ask further questions? Do so.

Although it's fairly easy, even with this exercise, to recognize images that reappear again and again, every staff makes something different of the images as they appear, and it's where a staff is, and what I want to teach them and what they'd like to teach one another, that drives our conversation. The point is to use the pictures to see what they might reveal that we might not otherwise say or might not yet be able to say. With pictures there is some play (as in the slippage Weber and Mitchell describe) in what we reveal about ourselves and about our practice.

The first pictures shared in this particular meeting were, not surprisingly, about the more positive, satisfying conferences of the week. For example, in Ing's picture,[5] two stick figures sit side by side at one of the WC's round tables. Both have positive expressions. Both hold pens. A text sits on the table right between them. Ing said she chose this moment from the week because it represented a moment in conference when she was aware of how collaborative the work was, and she was aware of how good she

Ing's drawing.

felt that she and the student writer had found a way to work together so well. We asked and heard her tell us about the conditions that had made that possible.

In retrospect, it isn't surprising that Davia said she'd like to follow those who had shown drawings of engaged, collaborative conferences. Davia held up a drawing with small stick figures, texts, and lots of dialogue. "I need a better grade," the student says, along with "The teacher hates me," and "I wrote what I thought made sense," and Davia's all-encompassing addition of all else the student said, the "Wha, Wha" of a whine. In bubbles above Davia are her thoughts. "I wonder if I'm helping too much," and "This is so hard." Out loud she seems to say "Lord help me" and "Okay, what do you want me to help with."

We laughed and laughed as we looked at that picture, but "at what?" is the question I posed. At what is what I wanted this staff to confront and name. Was it the whining student?—a familiar experience at the end of the semester, or a familiar, frustrated feeling that washes over all of us as the semester nears its close. Was it just that Davia had written in "Lord help me" exactly as she might say it with her Caribbean accent? Was it that the student feels so sure her teacher hates her, and we knew that feeling and thought it was ridiculous all at the same time? Or was it, most of all, that each of us knew just what Davia felt like as she said to herself, "This is so hard"?

As we talked, we realized we knew a variety of alternate answers to each question, and we spent the most time talking about how and why we might address the student's belief that her teacher hates her. Some felt it was a comment to avoid responding to; others felt responding to that comment, addressing it and releasing the writer from the feeling might be crucial to the writer getting the work done with authority and ownership. From Davia's picture, I can't stop thinking about the bubble that says "This is so hard," and I remember that a part of why my staff is scrappy and seems to get involved in struggles with writers is that they're inexperienced, most of them new to writing center tutoring. The images show me—show all of us on staff, for that matter—the exact situations that still feel surprising and uncomfortable to those who are new.

In "Playing With Reality: Writing Centers After the Mirror Stage," Nancy Welch (1999) describes encouraging her staff to "play" in writing conferences, working always "within a creative tension between genuine constraint and genuine opportunity" (p. 64). Hearing a student writer say

Davia's drawing.

"my teacher hates me" and "I need a better grade" feels as if it sets up just that type of creative tension. Writers have needs and struggles and demands they must meet, but Welch points out that creative tutors can think about possibilities in conferences, and when they do, every conference becomes "a potential space for trying out, not closing out, different constructions of reality" (p. 64). Every conference, we might say, has opportunity for worldmaking for tutor and student writer. But tutors cannot play in conferences, cannot be expected to be ready to think about possible and potential choices in conferences, if they do not have opportunities to play and try out those choices in spaces outside of conferences, without the time pressure and performance pressure they'll feel in conferences. As Welch (1999) notes: "This kind of play does take practice" (p. 64).

She explains that the "pedagogical moves" of the tutors she's profiled in her essay "didn't happen through chance but resulted from ongoing consideration of how to play against apparent limits. In weekly staff meetings, the tutors examine a particular tutorial and imagine what other stories might be told" (p. 64). She recounts a meeting conversation that ends with a tutor saying "So now I'm wondering what would have happened if I had asked that question earlier" (p. 64), and it's in meetings, Welch (1999) says:

> the tutors consider how through a seemingly simple question or prompt (*When do you . . . Tell me about a time when . . .*) the tutorial can shift from protest to examination and critique, from a sense of futility (*Well, you just have to buckle down and do this*) to the discovery of possibility. Through storytelling and through playing with and against the stories told, the staff meeting becomes a potential space. It offers a view of and a space apart from the week's tutorials, a space for playing with tutoring realities, addressing the obstacles, reaching toward what else could be. (p. 65)

In that meeting, Shiva asked if she could follow Davia, and our conversation of Davia's drawing, with her own image. She held up a drawing that shows a series of triangles point to point. The sequence is numbered, as figures might be, 1 to 5, and through the sequence, the triangles change size in relation to one another. The triangle to the left (red in her drawing) is meant to represent the student writer. The triangle to the right is meant to represent Shiva herself. Across the page, the triangles look like two beaks, beak to beak, about to peck at one another. The student was writing for an advanced English course, and Shiva is an English graduate student.

In the first frame, the student writer's triangle is larger than the small triangle that represents Shiva. In the next frame, both the student writer's triangle and Shiva's triangle have grown in size. In the third frame, the triangles are almost equal in size. And then, in the fourth, the student writer's

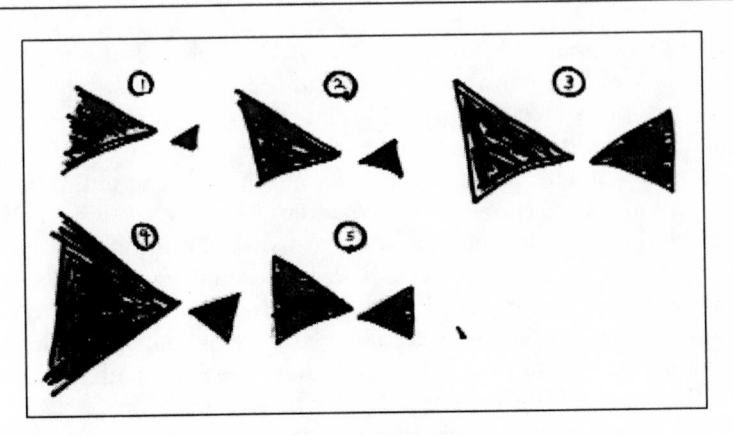

Shiva's drawing.

triangle grows larger still, and Shiva's triangle shrinks to as small as it was two frames earlier. In the final frame, Shiva's triangle shrinks even smaller. The red, growing triangle is meant, Shiva told us, to signify the student's growing annoyance with Shiva and the suggestions she was offering. Shiva pointed to the third frame, where her triangle grows, and said, "I started to get annoyed with her here, and I wanted her to hear me, so I began speaking more loudly. That's why my triangle gets larger." Shiva said that at that point in the conference she had suggested that the student, who she felt was already resisting her suggestions, take a bracketed personal joke with the professor out of the middle of an integrated quotation. "Why not place that joke in a footnote?" Shiva offered. Why inappropriately break up the integrated quotation? No, the student felt the professor would understand.

What is important is that Shiva remembered raising her voice. She knew she had made a decision to assert herself more loudly if not more boldly. But Shiva said that in that moment in conference she had also thought about how we had been talking in previous meetings about the confrontations consultants had found themselves in with students. Thinking of that, she paused, gave herself a moment to think in this conference, and, taking a breath, she realized there was no reason to be locked in such a strong conflict with the student writer. She backed down to change the tenor of the conference, and the image shows us the progression of her thinking and decision making.

Before we had time to comment very fully on Shiva's image, Saeromi raised her hand, and asked to show her drawing. She held it up, and Shiva began to laugh. We turned back and forth looking at one of them and then the other. "I saw the same student," Saeromi said.

In Saeromi's image, two faces float above four arms. One hand, the consultant's, is on the text that sits between them. The student grimaces, her eyebrows a single deep curved line above her eyes. She frowns a tight frown. To the right sits Saeromi. Her eyes are wide and bulging. Her mouth, too, is in a frown, but her frown is more crooked, more confused. Three lines of steam rise between the two figures. "I overheard that conference," Shiva said, "And the student did the same thing to Saeromi. She raised her voice and disagreed, just as she did with me."

Saeromi felt she should have picked up on the student writer's frustration right away. The student began by saying the professor would not accept her paper until she "worked on her writing." She reported that the professor said he couldn't understand her ideas on paper, though he said he knew she had good ideas because she had made insightful comments in class. Saeromi says the student made comments like: "He's giving me a lot of trouble. He's always been like this."

When Saeromi stumbled across sentences she noted as "grammatically cryptic," the student claimed she could not understand because she was not in the class. When Saeromi tried to explain what she felt wasn't working in the sentences, the writer insisted the sentences weren't unclear. And when the student became frustrated, she would say "What if I just erase this whole sentence?" Saeromi would say no, and she said the student would get frustrated all over again. Saeromi was frustrated, too. That look on her face in the drawing, she said, shows how defensive and angry she was feeling, and she realized as the conference went on that she was disengaging. She saw herself backing off, and she "didn't push on sentences that she would have negotiated with other students."

We were all still thinking about Saeromi's difficult conference when she said, "Look," and turned her drawing over, revealing a second image of the same conference. In this drawing, two faces, the faces of the previous picture floated side by side. A single sheet, to represent the text, is in front of the two faces, and above the heads of the two people float three hori-

Saeromi's first drawing.

Saeromi's second drawing.

zontal lines. Saeromi explained that 5 minutes before the end of the conference hour she had stopped the work, turned from the student's text, and said to the student writer, "This was a very uncomfortable conference for me. Could we talk about that?" Saeromi said she apologized for "getting caught up in the process and forgetting to pay attention to what a hard project this was for her and what a difficult history was attached to it." The student writer seemed "more vulnerable," Saeromi said. Her jaw relaxed, and she said she, too, was sorry.

In our meetings this semester we have often thought and talked about how consultants can be explicit as they work with student writers, and how they can be confident enough to name the work they have done in conference. I want to help the consultants see that they can take time in conferences to ask the questions they want to ask. They can take time to address non-text-related issues that are keeping them—or the student writer—from the text. And they should feel they can do the opposite too, and explicitly turn the work of the conference back to the text at hand.

What's important to me, and what I am particularly pleased that the entire staff saw, was the two-sided picture. These were not images of what was and what could be. These were *both* images of what was because of the work we had all been doing together in meetings. Represented in Saeromi's two images, and in Shiva's negotiation, were many, many of their consultant colleague's suggestions from previous weeks. Shiva, working on the other side of the high bookshelf that divides the writing center into two spaces, had heard all of Saeromi's conference as she (un)intentionally eavesdropped. Saeromi and Shiva had already talked and compared their conferences with this same writer, but were it not for this type of in-meeting sharing of experiences, no one else would have seen evidence of how Saeromi had learned from our meetings and carried what she learned into a conference. And no one else on staff would have seen how Shiva had learned from Saeromi's very similar and very different conference with the very same student writer she had struggled with. No one would have seen all the possible ways to conference under similar conditions.

Those conference moments, and that interaction between consultants, replayed before the eyes and ears of the rest of the staff, is what I seek in the work I do with my staff of graduate writing consultants. It's the type of interaction we think we can't plan for, the type of co-learning that we think happens by accident. But more and more I believe that's simply not true. If we want our tutors to feel encouraged to risk imaginative and creative thinking in conferences, we must build a deep listening, learning culture among our tutoring staff so they feel encouraged to imagine creative conference risks in one another's presence.

In fact, in a review of the literature on the social and contextual factors that can create or discourage creativity in the workplace, Christina Shalley and Lucy Gilson (2004) note "one common theme is that individuals need to feel they are working in a supportive work context" (p. 47). In other words, creativity needs company to flourish. When they are in these meetings, my staff needs to feel as if no one will judge their pictures, or the conference decisions they represent, without offering supportive response and additional possibilities left unconsidered in the conferences themselves.

ENCOURAGING CREATIVITY

Reflecting explicitly on the difficulty of a conference with a student while still in conference requires taking some risks, and the staff asked Saeromi if she had thought about those risks. What if the student hadn't wanted to talk? What if the student didn't feel she had been resistant or didn't feel the conference had been difficult? What did *I*, the consultants asked outright, think about what Saeromi did at the end of that conference? And, in positioning me, their director, as the expert who could proclaim Saeromi's conference strategy appropriate, or not, they tried to move away from play, away from considering possibilities, and away from thinking with and riffing off of one another.

Shalley and Gilson (2004) also suggest the research shows that "if leaders truly desire creativity, they need to, in some way communicate this to employees . . . by setting goals or role requirements for producing creative outcomes . . . [or] through modeling the types of behaviors that would be more likely to lead to creativity" (p. 47). When the staff reflects on one another's drawings, and one another's actions, imagining additional possibilities for the moment represented, we are explicitly noting when creative moves have been made in conferences and when they haven't. We are also noting when creative moves *could have* been made.

Additional research reveals that the presence of creative co-workers will do little to spur the creativity of those who work with them if employees feel their supervisors monitor them so closely they are pressured to "do certain things in certain ways," because those expected responses leave employees feeling as if there is an "external locus of causality for their behavior," which "undermines intrinsic motivation" (Zhou, 2003, p. 414). If supervisors offer employees "developmental feedback," however, "their enjoyment in the task and orientation toward learning and improvement enable them to seek challenge and to be persistent and not afraid of making mistakes," and this is what is "essential for their truly mastering and utilizing creativity skills and strategies" (p. 415). Interestingly, "employees with less creative personalities benefited more . . . than those with creative personalities" (p. 420). As Jing Zhou (2003) explains:

in addition to making creative role models such as creative co-workers available, supervisors needed to either not engage in close monitoring or provide developmental feedback. Under these joint conditions, opportunities for acquiring creativity skills and strategies are present, experimentation and exploration of new ideas and solutions are tolerated or encouraged, fear for criticism is diminished, and inhibitions and worries are loosened. Employees with less creative personalities especially benefited from these conditions, as they usually are much more in need of opportunities to learn creativity strategies and of support for experimentation and exploration. (p. 420)

I thought it was interesting that the consultants asked me to say what I thought about what Saeromi had done. Hadn't we been talking for weeks in our meetings about why we would want to encourage this type of explicit reflection? Others on staff had even offered strategies for promoting explicit reflection in conferences. This literature on professional creativity, however, helps me rethink my surprise. If we want WC tutors working together to learn creativity from one another, if we want our tutors taking creative risks, they need at all times to be reminded of that goal and encouraged to take on creative practices, especially from one another. My staff was asking, I realize, if they could take Saeromi's practice as their own. I not only gave them that permission, I once again asked them to offer one another some additional possibilities for how they might approach moments like those confrontational moments Davia and Shiva and Saeromi faced. In the conclusion of *Getting to Know City Kids*, Middlebrooks offers lessons for educators and one of these lessons is "Allow children to participate actively" (p. 146). "That teachers may stand in childrens' way even when the environment they provide is safe and well endowed reminds" Middlebrooks of a conversation she once had "with a fifth grader" who asked why Einstein and Edison "'got to invent everything and we don't'" (p. 146). Middlebrooks says she understood what that student was saying, for although his school and his classroom were conducive to invention and "students often worked in small groups"—"Their work, however, was all the same, often with paper and pencil, and almost every question the children worked on was posed by their teacher" (p. 146). "It is difficult for children to be inventive in teacher-centered classrooms," Middlebrooks notes, and the same is true of writing center tutors (p. 146). It is difficult for writing center tutors to be creative, problem posing thinkers and learners, when their worlds are director-centered. Middlebrooks calls on teachers to "co-construct an environment for learning and doing" (p. 146).

What I know is that if I were now asked to draw my most significant moment of that week in the writing center,[6] I would draw Saeromi holding her two-sided picture up for the other seven writing consultants around the table to see. I would show Shiva leaning forward. Asked to hold that drawing up and describe it, I would talk about how pleased I had been that Shiva had stepped back for a moment in her conference, learning from what we'd been talking about in previous meetings. I'd note how terrific it was that Shiva and Saeromi had talked about their conferences with the same student even before our meeting. And I'd say how much I liked the way the drawings that day picked up on themes we had been discussing all semester and showed moments when consultants were reaching out or grasping out for the most creative conferences strategies they could imagine, even when the conference had been frustrating or intellectually or pedagogically challenging. Then, I'd ask for developmental feedback. I'd say, let's go around once, as we always do at the end of our meetings, and say what we're each left thinking, asking, or wondering. I'd listen, and I'd hope that my staff would listen to me, because sometimes when they hear in that final meta-reflective round that I, too, have a pressing question, one or two of them will appear at my open office door later in the day, peek in, try to understand my worldmaking, and offer much needed encouragement and feedback.[7]

NOTES

1. One of Tamer Amin's early drawings was integral to my thinking about time in the WC. It appears in my essay (Geller, 2005). I had spent a lot of time looking at the Clark writing consultants' early drawings, because, until I began incorporating them into my research, they decorated the sides of the bookcases in my office.
2. I think here of Donald Schön's (1987) suggestive term *professional artistry* and his call, in *Educating the Reflective Practitioner,* that we should "study the experience of learning by doing and the artistry of good coaching" (p. 17). As he notes: "Perhaps, . . . learning *all* forms of professional artistry depends, at least in part, on conditions similar to those created in the studios and conservatories: freedom to learn by doing in a setting relatively low in risk, with access to coaches who initiate students into the 'traditions of the calling' and help them, by 'the right kind of telling,' to see on their own behalf and in their own way what they need most to see" (p. 17).
3. Weber and Mitchell (1996) incorporate wonderful images throughout their article, and, in that piece, they describe their own "critical reading" (p. 306) and theoretical analysis of 64 drawings created by undergraduate and graduate students enrolled in elementary education programs.
4. I learned to make room for that from graduate students Jonathan Lassen, an abstract thinker and geographer, and Shelby Ortega, a psychologist, who were, in previous semesters, both more comfortable with the notion that a visual image of a conference need not be a narrative of the scene and could be a more metaphorical representation of success or struggle. These more abstract drawings

often led to deeper conversations about the conference moments requiring the most consultant creativity.

5. What follows is a combination of what I remember from this meeting and what consultants told me or wrote to me about the conferences they had. I asked each tutor to read the section of this text describing her conference. For a description of this reviewing process see Seidman (1988, p. 54).

6. When the staff draws in a meeting, I, as director, draw too. Often I will not have held any WC conferences of my own, so I will draw a conference I held that week in my office with one of my own students, or a one-to-one WAC/WID consultation I had with a faculty member. That my drawings are usually *not* of writing center conferences helps my staff understand even more about what *I'm* trying to figure out in my work with students and colleagues.

7. Thanks to the Clark University writing consultants who have drawings in this chapter and who talked with me about their conference experiences and read through my description of their experiences: Shiva Aliabadi, Davia Davidson, Saeromi Kim, Ing Phansavath. Thanks, also, to those who generously read and responded to this chapter as I wrote and revised it—Shanti Bruce, Harry Denny, Rebecca Dezan, Gino DiIorio, Kevin Dvorak, Michele Eodice, and Neal Lerner. Thanks to Cheryl Elwell for her help with the chapter's images.

REFERENCES

Geller, A. (2005). Tick-tock, next: Finding epochal time in the writing center. *The Writing Center Journal, 25*(1), 5-24.

Gilewicz, M., and Thonus, T. (2003) Close vertical transcription in writing center training and research. *The Writing Center Journal, 24*(1), 25-48.

Middlebrooks, S. (1998). *Getting to know city kids: Understanding their thinking, imagining and socializing.* New York: Teachers College Press.

Seidman, I. (1998). *Interviewing as qualitative research: A guide for researchers in education and the social sciences.* New York: Teachers College Press.

Schön, D. (1987). *Educating the reflective practitioner: Toward a new design for teaching and learning.* San Francisco: Jossey-Bass.

Shalley, C. E., & Gilson, L. L. (2004). What leaders need to know: A review of social and contextual factors that can foster or hinder creativity. *The Leadership Quarterly, 15,* 33-53.

Weber, S., & Mitchell, C. (1996). Drawing ourselves into teaching: Studying the images that shape and distort teacher education. *Teaching and Teacher Education, 12*(3), 303-313.

Welch, N. (1999). Playing with reality. *College Composition and Communication, 51*(1), 51-69.

Zhou, J. (2003). When the presence of creative coworkers is related to creativity: Role of supervisor close monitoring, developmental feedback, and creative personality. *Journal of Applied Psychology, 88.*

PART III

The "Creative" Writing Center

11

CENTER STAGE

Performing the Culture of Writing at Stanford

Wendy Goldberg

PART I. SETTING THE STAGE

In Summer 2001, when I made my pilgrim's voyage to the site that was to become home to the new Stanford Writing Center, I experienced, I'll not deny it, a slight uneasiness. The 30 x 60-ft freight car-style room—a former science lab located in the basement of the building—was then undergoing extensive renovation: a mass of wires and cords were snaked haphazardly through a maze of musty set tubs and disintegrating lab stations. It was hard for me to imagine that this underground stronghold with its chemical scent would one day become a well-appointed writing center (WC), much less that it might serve as an inviting performance space. But I need not have been concerned: transformation and reinvention were key to the development of the Stanford Writing Center from the outset.

On November 6, 2001, with well wishers from throughout the university community on hand, the WC opened its doors for the first time. The metamorphosis of the Science, Math, and Engineering Lab into a state-of-the-art resource for writing, at once cutting-edge and homey, was as gratifying as it was remarkable. Supported by the Department of English, the School of Humanities and Sciences, and the Office of the Vice Provost for Undergraduate Education, and staffed by the Program in Writing and

Rhetoric, the new WC brought with it the good will, hopes, and energy of a formidable cross section of the university.

On first entering the WC today, one notices a well-lit wall of books at one end with a nest of sofas and armchairs at its base; at the opposite end of the room, a mounted plasma screen rises above a long conference table. Individual consultation carrels run along a third wall, and small offices line the back of the room. The architectural signature of the original space is best represented by a pair of massive concrete pillars that once dominated the lab: now encased in wood paneling from head-to-toe, each pillar sports a wooden "skirt," or circular desk, on which computers sit.

At the opening festivities for the center, the bare walls that greeted visitors contrasted starkly with the generous design and anti-institutional flavor of the whole. These blank surfaces confirmed the Center's status as a work in progress and spoke to far-ranging possibilities for creative self-definition. What kind of place would the Stanford Writing Center become? How might this space be used? One provisional answer to this question found expression in the abbreviated mission statement, spare and hopeful, which appeared in our first promotional brochure: "The Center assists students with all elements of academic writing while sustaining and celebrating the lively culture of writing at Stanford."

If the first part of this formulation was standard and accessible, the second made greater demands, requiring further parsing. What precisely did we have in mind when we proposed to "celebrate the culture of writing," and how did we intend to facilitate this celebration? Such questions and issues had, of course, occupied the attention of the center's new staff from the moment it became clear that this facility would be built. John Tinker and I—both longtime lecturers in Stanford's writing program—were appointed co-coordinators of the WC, with advanced graduate student Christine Holbo playing a significant role in WC planning. Andrea Lunsford, Professor of English and Director of the Program in Writing and Rhetoric (PWR), and PWR Associate Director, Marvin Diogenes, met with us regularly to discuss the philosophy and goals of the new Stanford Writing Center.

Well-known in WC circles for her endorsement of the WC as a locus of collaboration and diversity, Lunsford helped set the tone for this new resource. In her influential essay "Collaboration, Control, and the Idea of a Writing Center," Lunsford (1995) identifies and critiques two prototypes of the traditional WC—the center as "storehouse" and the center as "garret"— ultimately calling for an alternative design. Storehouse centers, Lunsford explains, function as "information centers," packaging and distributing "skills and strategies" for learning (p. 110). From the perspective of the storehouse, knowledge is an individual acquisition; collaboration, if at times tolerated, is not encouraged and may even be openly opposed. Garret centers likewise privilege the individual. However, as viewed from the garret, the individual self is the deep-rooted *source* of knowledge, an insular well of inchoate wisdom to be plumbed rather than the target or *receptor* toward which external knowledge is directed, as is the case with the storehouse.

For Lunsford, who has worked in both settings and acknowledges the strengths of each, neither model is fully satisfying. If the storehouse commodifies knowledge as a product to be "prescribed and handed out," the garret romanticizes it as that "individual and unique" inner voice that enlightened centers are expected to help students locate in themselves. Lunsford proposes, instead, a third perspective, a model of learning that understands knowledge as dynamic and constructed, "mediated . . . through language in social use . . ." (p. 110). Drawing on Kenneth Burke's image of the parlor in which endless discussion ensues even as successive participants move in—and then out—of the conversation, Lunsford envisions a shared space for learning where collaboration prevails, negotiation replaces directive, and difference fosters community as the conversation goes on . . . and on: the WC as "Burkean Parlor" (p. 112). Here, traditional hierarchies soften as academic discourse takes its place among other modes of expression that are likewise valued, and it is the *interplay* between multiple literacies that shapes meaning and invigorates users of language. By accommodating and validating different language-based needs and interests, the Burkean Parlor Center sends a message to all students—from the research writer preparing an abstract, to the creative writer composing a poem, to the junior statesperson rehearsing a speech—that it has something to offer each.

We embraced the challenge of importing this philosophy to our newborn WC. While John's primary administrative task was to coordinate the writing workshops that the WC conducts, my main charge was to help develop and implement the special events that would nurture the talents of our students and strengthen the ties between the WC and the wider community. Sharing resources with our students and providing support for their creative endeavors would enable us to carve out together an expanded arena of celebration in which a wide range of voices could be heard.

PART II. IT'S SHOWTIME: STUDENTS GIVING VOICE TO THEIR EXPERIENCE

Writers' Nights

The sustained attention to rhetoric and oral presentation that is integral to our writing courses contributed to the enthusiasm of the WC staff for the concept of *Writers' Nights*. These special evenings would demonstrate anew that the performance of writing, whether written or spoken, takes place in a rhetorical context that demands careful consideration. We use the term *Writers' Nights* broadly to designate all manner of creative readings and performances at the WC (including those few that have taken place well before dusk). Among the activities encompassed by this term have been poetry and fiction readings sponsored by campus literary magazines; an annual Parents' Weekend Celebration of Writing bringing parents and students together to read their work; an Open Mic reading on Admit Weekend that offers prospective students an opportunity to share their writing; a night of one-act plays; an evening of original song; a solemn recitation of poetry on Election Eve 2004; and a poetry slam featuring high school students from East Palo Alto. On occasion, we have taken our act on the road, in one instance bringing the Stanford Writing Center to the local cable TV station, where we held an Open Mic broadcast on a public access channel.

Our first Writers' Night, a pivotal event that lay the groundwork for the evenings to follow, took place at the initiative of *En!gma Magazine: Stanford's Journal of Black Expression*. Aware that we were interested in developing a performance program, *En!gma* writers proposed a poetry slam for the WC's inaugural reading. We readily agreed, offering to help with publicity and planning. As soon became clear, however, we were woefully ignorant of the protocols that define the institution of the slam. And we were equally clueless, by and large, about the conventions of spoken word, that edgy, street-smart, in-your-face poetry—often memorized and performed rather than read—that is the coin of the realm in slam competitions.

The night of the slam found us rarin' to go at 7 p.m. sharp. Neat rows of chairs in smart lines faced the bookcase that would serve as the backdrop for the reading. A podium stood in state, painstakingly centered. Lights blazed in welcome. Only when it became clear that we would, indeed, have a live audience—as students began trickling in at 7:30—did we dare to stop holding our breath. Not until later did we learn that it was customary, even *de rigeur*, to arrive fashionably late at a slam. When the student emcee took the stage and called for attention, a steady stream of students—multiethnic, of varied ages, with different majors, both men and women—came forward and shared their work. They bemoaned the disappointments of "watered-down love"; railed against "plurality election rules that make us fools"; riffed on the pleasures of "similes so sizzling that your mouth would water"; and lamented lost children "meandering from corner to coroner." The confluence of voices in sustained conversation underscored the role of the WC as a mediating agent and community-building force. Well-intentioned yokels, we clapped too long and too loud that night, at times applauding in the middle of a set to demonstrate our appreciation for a neat turn of phrase.

No more than 15 minutes elapsed before the Master of Ceremonies, perhaps unable to contain himself any longer, introduced a pause in the line-up and addressed the audience squarely. First, politely but insistently, he asked that the lights be dimmed. "Ah, much better," he murmured sotto voce in the darkened room, satisfied at last that the ambience was suitable to the occasion. Next, he suggested that in keeping with the conventions of slam, we register our pleasure and approval by rubbing our fingers together briskly, thumb against forefinger, rather than clapping our hands and disrupting a reading. And finally, clearly intending not only to create the vibe of a sensuous after-hours setting but at the same time to warm up the crowd and lighten the mood, he called on us all to close our eyes, roll our shoulders back and forth languorously, and recite aloud, together: "I feel sexy."

Which we did, rubbing our fingers in time with the beat he set in motion. Any self-consciousness people felt was outweighed by a shared delight in this radical change of mood that swept the room: suddenly, the Stanford Writing Center, the brightly lit home of the 40-minute tutorial, had modulated into a welcome and comfortable venue, more coffee house than classroom. The rigidly arranged rows of chairs now assumed more congenial patterns. The podium was displaced to the side by those who preferred to forego the mic. Best of all, perhaps, in a testimony to the inclusiveness of the event and the contagious good will of the evening, program director Lunsford surrendered joyfully to the occasion: chanting "I feel sexy" along with the rest of us (and more spiritedly than some), she rubbed her fingers together expertly.

On this night full of lively and memorable readings, one stood out among the others, earning its author a prize at the slam. First-year student Mark Otuteye, a self-described "middle-class Ghanaian/black male . . . from Orange County," reading his own work for the first time, inspired audience members to sit up and take notice when he performed what would become one of his signature poems: "What the Hell Do You Think the Stanford Admit Letter Said??" In this painful but cathartic meditation, Mark rehearses aloud the reply he imagines himself offering to a "close friend" of his, "a close friend no more," on "being told . . . flat out the only reason I got into Stanford was 'cause I'm black." At once chiding the "friend" and mocking the perverse mindset that seeks to diminish his achievement, he lets loose in the poem with successive versions of an irresistibly irreverent parody of the traditional Admit Letter. He suggests in one iteration, "Maybe you think it [the letter] went something like this:

Dear Negro,
Down with the white man!
Don't worry bout those SAT scores and damn AP scores
And damn those grades or those rec-o-mmen-da-tors

We don't look at none of that shit:
You're black! You're fly! You're J I double G Y
You eat your watermelon and you like your chicken fried!
....
You're ghetto. We know it! But we will never say
At Stanford University, you get in anyway.
You're stupid. We know it! Just sign the lie below and
You're in you're in we love your skin and this is how we show it!
Signed:
Sincerely whack,
Stanford

That this poem ultimately concludes in a stylized dramatic reversal on a note of affirmation—with Mark defiantly proclaiming his name and exhorting "y'all who worked your ass off to get in" to "fight back"—is only one of the reasons for the wild cheers that erupt whenever he performs this piece. Eschewing the niceties of PC, the poem speaks to a complex of concerns regarding issues of competence, bias, and identity that too often go unacknowledged in the dining hall though on the minds of many students. Nor is the charged question of "why did you get in" the exclusive province of underrepresented groups. What college student newly arrived in the halls of academe hasn't wondered silently or aloud: am I part of the geographical distribution quota? an Admissions mistake? Surely among the students gathered to hear Mark that evening were those wrestling with similar issues through the more traditional vehicle of the personal essay. The opportunity to hear familiar feelings expressed aloud in an alternative mode may have added depth to their understanding of the subject and greater texture to their compositions. The shared release of tension that the "Admit Letter" encourages is well served by Mark's delivery. He imparts his message with just the right style—the wry inflection, the well-timed pause, the eloquent gesture required to reach his intended audience. The hour grew late but no one wanted to be the first to leave the circle in the parlor.

Parents' Weekend Celebration of Writing

Emboldened by the success of our first Writers' Night at the WC, we continued to coordinate readings with campus literary magazines and to think about the various ways we might enlist and support the rich array of writing talent in the university community. We got lucky when husband and wife writers Thomas Pope and Freya Manfred, he a screenwriter, she a poet and memoirist, wrote to say they planned to visit their sons on Parents' Weekend and would be happy to conduct small writing workshops on campus. While assorted logistics precluded our taking advantage of this offer, we were reluctant that the pair should leave town without first having shared their interest and expertise in writing with our students. We conveyed these sentiments to them and thus set in motion the chain of events that would culminate in our first annual Parents' Weekend Celebration of Writing.

Why not, we reasoned, bring parents and students together for this special weekend in a single well-orchestrated event to learn from and enjoy one another's writing? Such a prospect held multiple attractions. A reading providing parents and children with the opportunity to share their writing would prove mutually validating as each acknowledged the other's voice and efforts to be heard. Additionally, students who needed further evidence that writing plays a meaningful role in the world beyond the ivory tower would have a chance to hear from practicing adult writers, both career writers and those for whom writing serves as a valued professional tool. Finally, the Celebration would expand the compass of the WC, drawing in visiting Stanford families while permitting alumni parents a second chance to make their voices heard at the university.

After making the necessary calls to ensure that the WC reading would be included on the official Parents' Weekend agenda, we set to work on publicity and planning. Communications inviting parents to participate in the event would be handled through the university press office. With the assistance of our student services specialist, we designed flyers announcing the reading, to be posted in dining halls and dorms and distributed to students by their writing instructors. It soon became apparent that recruiting students personally and urging them to bring their parents aboard was the optimal way to proceed. The personal invitation to participate in events represented a vote of confidence. The one-to-one contact reminded students that WC staff members knew them individually and had watched their writing skills develop. Not surprisingly, students who enjoyed a sense of identification with the WC were genuinely motivated to bring their parents by to see their work—and willingly encouraged the folks to share their own writing. And so the process began.

This time, when people drifted into the WC in a leisurely manner, we were prepared. Experience had taught us that it is not only slams that call for a stylishly late entrance at Stanford. Lights were dimmed appropriately, leaving the WC neither too bright nor too dark, and flowers and refreshments graced a corner table. The once bare walls now bore a portrait of Sappho wielding a stylus. More than 90 people gathered in the WC that evening to hear original writings that conveyed a shared love of language, a desire to connect, and pride in the work being celebrated.

Not surprisingly, student readers outnumbered participating parents and were representative of diverse backgrounds and political perspectives. A meditation on gay rights by Ellen Freytag, editor of *Masque: Stanford's Journal of Gay Expression*, climaxed in the rueful observation, "Sometimes it's easy to forget that you're the one that marriage needs protection from." In "Latin Lover," Caroline Kuntz dramatized the ambivalence a mixed heritage can produce: "I don't want a Latino Lover. . . . but who else will love me . . . who will bring me back. . . ." Shahid Buttar, already well known on campus for his political activism and the elastic and loose-limbed delivery he brought to spoken word poetry, repeatedly invoked "Big Brother Ashcroft" and cautioned listeners, "We're at war over what we stand for."

The Pope family came through ensemble, with twins Rowan and Bly joining their father, author of *Good Scripts, Bad Scripts: Learning the Craft of Screenwriting Through 25 of the Best and Worst Films in History*, in reading a short scene he had written expressly for the occasion. Intent on offering advice to young writers, Freya Manfred shared selections from *Frederick Manfred, a Daughter Remembers*, her account of the life of her novelist father, author of 24 published novels. Other parents and children partnered as well: sophomore Josh Benson, who would become, on graduating, chief speech writer for California gubernatorial candidate Steve Wesley, dusted off the eloquent introspective piece that he'd composed for his first-year writing class. In this essay he recalls the letter he painstakingly composed at age 9 to his hero Carney Lansford, Angels third baseman, who was retiring. Benson Sr. followed up with an essay of his own.

Few of us present at the WC that night will forget the experience of hearing Elizabeth (Liz) Phillips read her poem "Socrates." Then a first-year student who would go on to participate in virtually every Writers' Night we hosted at the WC until she graduated, Liz has been blind since the age of 6 months, a victim of "Shaken Baby" syndrome. Whether reading a poem or story or singing the eerily beautiful and original songs she treated us to regularly, she enriched the creative life of the WC (thereby enriching her own, she reminded us). What follows is the first stanza from her poem "Socrates":

"What is virtue?" he asks,
And I begin
To stare at the sun and tell him
And turn blind.
I say virtue is water
That fills my fixed eyes so I
Don't notice true things about light.
He persists. "What do we know about virtue," he asks.
I tell him, what do we know about ourselves?

Mark Otuteye, our slam champ and prince of spoken word, was on hand to conclude the evening, his pleasure in the performance of writing unmistakable and contagious. In the audience that night, waiting patiently for a glimpse of their son, were Mark's parents, who by their own account and to the wonder of all had no idea that Mark wrote poetry, much less that he read it aloud to packed rooms. Imagine, then, their surprise when he dazzled us all with the tribute he offered them that evening. Asking the audience to chime in with the refrain that gave his poem its name, he turned to face his parents and let them know how it felt to be raised in the circle of their care: "IT'S ALL GOOD!" we shouted aloud together as he began his piece. Echoing this same sentiment, the father of one poet-reader rose to his feet when Mark was through to thank the students and salute the WC for making such a joyful celebration possible.

The gratifying response of parents and students, spectators and participants, to our inaugural slam and our first Celebration of Writing reinforced our conviction that *creativity has a defining role to play in the life of the writing center.* E-mail that arrived in the wake of Parents' Weekend brought appreciative comments from students describing the reading as "inspiring." "It left me awestruck," offered one, "at the depth and talent of my peers— it is a side of Stanford that I value the most, but have a hard time finding." A young woman who had to be coaxed to read her short story by friends confided, "Even though I was nervous and intimidated, I'm glad I shared anyway, 'cause there was a very positive vibe in there." The reverberations of that "vibe"—an energy that has grown and spread—have yielded any number of outstanding initiatives and projects in the days, months, and now years, that have followed. Two such endeavors deserve special mention: the formation of the Stanford Spoken Word Collective and the production of *The Hip-Hopera.*

The Stanford Spoken Word Collective

For the Stanford Spoken Word Collective, the Stanford Writing Center is home: the place where it got its start, holds its weekly meetings, and most consistently performs. In Winter 2002, students Mark Otuteye and Shahid Buttar applied for and were awarded the university's prestigious Pierce Prize, a grant dedicated to the promotion of the arts. Using these funds to seed the Spoken Word Collective, the two formed a group comprising 16 poets with diverse backgrounds and contrasting academic majors who together have created the intensely collaborative repertoire that the Collective performs campus-wide and beyond. Also known as "Juiced Truth," the Stanford Spoken Word Collective competes nationally in college poetry slams (making it all the way to the semifinals in the Poetry

Slam Invitational) and has produced and released three of its own CDs, including "The Best of Juiced Truth: Spoken Not Slurred." Active political-ly, Collective members are often invited to do sets at local peace rallies.

Modeling the values of the WC itself, the group embraces innovation. Rejecting a conventional hierarchy that privileges academic discourse above all other modes of expression, Collective members reinforce one another in experimenting with multivocal literacies and collaborative writ-ing. At Thursday night meetings at the WC, open to anyone interested in spoken word, students can be found actively writing together, warming up for the evening with improvisational exercises that involve the entire group in a single round-robin composition. Those who might otherwise be reluc-tant to speak up or commit themselves to a written page will often find their comfort level in this group dynamic. At times, more than 30 people have shown up for these meetings; more than 85 students auditioned this spring to join the Collective.

At the end of the quarter, with the graduation of the group's senior members looming, the Collective decided to toast itself with a formal ban-quet. In what was a notable first for the WC, the students draped adjacent tables with elegant white cloth; imported flowers, candles, and cutlery; cooked, conveyed, and served—from soup to nuts—dinner for 20; and with jazz playing softly in the suitably dim light, transformed the Stanford Writing Center into a regal banquet hall. Fit for a Collective.

The Hip-Hopera

Although it might have been the lure of Writers' Nights that first drew Debbie Burke to the WC to read and perform, it was the amenities and feel of the place—the nest of computers, the open work space, the lively, easy-going atmosphere—that brought her back almost daily. Debbie soon became a familiar figure at the WC, always deeply immersed in what she was doing, and "what she was doin'" was exciting. Quietly and persistently, over the course of 2 years, Debbie composed a multiact original theatrical piece, a work she entitled *The Hip Hopera*, orchestrated through drama, song, and dance. This family saga, which its creator directed, staged, and per-formed in, probes the experience of three generations of African-American women who live in vastly different eras but share common wounds inflict-ed by prejudice. Magical interludes that fracture time enable Inka, Magnolia, and LaShelle, the work's three protagonists, along with a large multicultural cast that provides historical context, to commune together to remember and retell the painful stories that must precede healing.

During the extensive composition process that produced *The Hip-Hopera*, Debbie, by her own account, felt well-supported by the WC, whose writing instructors read her drafts regularly and carefully and responded to this unique project with encouragement and suggestions. The show played on campus in February 2004 to large sold-out crowds and exuberant reviews. In the weeks that followed, audience members formed study groups that met at the WC to screen and discuss selected scenes of the show. Debbie's love of writing and her ability to make things happen also expressed themselves in the debut of *Soul Sistah Magazine,* the Stanford journal she founded celebrating the spirituality of black women. We take special pride in the fact that Debbie regards the WC as the "birthing place" proper of *The Hip-Hopera.*

Research Forums

The cycle of activities that continues to flow from the "positive vibe" of our very first Writers' Nights has evolved and renewed itself more than once as the WC becomes a genuine center of writing. In addition to hosting a round of annual readings—including the Open Mic for prospective students that is now an Admit Weekend tradition—we continue to explore alternative avenues of creative expression, with special emphasis on those that help make academic writing practices more natural and accessible to students.

One program that marries formal and informal elements of academic exposition is our series of quarterly Research Forums: students nominated by their writing instructors for exceptional work give oral presentations on their projects, often supported by multimedia. Last fall, for example, in an alternately humorous and sobering talk entitled "My Monkey and Me," two students aired and analyzed their original audio essay evaluating the condition of monkeys living in an underground campus laboratory "behind surveillance cameras, air-locked doors, and security guards." Having first created a buzz around their project with a playful promotional blurb that left readers wondering exactly *where* these monkeys were being held and *why,* the two presenters proceeded to answer these questions with their audio essay, a cogent argument for specific modifications in the monkeys' living conditions. Analysis of the various rhetorical considerations that informed the production of the audiotape followed as the two young men explained why they chose the audio form for their project, reviewed the criteria they had used for determining which taped segments to include, and discussed the balance they'd sought to maintain between logical and emotional appeals. This spring, in a very different kind of presentation, a trio of students from one of our community service writing sections collaborated on a talk in which they used PowerPoint to illustrate and analyze the fire safety manual they'd prepared—and had accepted for distribution—by the neighboring town of Woodside.

Just as Writers' Nights recognize and validate alternative forms of expression, encouraging students to see spoken word and academic writing not as sworn rivals forever at odds but as neighbors with plenty to say to one another, so Research Forums ask students to recognize that academic writing itself is a flexible form that has varied applications. Our Research Forums help to demystify academic writing for students by demonstrating that effective prose is equally active and observable in a thoughtful well-organized oral presentation supported by multimedia that "rocks" as in a traditional academic essay.

"How I Write" Conversations

In collaboration with Undergraduate Research Programs, the WC also hosts "How I Write" sessions, informal interviews featuring Stanford professors conversing about their writing practices with Hi Hon Obenzinger, Undergraduate Research Program Associate Director. Very little is out of bounds in these discussions, as the professors describe how they write, when they write, where they write (one speaker explained that she was most inspired in the shower and had installed a waterproof greaseboard on the stall wall), even what they wear when they write, and so forth. The speakers also share reliable sources of inspiration and their chosen methods for combating writer's block if they are so cursed. A number of these writers move regularly between fiction and academic writing, and engineers and scientists are as abundantly represented as English professors and historians. For our students, listening to these professors talk about their writing practices not only renders the speakers less intimidating but also humanizes the writing process itself.

In the course of the 4 years since the WC opened, we have had the chance to work closely and productively with an ever-widening circle of students who make use of and appreciate the resources offered by the WC. These close relationships have made it possible for us to learn together from the inevitable tensions and challenges that arise in a community. When, for example, a student read a story on Parents' Weekend so sexually graphic that it would have surprised no one if an uncomfortable visitor had walked out, we were able to talk frankly and constructively—nonjudgmentally—about conventions of the rhetorical situation, philosophies of free speech, and strategies for pushing limits. On another occasion, when a casual conversation about Eminem devolved into a virtual plebiscite on whether "white men can rap," we used the opportunity to identify and critique complex and competing constructions of identity. Language can be contested in the Burkean Parlor, where it is possible for us to understand one another even while disagreeing.

PART III. ANOTHER OPENING, ANOTHER SHOW: COMMUNITY OUTREACH

Efforts on the part of the WC to reach out to the surrounding community beyond Stanford have taken a variety of forms. When a senior English teacher from neighboring Woodside High informed us that her students were passionately interested in the culture of spoken word, we arranged for her to bring her class to a daytime workshop led by the Collective. Not only did "Juiced Truth" wow the high school students with well-selected performance samples, but Collective members also treated the young students to a lively history of spoken word, part of the interactive workshop they had developed for the occasion. We learned a great deal that afternoon watching our students teach. As is often the case at the WC, learning became an ongoing, mutual conversation as distinctions between teachers and students grew hazy.

Without question, our most ambitious and rewarding community outreach program has been Project W.R.I.T.E. (Writing and Reading as Integral Tools for Education): this 10-week long creative enrichment program brings students from local high schools to the WC each Saturday during Winter quarter. Project W.R.I.T.E. grew out of the interest and commitment of Stanford students Ajani Husbands (2005) and Taurean Brown (2005), former co-presidents of *En!gma Magazine*. Determined to contribute meaningfully to the educational experience of students of color in East Palo alto and to strengthen the ties between Stanford and the surrounding community, Ajani and Taurean raised the funds necessary to enroll 15 students in a pilot workshop in 2003.

Taught by graduate students, undergraduate coordinators, and WC staff, the workshop culminated in its first year on Community Day (a biennial event bringing members of the larger community to campus) with a class poetry slam and the unveiling before friends and family of an eye-catching mural that the students had themselves designed and painted. A brilliant explosion of color composed of four free-standing panels, each with a multicultural motif, this glorious piece languished briefly in storage. Now, two panels look down from the walls of the Stanford Black House. The other two, luminous in splashed orange and green, have been installed on the walls of the WC.

Project W.R.I.T.E. has grown increasingly robust each year, enrolling additional students, bringing in undergraduate mentors, and undertaking a variety of ambitious final projects. Last year, after reading selected works on the theme of language and identity (with special reference to Gloria Anzaldua's "How to Tame a Wild Tongue" and John Baugh's "Linguistic Pride and Racial Prejudice"), the students produced a small literary magazine featuring their own creative writing and essays. Written evaluations collected at the end of each year make it clear that participating high school students derive great satisfaction, both socially and intellectually, from the Project W.R.I.T.E. experience. Most express a strong desire to see the program continue and report that they would be happy if it were also extended each spring. For many of the students active in the workshop, the famous institution in their backyard has now become a more familiar, accessible, and appealing place.

PART IV. CODA

Over the last 4 years, our Parents' Weekend Celebration of Writing has acquired the force and resonance of tradition. Looking back we see clearly that it was the debut of this event in 2002 that first signaled the WC's importance as a site of performance. This past February, our Parents' Weekend Reading included a tribute to four graduating seniors—Liz Phillips, Mark Otuteye, Debbie Burke, and Chelsea Steiner (also a member of the Collective)—all of whom cut their teeth in public performance at our Writers' Nights and have continued to figure prominently in the life of the WC. To reinforce the ceremonial flavor of the evening and duly acknowledge the graduates, we composed brief written tributes for each student and presented all four with gifts. In an effort to surprise and delight Liz, a philosophy major, we had the good fortune to locate a phrenological bust in the tradition of L. N. Fowler, master of the "science" of character divination: it is said that by carefully feeling the bumps on the head, the skilled phrenologist can read the psyche and its humors. Through the good offices of the Student Disability Resource Center, we were able to translate the explanatory labels on the bust, all of which identify functions of the brain, into Braille.

Nor was this the only surprise of the evening. Members of the Stanford Spoken Word Collective honored founding member Mark and "calendar tsar" Chelsea with a genuinely unexpected, custom-made spoken word tribute. Borrowing from the themes, rhythms, and diction of signature pieces by Chelsea and Mark, the Collective expressed admiration for the pair's poetic skills, and appreciation for the loving energy the two brought to their leadership of the group. "You gave me a voice and showed me how to use it," chanted one Collective member. "Without you, how would we name our children?" asked another.

On leaving the WC that night one parent observed aloud, "What an amazing program this was. And what a very special place the Writing Center is." An e-mail note received the next morning by members of the writing program carried the blunt message that was itself, perhaps, the best testimony to the evening's success. Writing under the subject line "o, baby, what a night," Andrea Lunsford exulted: "Eat your hearts out all you who missed last night's extravaganza in the Writing Center. . . . [T]o all in the Writing Center: this was surely one of our finest moments."

I am ultimately persuaded, of course, that what Lunsford and others were responding to that evening went well beyond a recognition of the talents and skills of our students, however impressive those abilities might be. Far more striking as the evening unfolded was the students' authentic ownership of the moment they had created together through diverse expressive styles and from different vantage points. Whatever the show was, it was their show, imbued with the meanings they had brought to it collectively, as authors and collaborators. Their shared love for language and mutual respect for one another's abilities produced a heady exuberance and a fruitful cross-fertilization: students were moving beyond their natural comfort zones, experimenting with alternative styles. Those inclined to confine themselves to academic forms began experimenting with creative modes of expression while students averse to academic writing began recognizing its possibilities and testing their own. The culture of writing at Stanford inhered in the very fabric of the evening's program. And clear to all was the role that the WC had played—and continues to play—in fostering this culture. The compact, we believe, is a good one: the Stanford Writing Center accommodates and facilitates our students' needs and aims, providing them with a vital space and context in which to write and perform; the students reciprocate abundantly, conferring on the WC its vibrant creative identity.

Still . . . those who were not present at the WC that evening need not worry or feel left out. There will be many more such moments to come. The WC will continue to evolve and reinvent itself, the celebration will proceed, and the conversation in the Burkean Parlor will go on and on . . .

REFERENCE

Lunsford, A. (1995). Collaboration, control, and the idea of the writing center. In C. Murphy & J. Law (Eds.), *Landmark essays on writing centers* (pp. 109-116). Davis, CA: Hermagoras.

12

BUILDING LABYRINTHS IN ORDER TO ESCAPE

A Guide to Making Play Work

Julie Reid

In this chapter I share how I bridged a gap between traditional writing center (WC) work and the traditional creative writing workshop. I show how and why I created and implemented a series of creative writing "playshops," where writers were invited to the WC to engage in writing games designed to generate ideas and texts while creating a community of writers. I also offer various games and methods other WCs can use in order to facilitate these playshops at their own institutions.

* * *

I was hired as a student tutor at Sonoma State University's WC in 2001 while pursuing an undergraduate degree in English literature. Being myself a creative writer, I was interested in the fact that, while the WC offered an abundance of constructive and individual support to the composition-based writer, it had nothing comparable in place for the creative writer. Being also very familiar with the traditional creative writing class or "workshop," in which students bring in their own work to be critiqued by fellow classmates, I believed quite sincerely that creative writers were in dire need of an environment in which they could feel a sense of community among themselves, and generate work within that safer haven.

In my opinion the "workshop" contributed very little to the effect of making better *writers*. By its design, it seemed more suited for making better *critics*. I noticed this first and foremost in my own development as a writer in these workshops; what seemed to improve the most during the course of them was my ability to discuss and navigate others' poems and stories, while my actual writing changed very little. It was a combination of my disenchantment with the workshop and the ideas I received while enrolled that same semester in a Writing Center Theory and Practice seminar, taught by Writing Center Director Scott Miller, which were the impetus for what was to become the antithesis of the workshop, what would come to be known as the Parlour Parlour "playshop."

My own experience of learning to write had been suffused with playfulness, and was largely influenced by the wealth of writing experiments, games and constraints invented by various Surrealists and members of Oulipo. These were beneficial to my own process of writing, especially as a way of delivering me from the initial guardedness and discomfort I often experienced at the beginning of writing, particularly when faced with that ever-daunting blank page. Early on in the semester I expressed to Scott my own sense of the absence of a play element in the academy. I tentatively asked his opinion of creating a space in the WC that would be essentially an environment in favor of experiment, play, and collaboration; a space for writers to participate in discovering what they mean to say, and in so doing, realize more of the true pleasures of writing.

The playshop would not critique work, but show students how to generate it. Lots of it. It would teach them a process by which "ideas" could be found at every turn, and through which language could be made new and surprising again. Scott was very supportive of the idea and granted me permission to flesh it out as my final project in his writing theory seminar.

My research into the field of writing and play yielded an inexhaustible source of material. Certainly, I was not the first person to think of such a pairing. And yet, if the history of writing was brimming with play, why was play still so curiously absent in the academic environment as I knew it? It was while I was still riddling over this question that I came across the particularly curious claim by Oulipo member Jacques Roubaud: that Oulipo, and the ideas that propelled it as a literary movement, had "nothing in common with the academy." The name Oulipo, deriving from an abbreviation of *Ouvroir de Litterature Potentialle*, or, in English, "Workshop for Potential Literature," was formed in 1960 by about a dozen mostly French mathematicians and writers committed to researching the formal devices used by writers throughout the centuries, as well as the potential patterns in formal languages (such as mathematics and chess) which could be "cannibalized" and put to use to create literary texts. As this kind of "play with constraints" had helped me so much personally, as a writer who was also a student, I didn't see why it couldn't also greatly benefit writers at the university level. This idea of "constrained freedom" inherent in play compelled me further when I found it linked to the form of the festival by sociologist Johan Huizinga (1950), in his study of the play element in culture. Both play and the festival, he wrote, "combine strict rules with genuine freedom" (p. 22). This seemed, to me, the very echo of Raymond Queneau's definition of an Oulipian: "a rat who builds the labyrinth from which he plans to escape."

An Oulipian constraint, for example, that of creating a text in which every word must begin with the same letter of the alphabet, requires that the writer "invent" a way out of the constraint, a self-assertive act that provides new knowledge and a sense of pleasure once the "problem" has been solved. In addition, the constraint requires that the writer not rely on his or her habitual mode of generating writing; he or she must get something meaningful across by using only words which begin with, say, the letter "A." It is ultimately when the usual modes of expression are roped off, that is, when the writer can no longer make meaning using words that begin with "B"-"Z" and must make do with only words that begin with "A," that an alternate and inevitably more playful and surprising level of expression can surface. Another Oulipian game known as "N + 7," invented by Jean Lescure, a kind of poets' version of Mad Libs, in which a poem's nouns (N) are all replaced by the system of finding each one in a dictionary and then counting seven nouns down to find the one which should replace it (+7), allows students to see for themselves how to generate surprising, vivid imagery and juxtapositions, which couldn't have been arrived at in a usual linear fashion of thinking.

Although its theories were fundamental to my desire to create a festive atmosphere for writers in the writing center, the Oulipian model of play in writing was far from the only one to yield rich material. The Surrealists, having invented an exuberant number of provocative writing games, are a source of endless playfulness and discovery, although somewhat in opposition to the ideas of the Oulipians. While the Oulipian game is constructed around specific strategies of writing which necessarily transform expression through the limitations of constraint, the Surrealist game embraces the limitless possibilities of language inherent in the process of chance. The Surrealist model relies on the spontaneous and automatic, whereas the Oulipian model swears by the generative power of adhering to a form. Both schools of thought have been indispensable in my own development as a writer; both maintain an unflagging dedication to the spirit of play and the power inherent in it. And both being in favor of the three things I wanted the playshop to encompass: collaboration, play, and experimentation, I elected to frame it along the borrowed principles of each.

I called the would-be playshop, "Parlour Parlour," so named partly for the pleasingly old-fashioned lilt of the word "parlour" itself—exponentially increased by the use of it twice—but also to conjure up the atmosphere of an intimate space where games are played in groups. This "atmosphere" would need to be further established, I felt, to make it festival-like. Something would be needed to initiate a separation between the world outside Parlour Parlour and the world inside of it. A way in which, as I had learned from Huizinga, a kind of "standstill" to ordinary life could be established, so that writers could lay aside their preconceived ideas of either "good" or "bad" writing and feel completely safe to become active enthusiastic participants. For this, I thought, something slightly silly might suffice, like passing around a little plate of children's vitamins. I must admit, I had personal reasons for making this decision. I hate swallowing any kind of pill, and have always secretly wished that adult medicines and vitamins were also chewable and sweetened like candy. So you could say I was looking for an excuse to bring children's vitamins into my life, although this is not to say I didn't also believe they would serve a more serious initiatory purpose in the playshop. After all, who knows the art of playing better than children? And how better to remember what it was like to be children than to repeat some of the actions we carried out back then?

As children, we played freely with other children we didn't know; conspired with them to create new and secret languages. We were natural poets then, because the world, and the words we were still in the process of learning as a way of describing the world, were still "playthings." If we look at it from this point of view, one doesn't need to learn *how* to be a poet, but rather, must be jogged into *remembering* what it was like to be one. Therefore, childlike activity is beneficial in a playshop because it helps recall the natural poetic ability of childhood.

> **"Childlike activity is beneficial in a playshop because it helps recall the natural poetic ability of childhood."**

Another playful activity I thought would be beneficial to each session would be the adoption of a pseudonym by each participant, the taking on of a "different identity" serving as another means of looking at the world from an unaccustomed standpoint. By opening each session with the same small "rituals," the participants of each playshop would have a means by which they were initiated into an atmosphere where it was deemed safe not to be themselves, a world in which they were safely ensconced and could feel free to experiment without the pressure of writing something "presentable" or "good." Each session could then be loosely led by myself and other fellow writing tutors, following a daily "menu" of writing activities for that day. Choosing from the multitudinous array of games and exercises which abounded would be the hardest part, but could be decided on based on similarities of theme, such as collaborative writing, or a particular writer who generates writing through games, such as Jackson MacLow or Bernadette Mayer. My finished project consisted of a flexible outline of a semester's worth of Parlour Parlour sessions, to be held once every 2 weeks for roughly 90 minutes each.

What resulted when the first Parlour Parlour playshop commenced in the spring semester of 2002 was thrilling beyond my expectations. I had harbored a secret worry that maybe no one would want to play, that maybe the playful spirit of it would be misunderstood, construed as too silly, that maybe I'd taken it a little too far with the Flintstones vitamins. But from one Parlour Parlour to the next, interest and attendance grew. Many tutors on the WC staff attended these meetings and reported that the playshop re-acquainted them with their own sense of playfulness and discovery and, in turn, deepened their capacity for successful tutoring. The assistant director, Kevin Dvorak, who was also very dedicated to integrating a larger aspect of play into the WC, and other fellow student tutors, were integral to Parlour Parlour's success. As the very essence of a playshop had taken its inspiration from the *playground*, an arena for children to invent, impersonate, perform and play games together, for the most part without regulation by teachers, it was key that Parlour Parlour be guided by students, each doing his or her own research on the nature of play and writing, and bringing it to the Parlour Parlour table in turn. Encouraging everyone, including university faculty as well as interested writers in the surrounding community to attend, promoted a spirit of friendliness and fostered an open exchange of knowledge and ideas. In this manner, our director, Scott Miller became one of Parlour Parlour's "students," who soon declared that the resulting heightening of his sense of play put him closer in touch with himself as a poet, and allowed him to re-explore aspects of himself as such which he had all but abandoned.

SETTING UP A PLAYSHOP

What follows is an in-depth guide to setting up and conducting a playshop. I am pleased to say that it is neither expensive nor difficult. The most difficult task may be procuring a private room, preferably the same one each time, in which the Parlour Parlour sessions may be held. A large rectangular table or series of tables that can be formed into a rectangle are ideal, although any table and chair arrangement will generally work fine. As far as materials are concerned, it will depend on your activities for that day, but you will want to always have enough paper to distribute to all participants for however many games you plan to play. If someone wants to use his or her own paper, it is not a problem, but you want to make sure there is enough for everybody. Also have extra pens or pencils on hand just in case anyone hasn't brought his or her own. You will also need to purchase ahead of time a packet or two of self-adhesive "*Hello, my name is . . .*" name tags, on which participants will write their pseudonyms for each session, and a bottle of children's vitamins, or hard candies, if preferred. The stickers are readily available in office supply stores and some drug stores, and the vitamins or candies can be found in any supermarket. Choose any brand you like; we found ourselves partial to Flintstones. Almost without exception, everyone at our sessions felt compelled to look and see what flavor and cartoon character he or she had chosen before eating it!

Once you have these basic materials, you will need to design a "menu" for each session and a flyer that you can post around the school inviting people to attend. The flyers can be as simple or creative as you like, but I always included some eye-catching image that ties in somehow with the text advertising the playshop. For instance, Parlour Parlour 4's flyer was centered around an old picture of the famous French funambulist Blondin, crossing Niagara Falls on a tightrope blindfolded. The caption beneath the picture read: "SSU's Writing Center Presents Parlour Parlour 4: For Writers Who are Serious About Taking Chances," and beneath that, in smaller type: "Put the danger back in your writing life. Join us Wednesday, March 27th, from 11:30 to 1:00, in Schulz 2019. Tightropes will be supplied. (Tights, however, will not)."

Be sure to post your flyer well enough in advance and in enough places so that people will notice it in plenty of time to make plans to attend.

Say you're planning a playshop, as we did, which concentrates on collaboration. The menu for that day might then be shaped as shown below. For this session, we began by taking vitamins and inventing our pseudonyms for the day. This was done by distributing a blank name tag to each participant. Everyone was given ample time to think of a name that conjured up something interesting, be it funny, literary, or otherwise. The pseudonyms would then be collected face-down into a pile, from which each person would then randomly choose one, and proceed, for the rest of the meeting, to allow that "identity," or whatever his or her idea of that identity might be, to influence his or her writing responses. For the first meeting, it helps to briefly discuss the pseudonym and the purpose it can serve us as writers, as one of the many instruments through which we can attempt to free ourselves from a habitual

> **Menu**
>
> Vitamins in Flintstone Sauce
> Pseudonyms (family style)
> Fake Poems/Real Poems
> Love Letter for Four—
> a cheese course
>
> Dessert:
>
> Fortune Cookie
> Split Many Ways

Menu for collaboration workshop.

state of mind. You can compile a list of authors who have written under assumed names throughout history, and discuss the various impetuses for this behavior. For our first meeting, I brought in a list of the 174 pseudonyms used by Voltaire.

The menu is a fun way of outlining the activities you have planned for your playshop, but it also works as a gauge to help you keep the session on track. Try to be realistic about how long a game may actually take to complete, but it is not the end of the world if you don't get to all the activities you have planned. You will also find that some activities work better than others. In my own experience I found that games with the least complicated directions seemed to yield the best results. You can also pretest games for playshops with a group of friends or fellow tutors.

In addition to making a menu, there are a few other simple things you can do to help set the tone of your playshop. A provocative quote, anecdote, and/or visual image on an additional handout can add infinitely to what you wish to communicate. For example, in addition to our collaborative "menu," we also distributed a handout headed with a quote by Roland Barthes: "I enwrap the other in my words." Below that were two anecdotes gleaned from Linda Tomol Pennisi and Patrick Lawler's (1994) "Without a Net: Collaborative Writing":

> When Man Ray and Marcel Duchamp first met in Ridgefield, N.J., they didn't have a common language with which to communicate. Duchamp could barely speak English while Man Ray knew nothing of French—so they played tennis, a game made more appealing because they slaved without a net. Though their game lacked the grammar of the game, it still contained its own language. Man Ray would call out the score while Duchamp would shake his head in agreement.
>
> To potluck suppers, my mother often brought Pittsburgh cake, a recipe given to her by an old Hungarian woman from, of course, Pittsburgh. There was a loose structure to these meals—each woman signed her name next to a category: salad, vegetable, dessert, on a clipboard in the church vestibule. What resulted was a meal which represented thirty or so different families. When placed together on the buffet table, though, these often basic dishes were transformed. They spoke of something larger—an agreement of cooperation. (p. 225)

By prefacing a playshop with examples of collaboration in the larger world, its participants are encouraged to see how experimenting with their own forms of collaboration brings them into the world's ongoing conversation of what collaboration is and what it means. It changes a roomful of writers playing childlike games into a small portion of a larger network grappling with the same daunting questions of relating to each other.

CREATING YOUR OWN PLAYSHOP

Playing Games

Outlined here are some detailed instructions for games we have played at
our Parlour Parlour sessions, but there is a wealth of ideas to be had just by
acquiring two books and logging on to one Web site. These three indispensable resources are:

- *Surrealist Games*. Compiled and presented by Alastair Brotchie
  and edited by Mel Gooding. Published by Shambhala Redstone
  Editions, Boston, 1993.
- *Oulipo Compendium*. Edited by Harry Matthews and Alastair
  Brotchie. Published by Atlas Press, London, 1998.
- Bernadette Mayer's list of writing experiments found on many
  Web sites, and at the time of this publication, on the following
  site http://www.spinelessbooks.com/mayer/index.html

"Carnival Ticket Haikus"

Materials needed are as follows:

- One roll of "carnival tickets": the ones that say ADMIT ONE on
  one side and are blank on the other. You can find them in sta-
  tionery or office supply stores. One roll lasts almost forever.
- Magazines for cutting words out of.
- Scissors and clear tape.
- Container for keeping the tickets in; we used an aluminum
  teapot, but anything with a little panache will do—a black hat,
  a vintage shoe, an old rickety colander, a velvet sack.

Prepare ahead of time as many tickets as you can. We made a lot of
ours during down time at the WC. Believe me, it's possible to sit around at
a table and cut parts of phrases out of magazines for *hours*. Cut out begin-
nings, middles, and ends of sentences. Cut out sections of sentences like
"looking quite eyelashy" and "is the work of sisters." These two fragments
came from different magazines but already we can see them becoming a
statement: *looking quite eyelashy is the work of sisters.* Already we're playing.
Cut out whatever fragments catch your eye: "expelled from the nostrils,"
"the salt and pepper disease," "milkweed attack," "behavior of plants," "to
turn around to be mistaken." Once you have a nice pile of these partial
phrases, you can begin affixing them to the tickets. Tear the tickets one by
one from the roll, and tape each phrase to the blank side of a ticket. Once

this is done, put the finished tickets into your designated container. You are ready to play carnival ticket haikus.

How to play: Have each player choose five tickets. No peeking. While this is happening, a short introduction to the haiku form of poetry can be explained. You can either make it mandatory that the players adhere to the traditional 17-syllable form of a haiku, or you can let them adopt a freer version of it. We have practiced both and ended up with delightful results each way. Let the players know that they may use the phrases any way they see fit: changing verb tense, omitting or adding words, changing singular words to plurals, and so on. In this way, five randomly chosen carnival tickets that read: "write on the mimeographed," "so that the birds cannot evaporate slowly in some," "nectar corridor," "suspiciously like hope," and "overshadowed by the floodlit" can become:

I cannot write about birds
in floodlit corridors
overshadowed by evaporated hope

This exercise usually goes pretty quickly, so you probably won't need to impose a time limit. If some people finish before others, you can encourage them to pick more tickets and write more. When everyone is finished, the poems can be shared, but no one should ever be forced to share what they have written. In our experience, however, we found that most people were very eager to share their results; in fact, there never seemed to be enough time to share everything they wanted to share. You can collect poems from participants, type them up, and make copies of them to distribute, or post them on your WC web site. We made a colorful display for ours on a wall in the WC. Some were little slips of poems like the one above, whereas others were much longer. For the following piece, our WC director, Scott Miller used his chosen phrases "darn off," "belgium in the fall," "odd around the shoulder area," "age romances," and "having to do with vineyards" only as starting points for a more fleshed out, narrative poem:

Those Darn Off-Age Romances

She thinks
his hair's too greasy
and he thinks
she's a little odd
around the shoulder area.
These are things they do not discuss.
"For practical purposes
having to do with vineyards,

we're not going to Belgium
this year,"
she tells him.
"Darn off!" he replies.
"Darn off yourself."
Age romances.
Romance ages.
That would bother me,
the practical purposes
of odd shoulder areas
and hair too greasy
for Belgium in the fall.

The joy of this game is in the endless magic it yields. The associations and suggestions packed in an image fragment like "nectar corridor" or "you used to hide" are multiplied when juxtaposed against others, such as "aching for sleep," or "rubber in the world." It is precisely in the process of bridging the gaps between disparate images that I believe we as writers may access some of the richest material inside of ourselves. The "accident" of drawing the words "write," "birds," "floodlit," "overshadow," and "hope" out of a "hat" of sorts results in the very deliberate delving into the part of one's memory which is essentially stored in those words. Learning how to gain access to this portion of our memories which resides outside of us, in specific objects and words we're not expecting to come our way, is a powerful tool for any writer, whether creative or composition-based, not because it teaches them how to write, but rather because it works to remind them of the abundance of things they already know, which they can then tap into and explore further, after the playshop is over, if they so wish.

Wheel of Fortune Cookie

The following materials are needed:

- Enough fortune cookies to go around. Be sure to have extras, as some may lack fortunes. No news may be good news, but for Parlour Parlour purposes, the fortune is important. You can buy them at Chinese restaurants or in the Asian section of supermarkets.
- Paper and pens.

How to play: This game is a kind of written version of "Telephone." For smaller sessions of 10 people or less, it is not necessary to break them down into groups, but larger sessions will be more manageable in groups of 4 or 5 players each. Everyone writes his or her original fortune at the top of a loose piece of paper. Underneath the original fortune, each player then writes a slightly changed version of that fortune. This means each player may change, add or subtract words from the original sentence. For example, a fortune may read, "If you continually give, you will continually have." It could be changed to, say, "If you continually give, you will continually have nothing." Once everyone has altered their fortune, the papers are passed, *either* to the right or to the left, and each player reads the two versions of the fortune in front of him or her, then changes the second version slightly, into a third version, which continues changing as it is passed around the table. If the players are broken into smaller groups, they may circulate their papers two or three times. As each player has visual access to all the stages each fortune undergoes, a cohesive and rhythmically compelling collaborative work is almost always the result.

For example:

You express yourself with charm and humor. (Original fortune.)
You express yourself with chicken and honor.
Chicken soup, well made, is an expression of self and honor.
Succulent soup makes for honorable humans.
Honorable humans are the secret ingredient, ask the Iron Chef.
The Iron Chef makes a great Soilent Green.
The Trojan Horse was actually an iron chicken
that laid a big golden egg
and inside was a fortune
so he screamed "I am fortune's fool!"
which truly puzzled the Trojans.

Games such as this one with its emphasis on collaboration play an enormous role in helping students learn to lay aside ideas of ownership and work together to create something from which they may all draw inspiration. Something we stressed from the very first Parlour Parlour session was that collaboratively created texts, in that they couldn't have been made without the creativity of everyone, "belonged" to *everyone*. These texts could then, in a sense, be regarded as community property, raw material from which everyone could draw, in much the same way from which a community shares the fruits and vegetables of a garden. Keeping this spirit in mind helped set the tone of cooperation and communal enthusiasm for what would "bloom" out of the "seeds" we had planted.

"Surrealist Question and Answer"

Materials needed are as follows:

- Paper and pens. Tear paper into rectangles about the size of index cards. Hand out several to each group.

How to play: This game is easy and yields quick, often astonishing results. Have players pair up, then each write a "what is?" question on his or her slip of paper. The "what is?" question can be any query, such as "what is ink?" or "what is the meaning of life?" or "what is the color red?" Each player should keep his or her question concealed by folding the slip of paper in half, then trading with his or her partner. Everyone then writes an answer in the form of "it is . . . ," in response to the concealed question, such as "it is a failed experiment," or "it is a tall bottle of lotion," or "it is above ground instead of under." When everyone has finished answering, the questions are revealed and read aloud to everyone's delight. Other versions of this game can also be played, substituting the "what is?" question format with "why?," and answering the question with a "because" answer. For instance "why is the sky blue?" may be mysteriously answered by "because of the paint on my paintbrush." The "if, then" version of this game operates in the same way, with one player writing the "if" half of the sentence, such as "if nudity was mandatory at supermarkets . . . ," concealing it by folding it, then trading with his partner, who then finishes the sentence by explaining what would happen in such a case, perhaps with: ". . . then a whistle would not be a whistle."

CONCLUSION

I believe that invention's more commonly used meaning, as a process of "creating," has led many of us to forget that for inspiration to arise it must do so out of a moment of discovery. Word games such as the Surrealist Question and Answer draw much of their power from the distance they manage to bridge in a single step, revealing the invisible threads existing between the most unlikely of subjects. In my original Parlour Parlour proposal, I confessed I wanted to be a homewrecker of language. To release words from their loveless and stagnant marriages by revealing the secret love affairs between all things which are not accompanied to being paired. A liberation like this, however, cannot be isolated within the realm of play. Inherent in teaching writing within the form of the game may lie the seed of an antidote against the established routine and increasingly standardized environment of our modern lives. Moreover, it may serve as a magnificent tool to be employed with other strategies for teaching and tutoring. In this arena the possibilities seem limitless; the Oulipian model could feasibly be handed back, with all its accoutrements, to the mathematicians, who could, in turn use it to help them bring the pleasure of math to their mathematically challenged, "writerly" students. When we, as students or as teachers, become accustomed to the certainty with which these techniques yield the hidden affinities between all things, we will have moved closer to a "festival" fluency and further from a habitual and non-playful state of mind, which is detrimental to the fluency of thought.

REFERENCES

Huizinga, J. (1950). *Homo ludens: A study of the play element in culture.* Boston: Beacon.

Matthews, H., & Brotchie, A. (Eds.). (1998). *Oulipo compendium.* London: Atlas.

Tomol Pennisi, L., & Lawler, P. (1994). Without a net: Collaborative writing. In W. Bishop & H. Ostrom (Eds.), *Colors of a different horse: Rethinking creative writing theory and pedagogy* (pp. 225-233). Urbana, IL: NCTE.

13

WRITING GROUPS FOR TEACHERS

Opportunities for Imagination, Creativity, and Renewal

Dawn Fels

Teachers in public schools give far more than they receive. Their individual and combined net worth to society sinks lower each year when government officials judge the quality of their efforts according to students' test scores and other performance indicators.[1] Proponents of No Child Left Behind (NCLB) legislation believe that more accurate measurement of student (and teacher) success will reform education. But the law's threatened sanctions for schools who do not meet adequate yearly progress requirements lay the groundwork for punitive measures and curricular catastrophes for everyone in a school building. No one feels the pressure more fiercely than students and their teachers.

Writing centers (WC), regardless of their institutional setting, sit poised to offer teachers some respite from the ill-effects of NCLB. For several years, I taught English in an urban-suburban high school where the majority of the student body was poor and African American. Our school was labeled a "school of concern" by the state, so the pressures to prepare students for the state test were immense. I loved my job and, like most of my colleagues, referred to my students as "my kids." I worked hard to preserve curiosity, discovery, and choice in the classroom while trying to rationalize (and avoid) using the manuals and released items administrators gave me to prepare students for the test. I grew quite adept at juggling the needs of my kids with the demands of my administrators. And in the end, I learned one thing: One can only juggle for so long.

What teachers need to reinvent themselves as teachers and learners awaits them in the WC. As a teacher, I shared the pressures my colleagues faced. As a WC director, I knew that quiet conversation with a caring individual could do wonders for a writer's well-being. As a writer, I longed for an audience. So, I approached several teachers and volunteers from our WC about forming a writing group. All that was promised was a casual atmosphere in which to relax and talk about writing, full support from participants, no pressure to share—and food. A diverse bunch, participants included two community members and five teachers who represented different departments: science, special education, vocational education, and communication arts.

Two of my former colleagues, Zora and Iris,[2] shared with me their reflections on our participation in the writing group. Vignettes of our experiences weave together the personal and professional discoveries we made as we lay claim to the intersection between our writing and teaching lives. We share these discoveries so that other teacher-writers, regardless of institutional setting, come to see the WC as a place of welcome, a place of comfort, a place where imagination and creativity can lead to renewal.

TEACHERS AS WRITERS

> Discovery and wonder is the heart of any discipline. However small, authorship is the first cousin of discovery. (Graves, 1994, p. 104)[3]

Standardization of curriculum and teaching methods can weary the most energetic, imaginative educator. Graves' (1994) assertion points to how writing might serve as a remedy, and certainly the ease with which I recruited teachers for our writing group points to a need for WCs to reach out to the weary. Any teacher, WC director, or tutor can easily do this on their own campus or by collaborating with a nearby university or K-12 school. All I did was e-mail an invitation.

The responses I received pointed to a need that could not be met through any of the professional development, team-building, and diversity efforts attempted by school administrators. We teachers needed critical friends who would listen without criticizing. We needed to be reacquainted with our own curiosity, creativity, and imagination. Above all, we needed to feel valued. As we found out, if given these necessities, teachers can prosper, and when teachers prosper, so do their students.

Our meetings energized and amazed us. We simultaneously engaged in knowledge *and* imagination—both necessary for an environment where the "best teaching and learning" take place (Osburg, 2003, p. 57). We took time to talk about writing as writers do. We helped each other overcome the same fears and insecurities writers experience. We listened not only to ourselves but to each other, responding carefully, thoughtfully, and sensitively, letting the reader and writer within us respond to what we saw and heard in another's text.

Our forays into authorship, just as Graves predicted, led us to several discoveries. We felt what our students feel when asked to share a piece of writing: the racing pulse, the beads of sweat forming on the brow, the constricting throat. We saw each other as people with lives outside the classroom. We saw ourselves as capable and creative.

IMAGINATION AND CREATIVITY AS ACADEMIC FREEDOMS

> Imagination, like all of our abilities, can be nurtured, developed, learned. (Osburg, 2003, p. 58)

Imagination standards do not exist on state curricula, but imagination is essential to life, learning, and teaching. Osburg (2003) described the importance of imagination in the classroom:

> All of our students are capable—to some degree—of imagining a world different from the one that greets them as they rise each day, a world different from the one they have been given, a world that might come to be through the force of their actions in this world. That is our triumph—that we can dream of an imagined future that differs from the present and the past. (p. 58)

What would happen to public education if teachers were invited to use *their* imagination to transform their classrooms from the "drill and drudgery" (p. 58) they have become since academic freedoms took a back seat to standard-

"While government officials continue to strip the teaching profession of its creativity, a writing center can help teachers reinvent themselves as creative, imaginative, intellectual teachers and writers."

ized strongholds? While government officials continue to strip the teaching profession of its creativity, a WC can help teachers reinvent themselves as creative, imaginative, intellectual teachers and writers.

CREATING WRITING LIVES

> . . . creativity grows, first, out of the relationships between an individual and the objective world of work and, second, out of the ties between an individual and other human beings. (Gardner, 1993, p. 9)[4]

Writing anchored many of us to what really mattered in our personal lives. One of our colleagues wrote a children's book about her grandmother's love for birds. Another wrote a series of letters to her daughter. Two members of the group wrote nonfiction that stood in stark contrast to each other's: One mused about the impending arrival of new grandchildren (twins), and the other reflected on the devastating stillborn death of a baby—more than two decades earlier. On one day, one participant wrote to release the overwhelming sadness she felt at her only child's leaving for college, but weeks later, she wrote to celebrate the comfort provided by her two beloved cats. We were not always so serious. We shared light-hearted poetry and macabre short stories that would make Poe shrink in horror. In sharing a bit of ourselves through our memoirs, letters, poetry, stories, we enriched each other's lives and achieved Lamott's (1994) standard for good writing: We told the truth. Working with the essential, we created the essential.

EMPATHY AND AFFIRMATION

> To be a good writer, you not only have to write a great deal but you have to care . . . a writer always tries, I think, to be a part of the solution, to understand a little about life and to pass this on. (Lamott, 1994, p. 107)[5]

Zora and Iris, two of my teacher colleagues in the group, care deeply about their students. Like most public school teachers, they are *so* much a part of the solution in some of their students' lives that their presence alone keeps some students from quietly slipping away. Caring as they do—as most teachers do—takes fathomless energy. To share their experiences from the writing group with me is one thing; to agree to publish their experience in the vignettes presented here takes courage. Courage, because they are sharing deeply personal experiences, admitting what they discovered about themselves and others, offering their observations about what they love most: students, learning, teaching. Courage, because teachers' voices, in general, are absent from discussions about school reform; they are often blamed for the state of public schools today, but rarely are they invited to school board meetings or legislative sessions to offer their ideas on school reform. Missing from too many articles about "failing schools" are the voices of Zora, Iris, and other public school teachers who want nothing more for their students than to be happy, healthy, and successful in their academic, personal, and public lives. Missing are the voices of students whose future "value" to society is determined by a test score.

We know students withdraw when they feel disconnected or slighted, but how often do we educators reflect on our own tendencies to withdraw? Palmer (1998) described a tendency of teachers to "disconnect from students, from subjects, and even from ourselves. We build a wall between inner truth and outer performance, and we play-act the teacher's part" (p. 17). Pressures imposed by NCLB leave teachers feeling caught between what they know will help their students and what they know they better do to keep their jobs. For about 2 hours every other week, our writing group encouraged participants to connect with their voice—their inner truth—and share it with others.

WC directors and tutors know well the value of writing conferences, but how many times are teachers invited to share and talk about their writing? When I first approached Zora about the possibility of pulling teachers together as writers, she loved the idea but felt apprehensive about sharing. So did others, and this surprised me. What did they fear? In describing the benefits of writing groups, Lamott (1994) wrote:

> Writers tend to be so paranoid about talking about their work because no one, including us, really understands how it works. . . . On a bad day, you also don't need a lot of advice. You just need a little empathy and affirmation. You need to feel once again that other people have confidence in you. The members of your writing group can often offer just that. (p. 157)

Ours did. The empathy and affirmation we displayed toward one another acted as a cooling salve for our fatigued teacher souls. Days whiz by so fast, their velocity often leaves little time for empathy and affirmation. Yet, empathy and affirmation are essential ingredients for good teaching, successful students, and harmonious relationships. In essence, we teachers created the perfect classroom setting within the writing group. We gave each other room to explore, to make mistakes, to be fully human. We promised and modeled safety. We affirmed.

TEACHERS AS ADVENTURE ENTHUSIASTS

Students will write if we give them understanding and support as they stumble toward discovery. How do we know how to do that? By experiencing the process of discovery ourselves. You cannot teach what you do not know. (Murray, 1989, p. 111)[6]

Our writing group gave teachers access to another ideology, the kind that adventure enthusiasts know so well. This ideology comes from gaining confidence after trying something new, something daring, something frightening, and then living to tell about it. Prior to our first meeting, Zora and I spoke many times of the apprehension she felt about sharing our work with others. I told her I felt apprehensive, too. I avoided humiliation by sharing most of my work with writers in online creative writing courses, and the first time I sat face to face with someone and read a poem I was working on, I felt like I did the first time I rappelled down the face of a cliff.

There I stood, frozen by fright. Before I could launch myself from the safety and security of terra firma, I had to clear a small shelf of rock that limited my view of the ground . . . so . . . far . . . down. What was I about to do? I couldn't see where my jump (or life) would end! But I also couldn't back out. My friend and I drove hours to get to this beautiful place, and he'd worked so hard to convince me that I would be safe from harm, assuring me over and over again that my ropes weren't frayed or tangled. He told me I'd be okay, and I trusted him. Standing on the edge of that shelf, trying to remember what he'd told me, wishing my gloves were a little tighter, I realized that no matter how much assurance he gave me, no matter how many times he checked the ropes and clips at my behest, I was . . . gulp . . . alone. If only my choking fear would recede long enough for me to send a message to my legs to bend, to my back to lean out a little, and to my feet to push gently off and away from the edge. Though I scarcely remember the moment, my jumping off point literally signaled my commitment to the task at hand. I could now see the ground (SO far down), and my survival skills took over. My friend, who ran down the back of the cliff to greet me upon landing, hollered words of encouragement and assurance, praising my new skills, never correcting me or focusing on my mistakes.

TRUST

You get your confidence and intuition back by trusting yourself, by being militantly on your own side. You need to trust yourself . . . where amid the anxiety and self-doubt, there should be a real sense of your

> imagination and your memories walking and woolgathering, tramping the hills, romping all over the place. Trust them. (Lamott, 1994, p. 112)[7]

The first day our writing group met was the first day many in our writing group read their work for others. Like my friend who convinced me to jump, I had a lot to lose if, say, things had not gone as desired. Like my friend who checked the clips and ropes every time I asked him to, I wanted my colleagues and friends to feel safe. Like my friend who cajoled and encouraged me to trust him, trust myself, I did the same for my colleagues. *Come on,* I beckoned to them from my position of safety, *you're gonna LOVE this!* To show how safe it was, I jumped first. I read the latest revision of a short story I had written for a creative writing class. I began confidently but then tripped over my words when alluding to a sexual relationship between the two characters. I kicked myself under the table for not having skipped that part or deleting it altogether—at least for the meeting. By the time I made it to the last page, my embarrassment turned to stone-cold dread: Where was my last page? *Some role model I was!* Fortunately, my writing partners disregarded my gaffe, and red-faced, I cobbled together the end of the story from memory. Having jumped and landed virtually unscathed, I beckoned to Zora to join me.

Going into the meeting, I knew Zora felt as if she too stood atop a rocky ledge willing herself to take the plunge:

> I was petrified of the Fall of 2003. My only child and best friend was off to USC and I was left alone but for two large cats. I love my cats, but they didn't talk baseball like my son. I was looking for anything to fill my time. When Dawn approached me about an adult writing group, I was thrilled. I have always felt like I expressed myself best in written form but I hadn't written much, other than IEPs for years. While I occasionally got creative with my IEPs, it wasn't exactly a satisfying endeavor. Because I had some overwhelming emotions about my son that seemed to require my attention, I decided to write to him. (Zora, personal communication, July 16, 2005)[8]

In her narrative, Zora indicates the source of her apprehensions: "The actual act of writing was a little more difficult than I expected . . . I had never written anything so personal that I was going to share with a group" (Zora, personal communication, July 16, 2005). I had known Zora for many years before that moment when she looked around the table at those gathered there. She was the strong, stoic type. And although she told me she may not "make it through" what she'd written, I was surprised when I heard her voice crack only minutes into her reading.

Oh, geez. What have I done? I thought. What should I do now? Zora slid her paper over to me, and I continued reading. As I read, most of the participants reached for the tissue box instead of the snacks. When I finished, we all exhaled. Surprisingly, Zora's emotions set participants at ease. We were moved by her courage to express such raw emotion (and perhaps glad that she was the first). When the tears dried, participants offered words of encouragement, consolation, and feedback about what worked particularly well in her piece. *Whew!*

Zora later reflected on this emotional moment: "The first time we met and read our work, I found that I was unable to read it aloud without crying and Dawn had to finish reading it for me . . . I really wasn't embarrassed by the show of emotion," she wrote, "but I was terribly nervous about reading (and then hearing) my words. It was of great assistance to me when I returned to my classroom and realized that I needed to be aware of my students' feelings when I so cavalierly ask them to read their writings out loud in class" (Zora, personal communication, July 16, 2005).

FEAR

> All writing is experimental. We don't know what works until we try it. Failure is normal and instructive. From failures we see ways to achieve success. (Murray, 1989, p. 123)

Most students avoid failure at all costs. With very few exceptions, my high school students saw failure—or the potential for failure—as a source of embarrassment and ridicule. Some felt their failures—or perceived failures—stemmed from teachers' complicity in a conspiracy to set them up for failure, whereas others saw failure as a certainty, fueled by any of the *-isms* they had experienced over time.

Teachers fear failure, too. Every time our writing group met, one or two people chose not to share, but they usually did at the next meeting. Iris never could summon the courage to read her work, although she gave thoughtful and supportive feedback. Her reservations surprised me. Iris exudes conviviality and creativity. Her short cropped hair, her funky jewelry, her hip eyeglasses, and her colorful clothing reflect her personality. Her sense of humor and wit, unmatchable. Yet she felt as most students do—inadequate: "I never had the nerve to write or share anything in the group, and not because people weren't warm and inviting either. It was a simple case of nerves . . . and the ever-present fear that I'm not good enough" (Iris, personal communication, July 30, 2005). Why did she join? In her narrative, Iris mentioned two reasons for joining the group. "I basically joined the group," she begins, "because I wanted to help my second graders. . . . All the research indicates that children do much better if they know that you are writing right along with them" (Iris, personal communication, July 30, 2005). She lamented, however, that she rarely shared her writing with students: "I guess I feel too self-conscious, which is ridiculous, but there you have it" (Iris, personal communication, July 30, 2005). Zora, Iris, and I all felt the irony of the double standard we created in our classrooms. Each of us, at one time or another, demanded, pushed, and sometimes begged our students to take risks we were too afraid to take.

MODELING SUCCESS AND FAILURE

> Sometimes the light's all shinin' on me, other times I can barely see
> Lately it occurs to me, what a long strange trip it's been . . .
> (*The Grateful Dead*, "Trucking," 1970)[9]

Facing our own fears as writers helped us identify with the personal risk students often connect with writing. Indeed, our writing group participants learned that it takes courage to write and to share. Troubled by the possibility of our own failure, we did not envision ourselves as successful writers. We occupied that uncomfortable space with which students are all too familiar. But with each other's support, we practiced what we always preached to our students: "from failures we see ways to achieve success" (Murray, 1989, p. 123). The answer to helping students see this is to model failure just as we model success.

Zora admitted in her narrative that being part of a writing group was a "humbling experience and teachers often times need to be humbled . . . when I was participating in a writing group of my peers, all the anxieties from my youth came back. Because I am theoretically in charge all day long, it's nice to turn the tables [*sic*]. It made me a more compassionate teacher" (Zora, personal communication, July 28, 2005). Iris later overcame her fear with the help of her son who challenged her to free her creativity by letting go of her fear. He was a junior in college at the time, no doubt an experienced workshop participant. Once her perspective changed, she felt more comfortable sharing her writing with peers in the creative writing class she took at a local university. She described in her narrative the benefits of writing with her second graders:

> With younger children, it's very helpful to do shared writing, where you write on a piece of chart paper as the class dictates what to say. Then by second grade, you can bring in your own writing and share bits

and pieces. You can write what the children are working on, say a piece
that is focusing on adjectives, . . . share your struggles with finding the
right words, or . . . ask the class's opinion about a phrase. That's one
thing I always am on the lookout for in my classes, how to encourage
the kids to not depend on me for all the answers, but to go to their
classmates. I constantly remind them that when they're on their own,
in either college or a job, there won't be a parent or a teacher to catch
their mistakes. Encouraging that independence in writing is one of the
hardest goals of a teacher. (Iris, personal communication, August 4,
2005)

Iris later mentioned that shared writing (or sharing writing, as we did in the
writing group) benefited another essential part of student and teacher success. "Another big reason for sharing your writing," wrote Iris, "is that it's
another means of connecting with your students. It's astounding what the
kids remember that you said, or what happened to you at a certain point
in your life. Writing is a really good way of connecting with your students"
(Iris, personal communication, August 4, 2005).

REVERENCE

Literacy events do not take place in isolation, but in relation to a discourse community of which the reader or writer is, or wishes to
become, a member. (Haneda & Wells, 2000, p. 432)

How can the WC engage more teachers who do not consider themselves
readers or writers? Aren't their efforts necessary to improving and enriching students' literacy lives? Teachers can recreate themselves as writers by
reaching back into the nooks and crannies of life to the truths that lie hidden beneath dusty layers of oppression, vulnerability, fear, confusion, pain,
and feelings of inadequacy. WCs can help.
And as participation in our writing group   **"When our perceptions
showed us, when our perceptions of our-   of ourselves as writers
selves as writers change, so do our percep-   change, so do our
tions of our students as writers. As Zora   perceptions of our
noted in her narrative, these changes can   students as writers."**
lead to changes in methods of teaching and
grading writing:

Writing for me is very personal and when my writing is read out loud
or I read it out loud, all the emotions that went into the writing sur-

face. Being in a writing group reminded me of this phenomenon. When a student turns in something so personal, we need to treat it as such. I have not always done this because when we don't do the exercise ourselves, we forget . . . just like administrators forget what it's like in a classroom, we forget what it's like to write and have it torn to pieces. (Zora, personal communication, July 28, 2005)

When teachers participate in a writing group, their students reap the rewards, too. Our writing group participants felt that what they had to say mattered. If we create assignments that help our students perceive themselves as problem posers and solvers rather than storage banks for formulae, then our students might feel as if we care about what they want to contribute. They will see that we value their ideas. Like we did, they will take risks and learn about themselves in ways that will surprise them and make them proud. All this, and more, they will reap. But not in a classroom with a curriculum that is devoid of curiosity, choice, discovery, imagination, and creativity—a classroom devoid of life and purpose.

According to Bomer and Bomer (2001), "Every classroom—elementary, secondary English, college history, whatever—creates a discourse initiated by the teacher and taken up to varying extents by the students" (p. 25). Imagine the possibilities in a classroom where curricular choices stem from students' and teachers' interests. Imagine teachers who share their successes and failures as writers with their students. Imagine teachers and students writing together. Teachers' discourse communities play a critical role in helping students adopt a healthy view toward learning, and writing centers can help create and strengthen those communities.

CONNECTING THROUGH WRITING

I miss the meaning of my own part
in the play of life
because I know not of the parts that others play.
(Tagore, 1928, p. 262)[10]

Reverence is critical to helping teachers take risks as writers. Lamott (1994) defined reverence as "awe, as presence in and openness to the world" (p. 99), and it is essential to learning. In order to be successful at what they do, teachers must feel a connection to other teachers. Zora indicated in her narrative that seeing her colleagues outside the context of their classrooms and teaching lives, sharing as they did in the writing group, changed her perception of them:

It was . . . a revelation for me to see my colleagues in such a different light. While I had always admired them for the work they did in their classrooms, hearing their writings was not unlike meeting a new person. Teachers get so wrapped up in their students that conversations often turn into staffings [*sic*]. We staff at happy hours, ball games, birthday parties and Saturday morning coffee. I think this gives us a very limited view of our friends and colleagues. (Zora, personal communication, July 28, 2005)

I could not have anticipated the shift in perspective to which Zora refers, but it too is important to teaching and learning. An avid baseball fan, Zora knows the difference between teams who have winning seasons and those who do not. Whether a team makes it to the playoffs has a lot to do with team chemistry, the commitment of every team member to win games, and the relationship between the manager and the team. Our writing group was a team. We participants came with different life experiences. We ranged in age from young to distinguished. We represented different curricular areas. Zora observed a valuable lesson we learned from our get-togethers:

I'm sorry to say that we all tend to stereotype people, and teachers are no different. You know . . . all English teachers are prima donnas, special ed teachers are crazy, math teachers are analytical, grade school teachers are perky. This experience made me look at them outside of their disciplines and just see them as writers. We are more alike than different. It was a bonding experience. (Zora, personal communication, July 28, 2005)

When teachers don't trust each other, or when morale is low, students feel it. When I asked Zora about the possibilities a writing group might have for forging relationships among faculty, she wrote, "If enough teachers were willing to have this experience, we would become a more gentle profession" (Zora, personal communication, July 28, 2005).

Who are these people we see every day? What and who is important to them? What are their dreams? What is the craziest thing they have ever done? We teachers get to know our students when we pass around the index cards each year and ask them to provide some basic facts about themselves: contact information, family members' names and ages, extracurricular activities, hobbies, favorite foods, favorite color, favorite song, what they hope to be some day, what they hope to learn in our class. We ask for this information not only to connect with our students and meet their individual needs but also because we recognize that what they bring to the classroom helps shape everyone in it. Knowing them well shows we care about them. What would happen to teacher morale, classroom instruction, and student achievement if more interest were paid to teachers' lives outside the classroom?

TICK . . . TOCK . . . TICK . . . TOCK

> All water has a perfect memory and is forever trying to get back to where it was. (Morrison, cited in Zinsser, 1987, p. 119)

Time drags on when you're nine and your mother makes you visit Great-aunt Lillisue on a day your favorite baseball team heads into what could be the last game of the playoffs. Each tick of the clock comes slower but louder than the last. In school, time races by as everyone counts down the days to testing. Pulses race, hearts pound, careers fizzle, futures whither. Each year, students drop out or graduate having sacrificed chunks of their former selves and their future selves, the truths of their lives, and the truths they could have lived—all in the name of testing. They seek safe haven for their imaginations outside of the core curricula—an art class, the darkroom, the stage, a poetry slam, a marching band competition, the dance studio, the choir room, or the writing center. Teachers, if they haven't already left the profession, lose their identities as teachers, lose their intellectual and academic freedoms. Constantly told they are not good enough, they recede, like the student who always hears the same. How long will futures be sacrificed?

Confidence is hard to create in someone who's been told time and again that their efforts fail to meet a standard or that their personal experiences and values have no place in a public school classroom. Nearly a decade before NCLB became law, Giroux (1993) painted a similar picture of the life of many classroom teachers today:

> The imposition of national testing and a standardized curriculum is not only an attack on the importance of allowing teachers to produce academic materials closely related to histories, interests, and voices of the students and communities in which the schools are located, it is also a proposal for further demoralizing those groups whose voices have been traditionally excluded from the dominant curriculum. Put bluntly, such a proposal is racist in its implications and represents an assault on the intelligence of teachers and parents and the importance of their role in exercising control over their schools and the curriculum. (p. 135)

More than a decade after Giroux called attention to America 2000's effect on teaching and learning, even less room exists in the school day for teachers and students to engage in inquiry and discovery about "social justice, responsible citizenship, the ethics of care, and the politics of solidarity, and other considerations that do not easily lend themselves to quantitative measurement" (p. 138). Yet these principles are intertwined with our most basic freedoms.

WCs serve as sites for educational reform, authentic teaching and learning, ethical care, and critical pedagogy in hosts of schools throughout the country. Much like their postsecondary kin, WCs in public schools should be valued as safe places where writers can go for assistance in expressing their own truths. They should be positioned as "places for honoring our students' [and teachers'] attempts at making their worlds more understandable, for creating ways of responding to these worlds, of being seen and heard when they are daily told in myriad, subtle, and not-so-subtle ways that they won't be" (Blitz & Hurlbert, 2002, p. 88). WCs hold promise for success not measured by test scores, success that depends on and honors each of the multifarious representations that exist within the school community. WCs and classrooms where writing instruction does not aim to decontextualize the writing lives of students and teachers develop into sites where strange bedfellows—knowledge and power—meet "to provide students with the conditions that enable them to be critical, ethical agents, to assume a leadership role, to learn how to govern rather than be governed" (Giroux, 1993, pp. 139-140).

Our writing group made us better writers and better teachers. We laid claim to what we thought, what we knew, and in some cases what we didn't know. We faced our fears. Sharing our writing allowed us to shed the burdens of the day, connect, trust, learn, and honor. We laughed. Our conversations were devoid of words that serve to punish, to separate, to judge or to single out—language that Bomer and Bomer (2001) said "traps" our profession: test scores, adequate yearly progress, failing schools. We moved beyond the language of measurement (Giroux, 1993) and practiced a discourse of affirmation and empathy, characteristic of our WC pedagogy and tutoring methods.

We teachers in the writing group were now more than just colleagues. We were friends who knew each other's attachments outside the school building, attachments that affected our lives within it. When Zora (personal communication, August 24, 2005) read two poems she wrote about her cats, there were no tears. Only laughter. We commented on the poems' Zen-like simplicity and Zora's gentle rendering of the depth of her cats' devotion, so important to her now that her son was off to college. Their lightheartedness signaled to the rest of us that Zora's melancholy, so apparent during our first meeting, was beginning to lift—a renewal we all wanted for her.

Teachers and students deserve more. Deny them access to essential elements of learning—choice, curiosity, creativity, discovery, and imagination—and no one wins. It's time to stop juggling, start enjoying, and stake our claims to brighter futures.

NOTES

1. For an explanation of NCLB go to the Department of Elementary and Secondary Education for your state.
2. Zora and Iris are pseudonyms.
3. Graves' book *Bring Life into Learning* can help teachers from many curricular areas design writing assignments that engage creativity and imagination.
4. Many teachers will be familiar with Howard Gardner's Multiple Intelligences theory. His book, *Creating Minds* looks deeply at creativity in the lives of seven individuals. Each was chosen for their contributions to their fields but also for how they represented one of Gardner's original seven intelligences. Only two of the seven were outstanding students, and Gardner looks at how creativity and other factors led to the others' success despite their scholastic performance and apparent lack of interest in school.
5. Anne Lamott's book, *Bird by Bird*, is an excellent source for the personal and professional lives of classroom teachers. Every WC and teacher in public schools should have a copy.
6. Teachers would enjoy reading any of Murray's books. *A Writer Teaches Writing* served us well in our high school WC, providing many of our methods and contributing to our guiding philosophy. *Expecting the Unexpected* points directly to how essential surprise and discovery are in teaching writing and learning to write. Murray's point holds implications for authentic learning and teaching. I use it here to raise the possibility that too much focus on students' and teachers' "failure" on state tests is doing more harm than good to writers, writing instruction, student achievement and teacher effectiveness.
7. Lamott and Gardner both speak to the importance of allowing our "inner child" to lead us back to curiosity. Moreover, Gardner points to specific childhood events that served the seven individuals into their adult lives and led to their successes.
8. An Individual Education Plan (IEP) is required for each student receiving special services, such as modified instruction, to accommodate for special learning needs, such as a learning disability.
9. As writers and teachers of writing, we can learn a lot about creativity and imagination from artists, musicians, and dancers. Both Graves and Gardner allude to this in their books. I thought these lyrics from The Grateful Dead incredibly appropriate for this piece. Besides, Jerry Garcia had a nice smile.
10. My literature and composition students loved Tagore's essays on art and artists' roles in society. Of interest to them was also Tagore's conversations with Einstein. These essays can be found in the *Tagore Reader* published in 1961 and edited by Amiya Chakravarly.

REFERENCES

Blitz, M., & Hurlbert, C.M. (2000). If you have ghosts. In L.C. Briggs & M. Woolbright (Eds.), *Stories from the center: Connecting narrative and theory in the writing center* (pp. 84-93). Urbana, IL: NCTE.

Bomer, R., & Bomer, K. (2001). *For a better world: Reading and writing for social action.* Portsmouth, NH: Heinemann.

Gardner, H. (1993). *Creating minds: An anatomy of creativity seen through the lives of Freud, Picasso, Stravinsky, Eliot, Graham, and Gandhi.* New York: Basic Books.

Giroux, H. (1993). *Living dangerously: Multiculturalism and the politics of difference.* New York: Peter Lang.

Graves, D. (1994). *Bring life into learning: Create a lasting literacy.* Portsmouth, NH: Heinemann.

Haneda, M., & Wells, G. (2000). Writing in knowledge-building communities. *Research in the Teaching of English, 34,* 430-457.

Hunter, R. (1970). Truckin' [Recorded by The Grateful Dead]. On *American Beauty* [CD]. Warner Bros. (1990).

Lamott, A. (1994). *Bird by bird: Some instructions on writing and life.* New York: Anchor Books.

Murray, D. M. (1989). *Expecting the unexpected: Teaching myself—and others—to read and write.* Portsmouth, NH: Boynton/Cook.

Osburg, B. (2003). A failure of the imagination. *English Journal, 92*(5), 56-59.

Palmer, P. (1998). *The courage to teach.* San Francisco: Jossey-Bass.

Tagore, R. (1928). *Fireflies.* New York: Macmillan.

Zinsser, W. (Ed.). (1987). *Inventing the truth: The art and craft of memoir.* New York: Houghton Mifflin.

14

PORTFOLIO PANDEMONIUM

More Than a Practical Solution

Jill Pennington and Timothy A. Miank

All writing centers (WC) face challenges handling the end-of-semester rush, but at Lansing Community College (LCC), the challenge is compounded by the portfolio evaluation system used in the writing program. Approximately 2,000 students submit portfolios within 3 or 4 days, and the 2 weeks leading up to submission create a serious challenge for a small WC staff. Addressing this challenge has required creativity.

LCC'S EXTERNAL PORTFOLIO EVALUATION PROCESS

The writing program at LCC began requiring external portfolio assessment in developmental and first-year composition courses in 1998. Two weeks before the end of the semester, students submit portfolios that are then holistically evaluated by their own instructor and two other instructors teaching the course that semester. The portfolio is graded anonymously and counts 70% toward the student's final course grade, and students cannot earn exit competency in the course without earning a minimum grade of a 2.0 (on a 4.0 numeric scale) on the portfolio.

This assessment involves as many as 100 faculty members, and, as mentioned earlier, approximately 2,000 students each semester. Although approximately 80% of students submitting portfolios earn exit competency, it is a high-stakes, high-stress experience for students, as well as for faculty and for LCC's WC. Although the WC serves the entire campus, students in composition classes requiring portfolios comprise 70% to 75% of the clientele. In the final weeks before portfolios are due, students flock to the WC, quickly exceeding the number of available appointments and walk-ins the WC can accommodate.

In an attempt to address this problem, WC staff are asked to add as many hours to their work schedules as possible, and waiting lists are made for students so they can be contacted when appointments are cancelled. Even so, these efforts offer little relief in addressing the overload. The small staff of eight peer writing assistants (PWAs) can spread themselves only so far. The result is a frustrating scenario for students who are turned away from the WC and for the PWAs, who wish to accommodate everyone.

MIDNIGHT MADNESS PORTFOLIO PANDEMONIUM

In Fall 2001, the WC staff decided to conduct an experiment in more creatively addressing the end-of-semester rush. Both of us had attended colleges that held finals week "midnight breakfasts" designed to support students as they studied for exams, and this gave us an idea: Maybe a late night revision workshop would help us accommodate significantly more students making last-minute revisions on their portfolios. Soon the idea turned into reality, as we discussed it in a staff meeting with eager PWAs, one of whom immediately came up with a name for the workshop: "Portfolio Pandemonium." To that name, another staff member added the words "Midnight Madness."

Our first Midnight Madness Portfolio Pandemonium was offered just a few weeks later. Having no idea what to expect or whether many students would even be interested in attending such an event, we publicized it widely among composition classes. Faculty were asked to share a flyer with their classes, advertising the time and place, as well as the purpose for the workshop. They were also asked to direct students to a "What You Should Know" section on its reverse side of the flyer, which explained that students should (a) bring the most recent drafts of their essays as well as questions about them, (b) bring any textbooks or relevant resources or research materials, and (c) be prepared to take an active role. The reverse side of the flyer also informed students that they could not expect last-minute "quick fixes," that Pandemonium staff may not have time to address all of their concerns on all of their essays, and that neither WC staff nor faculty volunteers could predict the grades they might receive on their portfolios. In addition to advertising the event, we asked that the entire WC staff be on hand, and we solicited as many writing faculty volunteers who were currently teaching portfolio-based classes as possible, deciding to run the workshop from 7 p.m. to midnight. A few faculty who could not attend took up a collection to buy pizza for everyone.

To our surprise, when the WC staff and volunteer instructors arrived at 6:30 that evening to prepare, 40 anxious students were already lined up in the hallway. It looked as though they were waiting to buy tickets for a rock concert! Some lounged on the floor, their heads supported on huge backpacks, some stood eagerly, crowding the doorway with essays in hand. All of them looked tired and hungry. At this point, we began to suspect that we had bitten off more than we could chew, that we needed to adjust our thinking—and quickly, as students waited impatiently and knew we'd planned to open at 7 p.m.

After exchanging nervous glances, we quickly began brainstorming how we would work with so many students at once. The one-on-one approach we traditionally used in our WC sessions would clearly not suffice; instead we would set up "stations" around the room for students who wished to focus on specific concerns that we would categorize broadly as content and ideas, organization, style, mechanics, and MLA documentation. A sign would identify the focus of each station, and stations would be operated by at least one writing assistant and one faculty member, with enough seating for five or six students. Additionally, students would be told upon coming in to the room to be prepared with specific questions and to work with each other while they awaited assistance. Lists of possible questions were made available on handouts at each station for students who needed assistance determining what questions seemed most relevant to their concerns.

Pandemonium staff were then asked to choose stations at which they felt most comfortable. Some, who had already been identified within the WC as "experts" in certain areas, gravitated toward stations that seemed natural choices. Others, WC staff and faculty alike, avoided certain stations. Choosing stations was somewhat akin to playing duck–duck–goose. When Jill asked, "Who wants to handle the MLA documentation station?" one faculty member yelled, "Not it!" and quickly sat down at an adjacent station. Another veteran faculty member who proclaimed he had been teaching MLA "since the earth cooled" gladly took up the task, relieved to have the opportunity to focus on something more specific than content or organization.

When 7 p.m. arrived, we all huddled in the middle of the room nervously to take a deep breath before opening the door. One of our PWAs shouted, "Let the Pandemonium begin!" The staff took their stations, and students began pouring through the door. As overseers of the workshop, we took a seat at a table near the front door and began checking students in, asking them to report which class they were in (WRIT 117: Preparation for College Writing, WRIT 121: Composition 1, or WRIT 122: Composition II, all classes requiring portfolios), and whether they had visited the WC previously. In between checking in students, and as time allowed, we also worked with students directly, attempting to offer some relief to those who had been waiting at stations that were overcrowded.

A NEW TRADITION RICH
WITH BENEFITS

One hundred and twenty five students and 5 hours later, we left the workshop knowing we had just begun a new tradition as well as solved a practical problem of serving more students at the end of the semester. We also began to realize and discuss many additional benefits of the Midnight Madness Portfolio Pandemonium that we could not have anticipated prior to the event.

We discovered that the Pandemonium, in addition to meeting our major objective—to serve more students in less time—is an especially effective means of helping our students improve their essays as they prepare for portfolio assessment. One reason the Pandemonium works so well is it provides students with assistance when stakes are highest—during those final 2 weeks of the semester, when they are completely focused on revision, when everything they do will "count," when it becomes most critical that they "get it right." Thus, students who attend are highly receptive to the feedback they receive and very open to ideas provided during their sessions. It's an ideal setting for reader–writer collaboration.

Another reason the Pandemonium works well for students is because it happens late in the semester, after much classroom instruction and a considerable amount of practice working in peer review groups within their writing classrooms (as well as previous visits to the WC in many cases). By this time, our students tend to understand the language of revision and the basic course requirements readers' suggestions are aiming at—thus furthering their ability to implement the suggestions they are given. Additionally, their prior coursework and constant practice with peer review provide them with the skills to ask very good questions—the kinds of questions that help readers provide useful feedback. Their previous course work allows them to participate fully in the session and, often, to make discoveries themselves about how their essays might improve.

Additionally, because the workshop is offered almost precisely in the middle of our students' 2-week revision process, it allows them adequate time to prepare their essays for the Pandemonium by making preliminary revisions and then time to revise (approximately 1 week) before submitting their portfolios. This timing works quite well for our students, and it subtly reinforces the notion that revision is time consuming, that it happens in stages, and so on.

It is important to emphasize, as well, that although the feedback students receive at the Pandemonium is generally similar to what they have been given by their classroom instructor and/or their classmates during the semester, the person or persons reading and responding to their essays at the Pandemonium are often strangers—certainly not their classmates or their classroom instructor. The Pandemonium staff are almost always reading the student's work for the first time and reacting to it as any new, objective external reader would. Thus, in this sense, the Pandemonium provides them with a practical rather than theoretical example of external audience—and, again, it provides this example at perhaps the most crucial stage of their course experience, at a time when readers have their undivided attention.

A story from a PWA at the conclusion of one Pandemonium serves as an excellent illustration. The PWA was seated at a station with one male student and three female students, who were all waiting for assistance with content and ideas. Determining that the male student was next in line, the PWA asked to see his draft and then asked him what questions he had about its content. The student commented that his instructor had said something about how he needed to do a better job reaching his intended audience, but he wasn't quite sure what that meant. The PWA began reading the essay aloud, asking the three female students at the table to listen along and offer their suggestions as well. He discovered in the process of reading aloud that this was an essay essentially blaming women for domestic violence incurred against them. When he paused briefly approximately two paragraphs into the essay to gather his thoughts about how to tactfully approach the student's question about audience, the three female students listening to the draft began to raise serious questions about his content and logic, giving the student likely the best lesson he had received in audience all semester, a very real, very passionate and on-the-spot reaction from an audience of anonymous peers.

This experience reinforced for the student in a very powerful manner a concept he had been hearing all semester—that he was, indeed, writing for an outside audience, someone other than himself. Although this point is emphasized in all portfolio-based writing courses, and practiced through peer review in the classroom and instructor review, we think nothing prepares students to recognize this concept quite as well as the experience of watching a perfect stranger read and comment on their work, while other strangers listen along and provide additional commentary. It is both discomforting and illuminating.

But beyond this very practical benefit, the Pandemonium helps students in other ways as well. Many students come feeling the need to vent—to discuss their frustrations, uncertainties, and fears about the portfolio evaluation process they are about to endure. It is not unusual, in fact, for a student to use the first several minutes of his or her time to "let loose" with unsolicited observations about his or her instructor, course requirements, and the general stress the entire portfolio revision process has caused. Fortunately, when this happens, despite the intensity and chaos inherent in the workshop, those who work the Pandemonium often provide a sounding board for the students when they most need it, allowing them to speak their minds, and supporting them as they do so. The PWAs are especially sensitive to student concerns because they are students themselves and all of them have been through the portfolio system in at least one class. Thus, they understand the importance of allowing students to vent briefly so they can then focus on the work that brought them to the Pandemonium in the first place. Faculty volunteers, too, are well-prepared to listen to students' anxieties about the portfolio evaluation process, often seeing it as an opportunity to demystify the process and explain the logic behind it. For students, just seeing that faculty members care enough to volunteer to help them at such an event sends a clear message that faculty are invested in student success on the portfolio. As a result, they frequently come away empowered to finish their work.

In addition to benefiting students, the Pandemonium also affords great benefits to our WC. First, it enables the WC to assist a greater number of students during the end-of-semester rush. On average, between 80 and 100 students attend the 5-hour workshop, far more than the number we could serve if we simply held the WC open and took appointments for an additional 5 hours during finals week. The Pandemonium also allows us to maximize the availability of our staff by enabling them to work with students more efficiently. Although we accommodate walk-ins in the WC whenever possible, more typically we schedule one-on-one appointments on the hour, lasting up to 50 minutes. The appointments are nearly always booked well in advance of the final week of the semester. However, like all WCs, we face a problem with a high rate of "no shows." This seems to result, at least in part, from students' tendencies to make appointments in advance but then either forget about them or fail to cancel them when their revision work is finished earlier than anticipated. Another trend in end-of-semester appointments is that often they do not take the entire 50 minutes allowed. Students may have questions about specific items like MLA documentation or grammar and usage, resulting in 15-minute sessions. Both of these scenarios unfortunately leave the PWAs with plenty of free time that could have been spent accommodating additional students. The Pandemonium allows us to answer students' quick questions without having to schedule a whole session.

The Pandemonium also affords good publicity for the WC. As the popularity of the event grows, students and faculty alike begin stopping at the front counter earlier in the semester to ask whether we have set a date yet for the workshop and when flyers will be available. The fact that our staff are willing to set aside an evening during the busiest time in their semester (not to mention an evening that does not wrap up until midnight!) also sends a clear message to students that the WC is "on their side" in terms of supporting them with revision efforts. Additionally, roughly half the students who attend the workshop have not visited the WC before, and this is an opportunity for them to be introduced to it as a resource.

Perhaps the greatest benefit of the Pandemonium for our WC is one we had not anticipated. The workshop creates an unusually strong bonding opportunity among our staff and between WC staff and faculty. Although the staff is small and they tend to already know each other quite well, they have very few opportunities, aside from staff meetings, to work simultaneously. The Pandemonium provides this rare opportunity. Faculty volunteers who attend the Pandemonium also bond with one another and with WC staff as they work alongside each other toward a common goal. Sometimes, the PWAs even have a chance to reconnect with their own, former writing instructors in very meaningful ways, working alongside them to assist student writers together therefore creating a powerful dynamic in which a community of writers is formed. It is also a great opportunity for faculty to be exposed to the philosophy of the WC and to witness the skill with which our PWAs handle students. Imagine, in this scenario, a PWA teaching a former teacher, albeit indirectly, about WC pedagogy.

> **"The workshop is a great opportunity for faculty to be exposed to the philosophy of the writing center and to witness the skill with which our peer writing assistants handle students."**

THE ATMOSPHERE

If one were to look into the room through a window on Pandemonium night, it may appear that a party was taking place. Some students would be milling around, eating pizza, drinking soda, and socializing with their friends, classmates, and faculty. Others would be sitting at tables huddled over their papers with a WC staff member or faculty member exchanging lively conversation. Many in the room would be smiling, laughing, and exchanging witty retorts to keep the mood fun and ease anxiety. At times, one would have to shout to be heard over the numerous simultaneous conversations taking place.

Even the signs placed at each station are designed with a sense of humor in mind, thanks to one of the WC staff. Not only are the signs colorful, but they contain light-hearted remarks about the task for each station. For example, one of the "Mechanics" signs contains the remark, "Periods, commas, and spark plugs, oh my!" An "MLA Documentation" sign reads "Let the tedium begin!" whereas another reads, "Because your teacher told you to, that's why!" The signs for the "Style" stations read, "And we'll do a little turn on the catwalk..." and "Not just for snappy dressers." The "Content and Ideas" signs read, "Where ideas achieve nirvana" and "Cause it's what's on the inside that counts!" It is safe to say that many students, although they may be feeling tired and apprehensive about passing their portfolios, have fun at the Pandemonium.

However, no matter what we do to create an atmosphere of fun, the workshop is often one of sobering reality for students, many of whom are under extreme pressure and need to be handled with a delicate mix of fortitude and care. Although we all strive to maintain our philosophy that a writer can learn just as much about how to improve an essay through positive feedback as through more critical feedback, we also realize that students will only have approximately 1 week before portfolios are due, and if their essays raise serious questions in terms of content, logic, approach, fulfillment of assignment, structure, and so on, they need to know. During the last Pandemonium, the first student who sat down to work with Tim eagerly handed him her lengthy argumentative essay for an advanced composition class, and a few minutes later, after some initial praise, heard his comment, "but I'm not sure I see an argument here." At this point, the previously enthusiastic student burst into tears, informing us that she had already spent hours revising the essay in response to her instructor's comment that it did not contain a clear argument. This student, like many others who attend the Pandemonium, was experiencing exhaustion, while still feeling pressured to master course concepts in order to pass her portfolio. After a few minutes, she calmed down and, she and Tim were able to construct a plan for revision. She was on her way to the all-night computer lab to produce another draft.

Like this young woman, several other students, who seem to seek out a "stamp of approval" response at the Pandemonium, often feel discouraged when they learn they need to go back to the drawing board with major revision work still lying ahead. A more humorous example comes to mind as another illustration of this issue. At approximately 11 p.m. during one

Pandemonium, one PWA sat down to work with a student who just wanted him to "look over" an essay and tell him "if it was alright." When the PWA began asking questions about the draft, he became perplexed by the student's apparent inability to answer them. Finally, he began to develop a theory that perhaps the essay had been plagiarized, at which point he asked the student, "Did you write this essay?" To this question, the student responded with exasperation, "Oh, no! This is my wife's essay. She went to bed after finishing it and asked me to bring it here to make sure it was OKed." After pausing a few minutes to write down some of the PWA's questions, the dutiful husband continued, "She's not going to like this!"

The Pandemonium can also be filled with stress, exhaustion, and discouragement for staff. Though we encourage staff to take 5- to 10-minute breaks as often as possible, the sheer volume of students makes it nearly impossible to take more than one break during the 5-hour workshop. In response, one PWA, after several failed attempts to refill her coffee cup, finally grabbed the entire carafe and a straw, positioning it beside her as she continued to respond to students' drafts. Many staff often find their voices hoarse by the end of the night and their minds awhirl with excerpts from students' essays still spinning in their thoughts. Although we ask staff to focus on answering students' specific questions at each station, inevitably they get roped into reading entire drafts, even entire portfolios, and giving holistic assessments of "what needs to be done." One adjunct faculty member, a former veteran high school English teacher of nearly thirty years, expressed at the end of the last Pandemonium that she could not remember a time when she felt so "overwhelmed" by the needs of student writers, needs which were all immediate and a matter of pass or fail. At the conclusion of our last Pandemonium, one PWA described the event as "writing triage," noting how incredibly taxing it was on her both mentally and physically.

It surprised us the first time we held the Pandemonium that student traffic was steady during the entire workshop. We had assumed that perhaps by later in the evening (at least by 11 p.m. or so), students would begin tapering off, and that perhaps we could begin dismissing some of our most tired volunteers and staff. But, quite to the contrary, traffic actually seemed to pick up after 11 p.m. We found ourselves almost literally pushing students out the door at midnight. After holding the workshop once and knowing more about what to expect, we decided it would be a good idea to initiate a "warning" to students when there was about 30 minutes left, and then another one when around 15 minutes remained, followed by another at 11:55 p.m., and finally, at midnight, one of us now walks around to each table where students remain and politely lets them know that the workshop is over, encouraging them to visit the WC the following day.

Several of these late-night students were ones who had visited the Pandemonium earlier in the evening, had gone to the computer lab and revised their drafts, and were returning for another round of feedback. But we also got students coming in the door for the first time as late as 11:30 or 11:45 p.m. Although we warned these students when they signed in that they had very limited time, and although we advised them to address our writing assistants with very specific questions (perhaps about lower-order concerns), we were still met with desperate questions like, "Can you please just read my portfolio 'real quick' and tell me if there is anything wrong?" Some of our staff, at this point in the evening, were too weary to resist, and engaged in taking up the task with whatever ounce of energy they had left, only to find themselves regretting this decision a few moments later. One example comes to mind from a previous Pandemonium during which one student, who had asked this very question, was still in the room at around 12:02 a.m. as staff were rearranging furniture around her, and the writing assistant with whom she worked was zipping the student's belongings into her backpack and helping her on with her coat while still answering questions about rephrasing her thesis statement.

AND TO ALL, A GOOD NIGHT . . .

And then it ends. When the last student of the evening has left, the atmosphere is noticeably silent. Remaining staff and volunteers mill about in a semi-catatonic state rearranging furniture, picking up pizza crusts and crumpled scraps of paper, and returning books and resources to shelves. After an initial 5-minute "decompression" time, conversation picks up again, and staff begin to exchange "war stories" about students they've encountered during the evening. These stories range from sharing descriptions of excellent writing as well as poor writing they have seen during the course of the evening to sharing stories of dismay over bizarre instructor assignments as well as stories about students who laughed, cried, and asked them out on dates (which ironically seems to happen to at least one writing assistant during every Pandemonium we have held). More often than not, after the room is put back together, the staff go out for a midnight breakfast, even though some of them have 8 a.m. classes.

Our Midnight Madness Portfolio Pandemonium, originally created to solve a workload problem within our WC, has given us more than we bargained for—more benefits for students, more benefits for the WC itself. Interestingly, although we have tinkered slightly with the original design we created on the fly that first night, the basic format of the Pandemonium has not changed—simply because it works, both for those who staff the event and those who attend it. And although to an outside observer looking in on the action, the Pandemonium might resemble a chaotic free for all, it really is a well-orchestrated evening in which students seem to realize that they are part of a larger community of writers and teachers, and, more importantly, that they are not alone in the struggle to produce a successful portfolio. It also reinforces the importance of WC work for students, PWAs, and faculty volunteers, and it has proven to us that sometimes the most profound benefits are born out of taking a creative approach to solving practical dilemmas.

> **"Sometimes, the most profound benefits are born out of taking a creative approach to solving practical dilemmas."**

15

INVITATIONS AND *VOICES*

Fostering Creative Expression

Carol Severino and Cinda Coggins Mosher

"AN INVITATION TO WRITE?"

You are excited but nervous about your first writing center (WC) meeting. Your high school teachers often noted your lack of organization and clarity, and you want to get off to a good start in your college classes, many of which require essays. Yesterday, when you enrolled in your first semester Rhetoric class, the receptionist gave you a calling card with your assigned days and time (Tuesdays and Thursdays 9:30-10:20 a.m.) and the name of your teacher, Dave. At the bottom of the card was the slogan: "An Invitation to Write." "What's that all about? What's this business about an invitation?" you wonder as you walk into the large, bright room, head toward the front desk, and ask for Dave.

"There he is," the receptionist says pointing to a young man not much older than you, sitting by the window scribbling in a notebook. Dave stands, smiles, and shakes your hand, "Welcome to the writing center. Where are you from?" After chatting with you about the Chicago suburbs, the Cubs, and the Sox, he looks over the enrollment card you filled out. "Do you have other courses with papers besides Rhetoric?"

"My social problems course has writing and so does environmental issues, but we don't have any assignments yet."

"Not a problem," says Dave. "Whenever you don't have course work, I'll give you informal writing prompts called 'Invitations' that you'll write during your writing center session. With Invitations, you will be free to express yourself and try some different types of writing than what you're accustomed to. And when I read your work, I'll get to know more about you and how you write—your strengths and weaknesses. Here's the first Invitation, kind of a stream-of-consciousness exercise," he says handing you a typed page. "It's called 'Talking on Paper.' Just pretend you're talking to me so we can start a dialogue in writing that will continue all semester. I'll go get my other student started, and you can let me know when you're done so we can talk about what you've written."

You look down and read:

Invitation to Talk on Paper

Whatever your style of talking, whatever the variety of English you speak, I hope you feel free to find your own language as you write. Whatever the range of your vocabulary, whatever the values that have shaped your life, I hope you feel free to say whatever you're thinking.

One of my students once told me, in writing, "The best thing that happened to me in this class was learning to respect my own writing."

That student, that writer, had discovered that writing is not a dreary, sometimes painful academic routine. For him, writing had become talking. In his own voice, with his own everyday language, he was saying something, in writing, for me, his tutor, and classmates to read. Saying something that was worth saying because it was important to him. And as I read his writing, as I listened to the personal knowledge of human experience that he was sharing, his ideas became important to me.

Though a sense of failure may sometimes diminish your self-respect, you can rediscover a sense of self-worth through writing. If you're saying what you think and feel, and if your reader is hearing and responding, with understanding, to what you're saying, then writing enables you to define your individuality, and your relations with others.

With the language you know and use every day, with the voice that expresses your individuality, you can *be* your own self. And you can *become* the writer you want to be.

As soon as you finish reading this invitation, I hope you'll start talking. On paper. Just as you do when you leap into a light-hearted conversation, or cautiously edge your way into a heavy discussion to add your knowledge and opinions to what other folks say.

Maybe you'll want to begin by responding to what I'm saying on paper to you. But that is not an *assigned* topic. You can't begin with your own everyday language unless you begin with your own personal knowledge, and with your own ideas about something you want to talk about with your tutor.

If you feel your mind turning off when you pick up your pencil to respond to this invitation to write, just remember that writing—like talking—is human behavior. Human communication and interaction. People talking and relating to each other.

So forget the "rules" you've learned about topic sentences or introductions and just start talking—on paper. Don't worry about the surface errors you sometimes or always make in spelling and punctuation. Don't stop to correct your "bad" grammar. And don't cross out the "inappropriate" words that you depend on to say what you feel. If you talk like that, write like that. So your reader can hear the sound of your own voice. Talking on paper.

As your pencil moves along the empty lines, try to say what you're thinking and how you're feeling at this very moment. Try to say, as honestly as you can, what's going on inside your own head. Right now.

Just talk on paper. For 30 or 40 minutes. Longer, if your mind and pencil are still spinning off words.

Wow, this WC isn't what you expected. "Forget about the rules?" "Don't worry about surface errors?" This is certainly not the advice your high school teachers gave you. And whoever heard of choosing your own topics and writing like you talk? You're a good sport, however, and although it sounds a little like a new-age therapy, you start free-writing, jotting down your first impressions of college, clicking away at the keys. Gradually you get carried away, lose track of time, and when Dave comes to see how you're doing, you're already on the fourth page, describing in great detail the electronic appliances brought from home with which your roommate has filled your dorm room. Amazing—you're writing and you're actually enjoying yourself! Dave praises the verbs and adjectives that make your descriptions vivid and compares his first week at college years ago with yours. You discuss different approaches to responding to Invitations—from plunging in to first making a list of what you might include.

That's what Invitations are.

INVITATIONS AND *VOICES*: THE UIWC

Browsing the current version of The University of Iowa Writing Center (UIWC) Web site (www.uiowa.ed/~writingc/), one is immediately struck by the absence of On-Line Writing Center (OWL) handouts in favor of

Invitations and issues of *Voices from the University of Iowa Writing Center*—
the UIWC's semi-annual publication composed largely of pieces written by
WC students in response to those Invitations and course assignments that
allow for creative expression. Because many WC Web sites feature helpful
handouts on every imaginable writing issue from the composing process to
citations, but few sponsor in-house publications, and even fewer, if any,
offer Invitations, we can point to our combination of Invitations and *Voices*
as expressions of our unique identity and contribution to the WC world.
Here, we share our experiences with Invitations and *Voices* so that other
WCs can consider adapting a version of both to their own institutional situations, constructing informal writing prompts that in turn would produce
material for their local WC publications.

THE HISTORY OF INVITATIONS

Some might speculate that the well-known UI Writers' Workshop has
helped foster this "creative" identity for our WC, but historically, the workshop's influence on the WC's ethos has been only indirect. In fact, the practice of composing Invitations and having WC students respond to them
originates not from a primarily creative impulse but from a rhetorical one;
our WC is housed in the Rhetoric Department, which stresses above all
else the importance of purpose and audience in communication.

When Lou Kelly, then Professor of Rhetoric (now Emeritus), started
using Invitations with her students in the 1960s, she was attempting to
counteract the formulaic and impersonal (but highly organized) writing
students had to do in order to pass an exit exam they had previously failed.
Gaining requisite skills to pass this exit exam was the reason most were
working in the WC. Others were assigned to work in the WC before taking Rhetoric because of low standardized test scores. As Kelly (1980) herself explained in "One-on-One Iowa City Style," the "pass out theme,"
unlike most writing deemed creative, was formula-driven. The recipe for
the core paragraph consisted of "an attitude sentence" (a sentence that
expressed an attitude), followed by a sentence with a supportive example
of that attitude, and a concluding sentence of interpretation. The students
then elaborated on these three sentences to build a passing essay. In
response to attitude essays that were as tedious and boring to read as they
were to write, Kelly wanted to create a live rhetorical situation in which
students were saying something important to someone important who
wanted to hear it, in other words, a dialogue. She created the first
Invitation to solicit students' reactions to failing the exam. She asked them

how they felt about having to do remedial work in the WC after 12-plus years of education.

The students' responses were emotionally powerful, passionate, engaged, fluent, and voiced—in striking contrast to their voiceless, mechanical attitude essays. To elicit more such engaged and fluent writing, Kelly developed a series of Invitations that she also used in her Rhetoric courses. As she (Kelly, 2001) explained in her keynote speech at the Midwest Writing Center Association Conference, "I couldn't resist giving students an opportunity to respond whenever I thought of another set of questions, or a current situation, that would further their understanding of writing as a personal interaction between themselves and their readers." Her textbook, *From Dialogues to Discourse: An Open Approach* (Kelly, 1972), which many Rhetoric teachers used in the classroom, and her in-house publication *Context and Response*, consist of more than 100 finely crafted and inspiring Invitations on topics ranging from "A Special Place" to "Talking about TV." In a recent interview, Kelly explained that Invitations only work in the context of a dialogue or relationship between writer and reader. Students must be writing to communicate, not just to fulfill an assignment or pass an exam (personal communication, November 25, 2005).

This sequence of Invitations evolved into a kind of curriculum for the WC for students at all levels of study, not only those taking or preparing to take Rhetoric. Thus, the semester-long WC experience was based on a sequence of Invitations and subsequent improvised Invitations that individual tutors devised that asked what Kelly called "tell-more-questions" about what the student wrote. For example, if in the Self-as-Writer Invitation in which a student is asked to offer an autobiographical account of his or her writing experiences, strengths, and weaknesses, a student mentions a favorite English teacher, subsequent spin-off Invitations might ask the student for an anecdotal profile that brings that teacher to life.

It is important to point out to those involved in appointment-based centers that a WC that is Invitation-and-dialogue-based, rather than individual course project-based, needs continuity over time with the same tutor, rather than periodic appointments with different tutors; otherwise, the written dialogue and collaborative relationship between tutor and student cannot evolve. Until 2000, when the UIWC added the Evening and Friday Appointment Program, every WC student who enrolled made a commitment to working twice a week on his or her writing with the same tutor, who became that student's writing mentor. As Severino (1993a) described in "Writers Writing," only after a student and tutor had worked on what was called the opening sequence of Invitations ("Talking on Paper"; "Self as Writer"; "Self as Reader"; "Where do y'all come from?"; "A Special Place"; and "Skills Exchange." See appendix for sample Invitations), could they commence work on papers assigned in Rhetoric and other courses.

INVITATIONS TODAY:
HOW THEY WORK TO BENEFIT STUDENTS

As the WC gradually evolved into the kind of Research I university WC that works with multiple university populations, including upper level and international undergraduates and graduate students, on multiple writing projects, including personal statements, proposals, and dissertations, we realized that Invitations should not interrupt or replace guidance with the professional or course work that many students find more urgent. And although the exit exam and the basic Rhetoric classroom course, the two principal motivating conditions for Invitations, no longer exist (the exit exam was abolished in the 1970s, the basic Rhetoric course in the 1990s), we did not want to eliminate the Invitations, which continue to benefit students and tutors in the following ways.

First, Invitations serve an excellent diagnostic function. Twice-per-week tutors learn much about their students' backgrounds, interests, strengths, and weaknesses in writing from reading a few responses to Invitations, which students usually write in the WC with no assistance from spellcheck features, dorm or housemates, or parents. Second, the more tutors know about their students' cultural and educational backgrounds and academic and extracurricular interests, the more they can help them find material for their later academic assignments and connect their academic learning to their own lives, as WC tutor Elizabeth Robertson (1988) did with her student Colleen and as Carol (Severino, 2005) did with Lin. A tutor who has worked with Invitations is more able to help his or her students find "ways in" to assignments—to make personally meaningful what can sometimes seem like meaningless "hoop-jumping."

Third, and most important, using Invitations in a twice-a-week setting communicates to students a much broader view of writing than only helping with individual course papers during appointments. Invitations demonstrate to students that the WC focuses on the overall writing process rather than privileging disconnected individual products. Students who do not already consider themselves writers realize through their own WC experience that one writes for other purposes than solely to fulfill course requirements. One writes to express and create identity, to discover personal meaning, and to reflect on experience, especially academic writing and learning experiences. The informal nature of Invitations and the fact that they are often revised multiple times reinforces the idea of writing as a process that evolves over a period of time. Invitations about academic assignments make use of freewriting in order to generate, discover, and clarify ideas, a technique that might be new to students, especially those who procrastinate.

DIVERSIFYING INVITATIONS

Every year, a new class of graduate students in the seminar practicum, Teaching in a Writing Center, has the opportunity to use Invitations with their WC students. Some of their students with a steady stream of course work, for example two papers per week, balk at using Invitations, so rather than force them on students, we offer them as options. After all, "invitation," unlike "assignment," implies that one can decline, that it is not "required writing." New tutors have discovered that the set of original Invitations geared primarily to first-semester students does not always work for other populations, for example, international students, upper-level undergraduates writing in their major, Rhetoric or sociology students studying arguments in social controversies, or students who are taking or are interested in creative writing—fiction or nonfiction. For example, in the early 1990s, tutors noticed that the majority of the international students' responses to the popular Self-as-Writer Invitation were depressing and self-deprecatory, emphasizing their faulty second language writing, even though many were fluent, even published writers in their first language. In response, we composed another version of the Invitation, Self-as-Writer II, for international students so they could discuss their writing in their native language as well as their writing in English and compare the two in terms of what features constitute "good" writing in each language (Severino, 1993b).

Additionally, because the original Invitations were more personally oriented, we came up with ones that were more academic—for example, about social controversies (the basis of the revised Rhetoric curriculum), injustices, and academic jargon. Other tutors composed Invitations that were visually based (see Invitations: "What Do You See?" on our Web site), some of which we also store as pictures on index cards in a file box. An art student tutoring in the WC course chose paintings from the UI thesis gallery and composed a set of Invitations to go with them. These visual Invitations complement the first-year Rhetoric curriculum which emphasizes visual and media literacy. A WC tutor who is also a religion instructor assembled a CD with music of different styles and moods with accompanying writing prompts to help students meditate while writing. A tutor in an English M.A.T. program composed a sequence of Invitations that build toward a short story (see "Creative Writing" under Invitations); and a tutor in the nonfiction writing program added a component (see "More Creative Writing") to generate ideas for 101 different creative pieces. The last Invitation a student writes at the end of the semester is the Invitation to evaluate the writing center experience, which we use to improve our programs and services and which the WC director excerpts from when she writes letters of recommendation for tutors on the job market.

INVITATIONS AND PROGRAM CONNECTIONS

Currently, instructors of Rhetoric and other courses use the Invitations from our files and our Web site in their credit-bearing classroom courses, but more as informal assignments rather than formal or major assignments. For example, many Rhetoric teachers use "Self-as-Writer" as the first week in-class diagnostic writing to assess their students' writing skills—to gauge how many lessons in organizational and sentence-level skills they will have to teach and to discover if anyone in their class has writing apprehension or writer's block. A common general education literature diagnostic assignment is a version of the two Invitations "Self-as-Reader" and "Autobiography of a Reader." When Carol teaches creative nonfiction travel writing, she uses the visual Invitations "What Do You See." Students who are held for pre-Rhetoric 10:09, a two-credit course taught one-to-one in the WC, work on Invitations before and during writing about reading and controversy-based assignments to prepare for Rhetoric. The purpose of the Web-based Invitations is to create a self-paced individualized program for writers primarily working on their own, outside of institutionalized, credit-bearing structures.

Similarly, Cinda and other tutors tailor their writing Invitations to each individual student. In the first week of the tutorial, Cinda has her students spend one or two sessions listing and describing their interests. Students generally begin by listing 10 issues of interest to them—often political, social, environmental, cultural, professional, and/or leisure interests. She then has them select five of these and write a developed paragraph on each, detailing how they became interested in the subject, what experience they have had with it, and what more they would like to learn about the topic. One of her students, Li, narrowed her initial list of 10 interests to 5 that she wished to pursue in more detail: the sudden failure of the Asian economy, gender roles in American society, crime in America and its relationship to gun accessibility, standards of beauty, and assisted suicide. Li spent the rest of the semester coming back to these topics on days when she did not have pressing coursework. These five topics provided many opportunities for Cinda to ask Li more questions pertaining to cultural differences she was experiencing and her reactions to these differences. This dialogue in writing allowed Li to work through not only her apprehension about writing in a second language but also her initial reservations about perceived dangers and unfamiliar gender interaction in American society.

Cinda also often provides relevant articles or has her students find sources that can enhance their command of the subject or that can offer perspectives they may not have already considered. Students often end the semester tutorial with several well-developed pieces of writing on controversial issues that they have expressed interest in pursuing. These pieces empower students in terms of their feeling better-educated on world issues and events, their gaining better command of the English language in the case of English as a Second Language (ESL) students, and/or their enhanced analytical abilities. Often, these pieces find their way into our publication, *Voices from the University of Iowa Writing Center*, a collection of pieces that has had a remarkable impact on a number of our WC students from around the world.

PUBLISHING AND READING *VOICES*

Voices from the University of Iowa Writing Center provides a crucial venue for students to see themselves as published writers who have an interested, although perhaps small, audience. Each semester, WC tutors are asked to help interested students craft contributions to this in-house publication so that students who are often not in communication with each other during the semester can come together at the end of the term and read what fellow students have created. Our focus on creativity is apparent in every issue of *Voices*. Students are encouraged to pursue any area of interest in their submissions. Although some students prefer to respond to a written invitation, others choose to submit fiction, poetry, or essays for courses they are taking. This freedom for students to choose their own subject matter is what makes *Voices* such a dynamic and diverse publication. Readers of *Voices* are able to enjoy a range of genres and subjects from a group of writers from radically different academic and cultural backgrounds.

    Voices has evolved considerably over time. Twenty years ago, it was a few typed mimeographed pages of sentences, paragraphs, or sometimes whole pieces, mostly from the Invitations of basic writers. Over time and due in large part to technological innovations, *Voices* has expanded to include entries from all levels of students from many different academic programs across campus. Its collage format, in which it is not unusual for a single issue to include essays and poetry by students from 10 or 15 different countries and as many different departments, has fostered a truly interdisciplinary, multicultural forum for creative expression at the university. The *Voices* experience has many powerful effects on the community of its readers and writers. For example, one issue of *Voices* includes the following submissions:

"From nowhere to somewhere," by Ronelle Langley, South Africa
"To Be Like an Eagle," by Joon Young Kwak, Korea
"Soul of a Woman," by Bethany Miller, Bolivar, Tennessee

"Remembrances of a Special Place," by Juei-Ju Cheng, Taiwan
"A little bit of everything," by Sheyla Shrek, Sao Paolo, Brazil
"Americans' Obsession with Thinness," by Amanda Hamilton,
    Sioux City, Iowa
"As Usual," by Naomi Yoshioka, Kyoto, Japan.

As they read through the issue, readers grow familiar with various memories and observations of the authors, and there are often illuminating areas
of overlap that give a sense that these students from all over the world are
in a form of conversation with each other. Because a number of our students respond to similar invitations in which they are asked to describe a
special place, compare their hometown to Iowa City, or introduce the reader to an influential person in their lives, the *Voices* submissions often seem
to speak to each other as well as to the audience (Coggins, 2001). Consider,
for example, Naomi Yoshioka's (1999) observation in "As Usual" that
"[w]hen I stepped into the home that I was away from these three years, I
immediately recognized the smell of home, which triggered my memories.
I was suddenly nostalgic. The years disappeared when I was surrounded by
the familiar atmosphere. Nothing had changed" (p. 22) alongside Yu-fang
Tsai's (1999) experience in which, "[n]ow, almost a year has passed by and
I keep calling home once a week. I worry about my parents' health; I worry
when my brother fools around all day and doesn't concentrate on his studies . . . I cannot help worrying a lot because I am the oldest child in my family" (p. 42). These two student pieces collectively echo feelings of nostalgia
or homesickness many international students express when responding to
Invitations or when asked to free-write.
    Threads of family, being away from home for the first time, memories,
and cultural differences permeate most issues of *Voices* and encourage an
appreciation of similarity as much as an appreciation of difference. When
Yanrong Chang (1994) explained in "Be Confident, ESL Writers!" that
"there are moments of over self-consciousness which virtually beat me
down totally and I was almost deterred from writing at all. I was overwhelmed with thoughts, thousands of preventive thoughts—how could the
readers (my professors, my students or my classmates, for instance) react to
my writing? Have I expressed myself well?" (p. 29), many native speakers of
English as well as fellow ESL students are undoubtedly reminded of the
near paralyzing fear they too felt when their writing was evaluated by professors and fellow students (Coggins, 2001). Although they usually study in
demanding academic programs that don't use personal essays, international
students are often enthusiastic responders to Invitations and contributors to
Voices. The assignments not only enable them to reflect on experience and
discover meaning, but also in terms of second language acquisition, to push
their linguistic output (Swain & Lapkin, 1995) and thus learn more English.

Some pieces for *Voices* originate from a tutor–student relationship in which a student writes to dispel a stereotype that the tutor or another American might have about his or her culture or to disclose a stereotype he or she had about American culture or the White race prior to coming to Iowa to study. For example, Lin wrote to counter the prejudice Carol had developed about her hometown in China from her limited reading (Severino, 2005). Similarly, a Taiwanese student wrote her *Voices* entry in response to American ideas of what constitutes edible meat, comparing her eating snake to Americans eating rare steak (Severino, 2002). A particularly compelling entry in the Spring 1997 *Voices* came from Boster Kazembe (1997), a student from Malawi, Africa:

> When I was little, about 10 years old, I first came across white people. My parents and I knew a little about the white people because there were a few of them in Malawi staying in main towns. Most people in my village believed that whites were spirits who came from the unknown. Some people believed that whites were normal people just as black people were.
>
> By this time, I was interested to know about white people, but it was difficult for me. Lucky enough, my parents knew a little bit about the whites, since we were living along the lake where most of the whites came to swim. My parents told me that they were normal people as we were. I asked my parents, "Where do those people come from?" They said, "We don't know yet, but we believe that they came from mbwani (meaning the ocean in my language) or the other side of it."
>
> Maybe that's why people believed that they were spirits. I also asked my parents, "Is this the only reason people think that they are spirits?" They said, "Another reason is that they are red." My parents could not say white. They thought whites were red, as they usually appear in Africa due to the sun.
>
> The most interesting part of this was that they thought red people, as they called the whites, had been skinned or peeled. We all felt sorry for the whites because we didn't know that they were born white. I also asked my parents again, "Why do people think that the whites have been skinned?" My father said, "It's because if we peeled our skin, it would look as red as their skin does, so people think that they have been peeled." But my father did not believe that red people had been peeled because he had met a lot of white people along the lake.
>
> Another interesting aspect which people thought about was the white man's nose. They had long, pointy noses, as most of the whites do. People could not understand how the nose could be so pointy naturally, as most blacks have flat noses. They thought that someone had pulled up their noses soon after birth.
>
> My father approached them nicely, but could not speak English. He could only speak Chichewa. Those whites were missionaries who

could speak rudimentary Chichewa and they had a conversation with my father. My father asked one of the whites where he came from and how he crossed the mbwani. He told my father that he came from Rome on a big ship which went around the world. Also my father asked how big the ship was and how long it took to come to Africa. He said that it was a big ship, many times bigger than those we had in Malawi, and that it took about three months to get to Africa.

My father also asked him why he was so red. He told my father that he was born white and the sun turned him red. My father asked him if he felt any pain in his body. My father explained that people believed that the whites had been peeled. The white man told my father that he didn't feel any pain, that he wasn't peeled, and that "white" was his natural color. But he never asked anything about us blacks. I guess he must have known a lot about us.

This was the first proof to me that whites were not spirits and did not come from the ocean. I learned that they came from the other side of the ocean, and that they came by boat. Some of the whites came to our village to buy farmland. Whites moving into our area really helped people from our village to understand them, because many villagers worked on their farms.

One time, when we were coming back from school, a white man stopped to give us a ride. But some of my friends ran away, because they had been told that the whites are killers. They white man felt sorry for the boys who ran away, because his only aim was to give us a ride home.

This was how people in my home village thought of the whites. Since then, despite the barrier of past misunderstandings between us, whites have been working hand in hand with the blacks. The Peace Corps plays a large role in increasing the understanding between whites and blacks, especially in the rural villages because they work with people directly in villages. Everybody is happy to see the white man and people would like to spend their time with them because they exchange ideas and learn from each other.

I've explained the many myths that the blacks in my village had about whites. Now, let me ask you: What did you first think about the black man? (pp. 9-11)

Boster's outstanding revelation of his initial impression of white-skinned people offers an excellent example of *Voices'* multicultural nature. His interrogative ending perfectly underscores the interactive nature of Invitations. His tutor undoubtedly met this thoughtful piece of writing with an equally earnest response that further strengthened the rapport between the tutor and student writer.

At present, our *Voices'* budget is quite small. So, Cinda assembles *Voices* as a Microsoft Word document and has around 30 colored copies made at the UI copy center, mainly for the contributors, their families, and

WC students and staff. A sample of several recent editions of *Voices* are also available on the WC Web site (http://www. uiowa.edu/~writingc/Voices/Voices-menu.html). Although *Voices* is not a high-profile or refereed publication, it has dramatically transformed many students' perceptions of themselves as writers. *Voices* affords contributing students the opportunity to see themselves as published authors. Students gain a tangible sense of accomplishment when they see their work in print alongside others' entries. Several students have commented that the experiences of contributing to *Voices* empowered them as writers and as students. One student wanted numerous copies to distribute to his family as Christmas presents. He was overjoyed that his work was in print and that his tutor and larger audience of readers had taken him seriously as a writer.

> "Students gain a tangible sense of accomplishment when they see their work in print alongside others' entries."

PSYCHOLOGICAL BENEFITS

Sometimes a student gains new insight from relating a monumental experience to an audience that extends beyond the student and his or her instructor (Coggins, 2001). For example, in Joon Young Kwak's (1999) "To be like an Eagle," the author discloses,

> I failed once to enter the university I wanted, in Korea. The reason was that I did not do as well as I wanted on my college entrance examination, which otherwise could have determined my whole life completely differently. The exam was held on November 13, 1996.
>
> Novels, movies, comic books—these were what I saw and read during the summer vacation right before the college entrance exam. The result? It was obvious. After a summer break, the scores of my practice exams, which were similar to the real exam, started to decrease, and this trend continued until the final exam. . . .
>
> Since the bitter experience of the university entrance exam, the first in my life, I feel I have awakened, can act independently and can decide what has to be done by myself. I changed my mind to be more aggressive than I was before in Korea. I have done fine so far. I have gained confidence and enjoy my life here. I do not regret coming to America. I am learning the way to survive in this world.
>
> When my plane landed at Chicago O'Hare International Airport, I felt I was not a thoughtless child anymore. I made one step toward my dream. Like a young eagle out from his mother's nest, I flew high toward the blue sky. (pp. 7-8)

The process of writing this contribution allowed Joon to work through what seemed at the time like the end of the road and recast the experience as a once-in-a-lifetime opportunity to study abroad. That this piece was published in English in *Voices* was a triumph unto itself, and this publication made it that much more clear to Joon how valuable the decision to study abroad was.

Other students feel empowered as they communicate to readers the essence of certain places or people who have had a profound impact on their lives. Bethany Miller (1999) tells of "the Palace of Hairstyles" in Bolivar, Tennessee, and "Teresa, the hairdresser, a healthy woman in her thirties who was well-educated, married with two children, and attended Antioch Baptist Church. Her hair was not done. She had a cape on, with her name and 'licensed beautician' on it also. She accepts about 60 percent of walk-ins or people without appointments" (p. 8). Responding to the same invitation to illustrate a "Special Place," Kuei-Ju Cheng (1999) chose to vividly describe the 8 months spent at her friend's house in Vancouver, where "the figures of the mountains are like perfect sculptures from the Creator and their expressions change every day with sunny days and cloudy days" (p. 14). When students such as Kuei-Ju and Bethany submit their essays, they feel proud of being part of a larger publication, a community of voices where they belong.

One student in the Spring 1996 edition chose to reflect on his progress as a writer and to pay homage to the WC. His heartfelt text speaks volumes about how many students come to fear the writing process because of baggage they've carried for the greater part of a lifetime. In "The Evolution of My Writing," Cinda's nontraditional student, Alan Unger (1996), writes,

> Writing has always been a losing game for me until the Writing Lab showed me how to spar. Through participating in the Writing Lab for three semesters, I have learned techniques that have helped me become a motivated writer. As a result of my academic advisor's encouragement and my lab mentoring, I have learned that writing requires invention, prewriting, drafting, composing, rewriting, and revising. From reading, I know now that effective writing also includes definition, analogy or comparison, consequence, testimony, clustering and sketching—all rhetorical elements.
>
> I now understand that good writing is not magically created by a gifted few. I previously thought that writers wrote perfectly without revision. But, upon reading Donald M. Murray's *The Craft of Revision*, I realized my error was caused by lack of modeling during my formative years. Additionally, I had writer's block because my inner mind heard my third-grade teacher speaking: "Alan, I know what you are saying, but you are not saying it the way I want you to." However, that blockage has thankfully passed. I can now write brief notes on Post-it slips! Years ago, if a card was passed around for a special occasion, I

could only sign my name. Maybe someday I will be able to write thoughts off the cuff like other people.

In a course taken with my advisor, I learned about maximizing student potential through liberal education. Four years ago, in a class I wrote a position paper on liberal education but it has only been through my experiences in the Writing Lab where I increased my ability to write coherent thoughts in one sitting that I have considered myself liberally educated. I no longer need writing rituals for the rhetorical process. I can just sit down practically anywhere and write. (p. 10)

Alan's ability to overcome his severe anxiety about the writing process was amazing to watch over the course of his years in the WC. When he first signed up for twice-per-week tutorials, it was clear that his past negative experiences with writing made him nearly panic stricken when faced with writing assignments that he knew others would critique. Of course, the transformation did not magically occur overnight, but his writing steadily and noticeably improved with practice combined with the positive feedback he was offered.

Occasionally, we are blessed with truly gifted and accomplished authors who could well be WC tutors. *Voices* contributors such as South American author Ronelle Langley have published essays in other, highly prestigious places. Langley's (1999) *Voices* essay, "From Nowhere to Somewhere," begins,

I smile at the idea that my husband David was a bit apprehensive at first when he told me he had inherited this piece of land from his parents. He did not want to take it, unless I was committed to the idea too. We drove for nearly five hours getting there to take a look at the land—semi-desert with a savanna type of grass, surrounded with indigenous trees as far as we could see—marulas, acadias, baobabs. The northern border of South Africa was close by, meeting with the southern borders of Botswana and Zimbabwe. South of the farm, we could see the Soutpan Mountains at a distance, where leopards and lions still roam, rising above the ground. We climbed a huge marula tree with long horizontal branches that invited us to sit down and have an aerial view of the farm and mountain range. (p. 1)

The essay progresses to tell the story of how Langley and her small children become stranded with two flat tires in what seems to them like the middle of nowhere. She details how she makes this disaster into an adventure for her children, all the while succumbing to negative stereotypes she has heard of rural people in this part of Africa. Surprisingly to both Langley and the reader, she is met with unbelievable acts of selflessness by a man named Sarel, and concludes with a life-altering observation:

In the end, it was the imperfections of this day, when things went terribly wrong in the middle of nowhere, that resulted in a lifelong, precious lesson for me: *There is still so much goodwill among my fellow human beings.* Enough goodwill to take back to the city where I lie, enough to inspire me for a long time to come. Enough to pass on to other human beings who cross my path. Enough for them to take it further and touch the lives of other fellow travelers. This road has led me to somewhere where I have a better understanding of what it means to be taken care of by a total stranger. Some place where preconceived, manmade boundaries no longer exist. (p. 4)

Although *Voices* necessarily reflects the wide range of abilities of our contributors, we do our best to prevent less experienced students from feeling self-conscious or inferior when their work appears alongside essays such as Langley's. Our desire for students to feel confident about their submissions drives us to pay close attention to each student's work and help them reach their individual potential. Contributors are always reassured that their individual piece will augment the collaborative publication and that it is more of a mosaic of different voices than a hierarchical contest.

READING *VOICES*

Although our students certainly enjoy seeing their words in print, nothing compares to their reading their work aloud in front of an attentive audience. When we assemble in the WC with food and refreshments, the sense of community established in the printed copy of *Voices* is magnified. The *Voices* reading brings students from different backgrounds and different departments together and allows the audience to put a face to the words on the page. It is amazing to hear the students' inflection and the emotion that accompanies their writing. Especially for students whose second language is English, the reading can seem intimidating at first, but tutors often help the students practice their oral presentation before the reading. Although some students initially feel nervous, they almost invariably feel proud of their accomplishments after they have presented their essays.

After each piece is read, the audience is encouraged to ask questions. The author is put in a position of authority and often elaborates on the motive for the writing, gives more information about an experience, and/or tells about the writing process itself and how he or she worked with the Invitation and his or her tutor to write and revise. When writers see the effect the writing has had on the audience, their confidence increases. They realize more than ever the power of language and their ability to reach their goals. This is a major step for many of our writers, like Alan, who come to us with little confidence in their writing ability. Others still carry with them the stigma of being placed in a remedial reading or writing group. Sometimes the positive attention we give students in the WC, especially the positive feedback of the *Voices* reading, can reverse some of the damage (Coggins, 2001).

Alan Unger was particularly elated after his *Voices* reading. He indicated that this experience had marked a turning point in his academic career and that being published was something he had never previously imagined possible. Although Alan was initially apprehensive about reading his "Evolution of My Writing" aloud, he read it extremely well and eagerly answered the audience members' questions afterward. His response, although particularly positive, is representative of students' responses to the *Voices* experience. In the many years of publishing *Voices* and having readings of the essays that are submitted, we can think of no negative student experiences that have come from the process. Even when an occasional student gets "stage fright" and doesn't want to read his or her piece aloud, WC tutors volunteer to read the piece for the student, and then the student answers questions after the reading.

Voices also provides the outside community with a glimpse of what we do in the WC. Because *Voices* is often distributed to students, instructors in various departments at Iowa and other institutions, family members, and so on and is published online, different readers take away different things from the publication. Some might deduce that we work primarily on personal writing in the WC, whereas others might be tempted to scrutinize the text's grammatical or organizational features, things we often don't significantly alter in contributors' writings. Parents of contributors might read solely for content or to discover their children's perspectives on a given topic. Other readers might choose to foreground the international make-up of our student population. Our hope is that the majority of people who read *Voices* find threads that resonate with their own interests and/or experiences and that they appreciate the empowerment the contributors experience when they see their entries in print and read their submissions aloud.

DEVELOPING YOUR
OWN IN-HOUSE PUBLICATION

Although The University of Iowa is conveniently situated to foster ongoing tutor–tutee relationships throughout the semester, we realize that not all colleges and universities can feasibly implement such a program. Yet there are other ways to sponsor informal and personal writing for publication.

WCs can sponsor writing groups and/or personal writing workshops, collect what the groups and workshops produce, and organize readings. Students who make appointments with the same tutors every week can be encouraged to take informal writing prompts home to work on and bring them to their tutoring session for the tutor to read if there is time or after the session. WCs might also solicit creative papers in the hope that students across campus will be inspired to contribute to a university wide publication.

> **"The writing center can sponsor writing groups and/or personal writing workshops, collect what the groups and workshops produce, and organize readings."**

INVITATIONS AND COURSE WORK

Although our Invitations and editions of *Voices* have been highly beneficial to numerous students from many different cultures and across many disciplines on campus, the last decade has marked a shift in our WC toward a greater emphasis on coursework. We are currently working hard to equalize this imbalance and re-emphasize the need for Invitations and creative expression. Unquestionably, course work has gradually taken priority over Invitations, a move that was hastened when the Rhetoric Department changed its curriculum from a personal to public sequence continuum, the first half of which conveniently corresponded to Invitations, to a curriculum that is controversy- and argument-based.

One gauge of the ascendancy of coursework over work with Invitations is the number of writing folders used in the twice-a-week enrollment program. Ten years ago, nearly every student had a weighty folder in which they saved their responses to Invitations. Now, fewer than half of the enrollment students have folders containing more than two responses to Invitations. One reason is that most writing for course papers is done at home rather than in the WC, and the drafts are largely discussed in the WC. Besides, with the advent of computer drives, discs, and sticks that save writing electronically, there is less need to physically save it in folders.

Another gauge of the importance of coursework is that the course paper-based Evening and Friday Appointment Program sees four times as many students as does the Twice-a-Week Enrollment Program, and the E-mail Tutoring program also helps twice as many students as the enrollment program. In the enrollment program, we struggle with those students who would rather take a break from writing than do informal writing in the WC when they don't have an assignment pending; despite our emphasis on the benefits of regular, informal writing, some call or e-mail in to cancel their enrollment hour because "I don't have a paper to work on." The upshot of all this is that fewer students are writing fewer responses to Invitations. The lack of Invitations, which constitute the major source of entries for *Voices*, has affected the frequency, length, and variety of its publication. Five years ago, a lengthy edition of *Voices* was published every semester; now we average one issue per year.

ELIMINATING THE FALSE DICHOTOMY BETWEEN ACADEMIC AND CREATIVE EXPRESSION

Although Invitations and *Voices* submissions are clearly billed as creative venues for expression, we in no way wish to establish a rigid dichotomy between creative writing and academic writing. If anything, the WC is committed to bridging this gap to create a space for greater creativity in academic expression. In fact, material from the personalized Invitations often find their way into academic papers in which students are asked to write essays on social or political issues in which they are personally invested. Furthermore, it is not unusual for essays students have written for courses to be included in *Voices*.

The University of Iowa Rhetoric Department's recent shift in curriculum away from Invitations-related essays in the first semester to argumentative reasoning, for example, need not mark the end of creative expression inside or outside of the WC. We strongly feel that there is always room for some degree of creative expression, and that argument-based writing often benefits from deep personal connections to the issues being addressed. We have seen a number of assignments in the WC in the past few years that ask students to adopt a creative approach to academic issues. One student, for instance, was asked to write a journal in which she assumed the voice of a working woman whose husband was fighting in World War II. The journal was to cover the period before, during, and after the war, and the purpose of the assignment was to provide insight into the role of women in the workplace when many men were fighting in the war.

Cinda has adapted her Rhetoric courses to include personal input from students on controversial issues of their choice. Her first major assignment asks students to choose an absolute value they were asked or encouraged (implicitly or explicitly) to accept without question as a child. Examples include, "Smoking is wrong," "Divorce is bad," "Fighting is wrong," and so forth. Her second assignment builds on the first, and students are required to research many positions on the topic. For example, a student who began with "Fighting is wrong" might discover perspectives that vary from absolute pacifism to support only for self defense to rationalization of offensive maneuvers such as the Gulf War. In the final assignment, students finally advocate their current position that has evolved over time as they have had relevant experiences and conducted research from a variety of angles. This blend of rigorous research and personal investment fits well with the aims of the WC, and we eagerly encourage creative approaches to assignments across the curriculum. Clearly, there are ways to get students personally invested in almost any course, and such an investment is likely to lead students to embrace, rather than merely fulfill, writing assignments.

AN ACTIVE RETURN TO INVITATIONS AND A COMMITMENT TO *VOICES*

While we clearly refuse to buy into the separation of creative and academic writing, we remain as committed as ever to the importance of Invitations and *Voices* publications and readings. We have seen first-hand the benefits of writing in a stress-free environment and have witnessed students' positive responses to ungraded invitations. For example, we recently enacted an attendance policy in which the benefits of Invitations are stressed, and students who nonetheless show up only on days when they have coursework are re-assigned to appointment hours so that students who are committed to the writing process can benefit from the twice-per-week appointments. Our ongoing diversification of Invitations to suit the interests and needs of students from all different backgrounds has also increased tutors' interest in and commitment to using Invitations with their twice-a-week enrollment students. We also recently hired a University of Iowa Writers' Workshop graduate as our new full-time e-mail tutor and outreach person. Matt Gilchrist has reached out to many different departments across campus, emphasizing our commitment to all forms of writing. His professional goals include bringing together a once-disparate community of writers in Iowa City—poets, fiction writers, scholarly writers, nonfiction essayists, community advocacy writers, and so on. His energetic approach in classrooms in the first 2 weeks of class has led to many eager undergraduates coming in to sign up for tutoring. Furthermore, because students are now submitting creative works to e-mail tutoring, we are also accepting online *Voices* submissions that have gone through multiple drafts with our e-mail tutor.

Although coursework will undoubtedly assume a much larger role in our WC than it did a decade or so ago, our future goals include outreach in which we offer interested professors suggestions for getting students more personally invested in writing assignments, more emphasis on the use of Invitations, and a thriving forum for a diverse group of student voices to be heard on this campus and beyond, thus embracing a more comprehensive definition of creative writing.

APPENDIX

The following is a sample of Invitations composed by Lou Kelly, professor of Rhetoric (Emeritus). These are a few of the most popular among tutors and students in the UIWC. For more Invitations, see http://www.uiowa.edu/~writingc/invitations/invitations.html

SELF AS WRITER

There are two versions of the "Self as Writer" invitation; the second is intended for ESL writers.

Self as Writer I: If you want your writing class to begin where you are, then you must let your tutor know how you see yourself as a writer. In fact, I would say you cannot become a better writer unless you're willing to take a careful look at writing abilities you already have. So please talk a while, on paper, about your concept of self as writer.

How do you feel, what thoughts fill your head, when you sit down to write what a teacher has asked you to? When you sit down to write a letter you want to write? A letter you don't feel like writing? Do you ever write simply because you feel a creative impulse? If so, what form does that writing take? What do you like about all, or some, of your writings? What do you see as occasional or recurring problems? Do you remember any specific writing experiences that left you feeling like a success—or failure?

Of course, these questions are not offered to test your memory as exam questions do. Instead, the intent is to help you see that your attitude toward writing is directly related to the continuing development of your writing abilities. So please hear and respond to them, in writing, just as you would if your tutor were asking them while talking with you face to face.

Since all your writing experiences are an important part of your concept of self as writer, your tutor may also wish to know something about the kinds of school writing you've done, and how frequently and how much you were asked to write. What kind of writing instruction do you remember? Did your teachers respond to your writing with compliments or corrections?

Whatever you remember about your previous writing experiences, whatever you feel as you try to respond to what I'm saying to you—just talk about it. On paper. Keep your mind and pencil moving until you've said whatever you think and feel about self as writer.

Self as Writer II: In your native country, you have probably had many experiences with writing in your first language that have shaped the way you think about writing. It's important for your tutor to know about your previous writing experiences and writing instruction so s/he can be of greater assistance to you.

So, using the following questions as a guide to get you started, please spend this hour talking about your experiences writing in your native language.

- When you were taught to write, did you learn any particular organizational structures or formats for your writing (for example, the four-part essay or the five-paragraph theme)? If so, please describe these formats in as much detail as possible.
- In your country, what qualities make a piece of writing good? What qualities make it beautiful?
- In school, were you encouraged to write about personal experiences or were you encouraged to write "objectively"? How did you feel when writing an assignment for school in your own language? A letter or something you chose to write? A diary or journal entry? A poem?
- What kinds of writing processes were encouraged in your country? Were you usually given a topic to write about or did you choose your own topic? Were you encouraged to make an outline or list before writing? Were you encouraged to pre-write or free-write first? How many drafts did you usually write for an assignment? Were you encouraged to revise your first drafts? What kinds of changes did teachers usually ask you to make? Did they ask for changes in ideas? In structure? In grammar? In phrasing?
- For students who have been at a U.S. college for a semester or more: Besides language, what do you find most different about writing a paper for a teacher in the U.S. compared with writing one in your native country?

AUTOBIOGRAPHY OF A READER

This is an invitation to talk, on paper, about what reading meant to you while you were growing up. It's an opportunity for you to recall, and record, the experiences that shaped your concept of what reading is, and the experiences that determined your attitude toward books and other forms of written language.

If you're a tireless, voracious reader, never stopping till you turn the last page of a book, you'll no doubt wish to focus on how your love of reading was born, and how it was nurtured. You'll write a different story, of course, if reading is not one of the joys of your life, and if you read only when a teacher tells you to.

Whatever kind of reader you are, I hope the questions asked here will take you into some self-involving writing. For writing this autobiography—and then listening attentively as you read it—could help you become a more perceptive and thoughtful reader.

Like most folks who write autobiography, you may wish to begin with your earliest memories—of the written language in this instance. For example:

- The word games you learned to play, and the reading lessons you saw and heard, while watching Sesame Street or another TV program.
- The brand names you learned to recognize—first on TV commercials, and then on the shelves of the supermarket.
- The first word games you played with your family, at home or on long trips.
- The sound and rhythm of a loving voice reading your favorite story, singsonging the nursery rhymes you loved, repeating the familiar words, talking about the familiar pictures. That voice may be your first memory of books. Listening to it, night after night, may be the first ritual you remember. If so, tell your reader about that significant reading experience.
- The first book you read all by yourself. or the first verse you memorized. If you remember, or if your parents have told you about it, talk about this happy experience.

WHERE DO Y'ALL COME FROM?

This is an invitation to talk about the place where you were born and raised. The place that shaped the beliefs and values you bring to your writing. The place that shaped your native dialect. (Will your tutor hear the sound of that dialect as he or she listens to you talking on paper? What regional dialect do you sometimes hear as you listen to this "talking" invitation?)

Instead of merely naming your hometown, please try to tell your tutor what that particular place has meant to you over the years, and what it means to you now. Of course, some families have lived in several or many different communities. So you may want to begin with the sense of loss you felt when you had to leave a place you loved and start over in a strange new place. Or did you leave an unpleasant or dangerous community for a happier and safer one?

As you recall the place(s) where you've spent most of your life, what do you see? What scenic views or ugly landscapes do you remember? Is your home community a small town or a spacious countryside? A big-city neighborhood, a suburban village, or miles of exurban sprawl? As your mind returns to the scenes of childhood and adolescence, what do you miss most? Maybe it's the sights and sounds of busy streets. Or the particular feel of the old neighborhood, even though it may not have escaped what sociologists and environmentalists would call urban or suburban blight.

Some of us feel nostalgic for the quiet beauty, but unbearable boredom, of a little country town. Or the still nights and busy days on a family farm. Others long to return to a homeland across the sea on another continent.

Whether your home is far away or across town, whether you return every weekend or won't see it again for a whole year, give your reader a brief but vivid glimpse of whatever you're remembering. Share with her/him your sense of the place you come from, the place you call home.

THE SKILLS EXCHANGE

Whether you feel like the best or the worst writer in class, I'm sure you can talk, with competence and confidence, about the skill it takes and the pleasure it gives you to do and be something else. So I invite you to share your enthusiasm for doing and being something you enjoy.

Just present yourself, in writing, in a role that permits you to talk about whatever you know and do best. Whatever language you prefer, here's your opportunity to introduce yourself as a skillful person by talking on paper for a few pages about something you know and enjoy.

For example: The old-fashioned board game of your childhood days, or the latest version of your favorite electronic competition. The child game you loved best. Or the games you love to play with your children. Or the ones you've played while babysitting. The musical instrument, or athletic game, you play every chance you get. The singing or dancing or acting that delights you. The fishing that takes you to a promising body of water, the hunting that takes you to an open field or the woods.

With the sound of your voice on paper, take your classmates with you to a place where you've spent many happy hours doing something you enjoy doing. Were you surrounded by the comforts of a family room, or the excitement of a club or gym? Or maybe you remember being all alone practicing for a concert, or memorizing your lines before the first rehearsal. Whatever your choice, let your readers see what happens on stage and backstage; while casting out and reeling in, while stalking your prey before sunup and after sundown. Let you readers see you showing off, or simply enjoying, the continuing development of your competence.

If my first suggestions sound frivolous to your studious ears, consider the possibility of talking about: The useful or beautiful, the useful and beautiful, things you enjoy making with your own skillful hands. Like the needlework that keeps you or somebody else warm, or something that adds an artistic touch to the place you call home. Your collection of stamps, or baseball cards, or antique cruets, and the purchase or trades you make to expand your collection. Or you may want people to know that you are: An ambitious, if not brilliant computer hacker. A collector of clothes and jewelry that reflect the latest fashion or express your own personal style. A mechanic with the skill and expertise it takes to keep your new motorcycle in top condition, or to extend the active life of your old clunker. Maybe your attention and affection are lavished upon your garden, either veggie or floral. Or you love to bake bread, or prepare delicious snacks and gourmet dinners.

Whatever you choose to talk about, whatever the skill you always enjoy, let your readers see you showing off your expertise. After participating in this exchange after listening to each others writings you'll all know each other a little, maybe a lot, better. Or in more academic terms as readers, you will have gained new appreciation of the interpersonal functions of writing; as writers, you will have gained new knowledge of the audience of readers you are expected to address as you continue writing for your class.

REFERENCES

Chang, Y. (1999). Be confident, ESL writers! In C. Coggins (Ed.), *Voices from the University of Iowa Writing Center* (pp. 29-31). Iowa City: The University of Iowa Writing Center.

Cheng, K. (1999). Remembrances of a special place. In C. Coggins (Ed.), *Voices from the University of Iowa Writing Center* (pp. 14-16). Iowa City: The University of Iowa Writing Center.

Coggins, C. (2001). A departure from the department: The writing center alternative to compartmental thinking. In *Traversing a landscape in flux: A disjunctive approach to identity constructs in academia and beyond* (Doctoral dissertation, University of Iowa, 2001). *Dissertation Abstracts International, 62/06,* 2113.

Kazembe, B. (1997). Skinned people in my village. In C. Coggins (Ed.), *Voices from the University of Iowa Writing Center* (pp. 9-11). Iowa City: The University of Iowa Writing Center.

Kelly, L. (1972). *From dialogue to discourse: An open approach to competence and creativity.* Glendale, IL: Scott, Foresman.

Kelly, L. (1980). One on one Iowa City style: Fifty years of individualized writing instruction. *Writing Center Journal, 1*(1), 4-19.

Kelly, L. (1987). *Context and response: An interactive approach to self—In writing and reading.* Coursepack for Introduction to College Reading and Writing, University of Iowa, Iowa City.

Kelly, L. (2001). *From Miss Stanley to the great writing lab in the sky.* Keynote address to the Midwest Writing Centers Association, Iowa City, IA.

Kwak, J. (1999).To be like an eagle. In C. Coggins (Ed.), *Voices from the University of Iowa Writing Center* (pp. 5-8). Iowa City: The University of Iowa Writing Center.

Langley, R. (1999). From nowhere to somewhere. In C. Coggins (Ed.), *Voices from the University of Iowa Writing Center* (pp. 1-5). Iowa City: The University of Iowa Writing Center.

Miller, B. (1999). Soul of a woman. In C. Coggins (Ed.), *Voices from the University of Iowa Writing Center* (pp. 8-10). Iowa City: The University of Iowa Writing Center.

Robertson, E. (1988). From expressive to academic discourse. *Writing Center Journal, 9*(1), 21-28.

Severino, C. (1993a). The "doodles" in context: Qualifying claims about contrastive rhetoric. *Writing Center Journal, 14*(1), 44-61.

Severino, C. (1993b). Writers writing. *Writing Lab Newsletter, 17*(6), 11-14.

Severino, C. (2002). Writing centers as linguistic contact zones and borderlands. In J. Wolff (Ed.), *Professing in the contact zone: Bringing theory and practice together.* (pp. 230-239). Urbana, IL: NCTE.

Severino, C. (2005). Crossing cultures with international ESL writers: The tutor as contact zone contact person. In B. Rafoth (Ed.), *A tutor's guide: Helping writers one to one* (2nd ed., pp. 41-53). Portsmouth, NH: Boynton/Cook.

Swain, M., & Lapkin, S. (1995). Problems in output and the cognitive processes they generate: A step towards second language learning. *Applied Linguistics, 16*(3), 371-391.

Tsai, Y. (1999). What it is like to grow up as the oldest child. In C. Coggins (Ed.), *Voices from the University of Iowa Writing Center* (pp. 41-42). Iowa City: The University of Iowa Writing Center.

Unger, A. (1996).The evolution of my writing. In C. Coggins (Ed.), *Voices from the University of Iowa Writing Center* (p. 10). Iowa City: The University of Iowa Writing Center.

Yoshioka, N. (1999). As usual. In C. Coggins (Ed.), *Voices from the University of Iowa Writing Center* (pp. 22-23). Iowa City: The University of Iowa Writing Center.

PUBLICITY, PLAY, PEDAGOGY

The Story of the Never-Ending Story

Derek Boczkowski, Ian Randall,
Truly Render, and Sarah Sinovic

Picture your ideal writing environment. Chances are you'll imagine a place that has adequate access to writing tools—although not necessarily a large pad of drawing paper and assorted colors of markers. You may envision proximal food and drink—although perhaps not steaming Chicago-style hot dogs, butter-drenched corn on the cob, and a variety of bite-sized candy. Perhaps the mood of your ideal writing environment is set by inspirational music—although most likely not played by a rock band at implausible sound levels. Do you picture yourself in solitude, or are you surrounded by, say, 500 of your peers, all laughing, shouting, weaving in and out of each other's way? Do you happen to see the guy on stilts?

This spectacular festival—the hot dogs, the ear-splitting rock, the stilt guy—plays out under a giant tent as part of Columbia College Chicago's (CCC's) circus-themed Convocation for incoming freshmen and transfer students. And this event, under the big top in a parking lot in the south side of Chicago's famed Loop, is the setting for the perpetual composition of the Columbia Writing Center's Never-Ending Story (NES). Upon making their way past the stage, beyond the free temporary tattoo stand, and around the various tables promoting Columbia offices, services, and student organizations, incoming freshmen are beckoned by CCC Writing Center (WC) writing consultants to the WC table. Here, the new students are invited to contribute a sentence to the ongoing narrative that is filling the pages of a large artist's sketch tablet.

STEP RIGHT UP!

An ongoing text currently composed only by incoming freshman during Convocation, the NES was piloted during freshman orientation in Summer 2002, scrapped the following year, and reintroduced during the newly adopted circus-themed orientation in Fall 2004. Because of the myriad contributors, the NES is a manuscript of disparate colors, styles, and print (or handwriting). However, as the contributors to the NES are instructed to take part in a perpetual, collaborative narrative, the different entries form an amalgamation of creativity and community, whether an author makes a conscious attempt to address the action of the preceding entry, chooses to move the story along a different path by purposely differing from the previous entry, or even salvages the NES from the blatant sales pitch of an exhibitor.[1]

The Never-Ending Story[2] is the CCCWC's frankly titled take on the Surrealist parlor game *le cadavre exquis* ("the exquisite corpse"), wherein a group of players would collectively create a collage of words by writing a word or phrase on a piece of paper, folding the paper so as to conceal part of what was written, and then passing the paper on to the next player.[3] The game was played by contemporary surrealists as an effort "to get rid of any semblance of rational control" over the creative act, thus making for the safe passage of "the stream of uninhibited verbal imagery," that is, *surreality* (Gauss, 1943, p. 39). Today, the exquisite corpse is often employed in writing classrooms as a method of invention or an introduction to a writing task or course itself, and it is not difficult to discern why: there is an element of ease to such a task. Creative writing instructor Tom Murphy (1989) assigns the exquisite corpse as a "playful exercise" on the first day of his course, suggesting it to be an effective introduction to creative writing in that students need only "a knowledge of the most basic parts of speech" and no "particular talent" to participate. Murphy also points out that the game is a sound classroom exercise in that it manages "to establish camaraderie in the group" (p. 24). And it is this collaborative nature of the exquisite corpse that prompted us at the WC to include it as our Convocation project.

We had been searching for a new way to present the WC at the Convocation; our giveaways—CCCWC pencils and Dum-Dum candies festooned with "Don't be a sucker; come to the writing center!" labels—had stirred only minor interest in previous years. And although we were concerned with attracting new writers, the WC was not hurting for visitors. The developmental writing courses at Columbia, an open admissions arts and communications school of more than 10,000 students, required weekly visits to the WC.[4] If anything, the WC is a victim of its brisk trade, as those whose composition courses do not require them to attend sessions at the WC are very likely to view the WC as a place only for remedial work. Like all WCs, we are faced with what Nancy Grimm (1996) identified as the "sticky history of remediation" (p. 530), a history that suggests to many that the college WC is a place to bring basic writers up to the academic code. Unlike some WCs, however, the specter of remediation is quite corporeal in our present.

Mindful of our historic and current place in the academy and the assumptions students must make about a center as large as ours, our primary mission in presenting the WC at Convocation was to assert ourselves as a service for all writers, no matter what experience or presumed skill level. Additionally, we were aware that many writers who would be required to visit us would be present at Convocation, so the event seemed to be the perfect opportunity to plant the notion that required visits does not equal a punishment. We looked to include these students in an activity for all writers and not "define them in terms of their separateness," as David Bartholomae (2005, p. 114) suggested is a hazard when introducing basic writers to the academy. Oh, and when competing for attention with freestyle rappers, rainbow-clad jugglers, and young co-eds offering free Slinkies, it perhaps goes without saying that we needed to offer something fun.

"IS THIS SOME KIND OF CLUB?"[5]

The fact that so many hours are spent in session with students who are institutionally recognized as basic writers has helped cultivate a resistance to the WC on the part of those who did not place in developmental composition courses. We knew that this resistance from "good writers" was an issue we needed to address, particularly during freshman Convocation. In their research on student and faculty attitudes toward the writing center, Frank Devlin and Nancy Schultz (1996) found that many instructors "hold a minimalist view of writing centers which assumes a focus on issues like grammar and mechanics." Observing that much of their WC's traffic was dependent on faculty recommendation, Devlin and Schultz noted that the assumptions faculty made about the center's ethos influenced who they would recommend: "Though faculty may acknowledge the value of writing centers for weak students, they seldom connect the center to the needs of the competent writer" (p. 159). By not presenting the WC as a viable option for all writers, faculty members were perpetuating the myth of the writing center as a remedial space. Although we were making efforts to address that attitude among Columbia's faculty, we were hoping to get the opportunity to make a strong first impression before the students began classes. So we decided to arouse their artistic proclivities.

Columbia's reputation as an arts and communication school is that it is a haven for the creative prodigy. Students are encouraged by the school brand to "create change" and by the school's mission statement to "author the culture of their times." The NES is an attempt to appeal to the students' creativity and *authority*. Without overt suppression of topic or language, the NES intends to attract those who are suspicious of institutional guidelines that are often seen as restraints to creativity. By distancing the WC from such guidelines and by championing the creativity of the student, we are suggesting to students—those required to meet with us and those not so required—that we see every student as a writer belonging to the network of CCC students.

It was clear that in order to make our participation in Convocation worthwhile, we had to prompt students to want to forgo a second hamburger and come visit our table; nevertheless, there persisted the nagging concern that the WC would not be able to maintain a reputation of professionalism if we, as a service, sponsored a thoroughly frivolous endeavor. Like most WCs, we are accustomed to scratching and clawing for institutional respectability and acclaim, working hard to portray a scholarly visage for administrators, announcing every professional achievement, no matter if the achievement is directly related to the work done in the center.[6] That said, we—like every WC that we know—are overall a jovial place, replete with inside jokes, folk tales, nicknames, and mascots: a comfortable and welcoming place for writers who may otherwise feel alienated by an unfamiliar college culture, a place where such writers are encouraged to experiment, to play.

In "Play and Game: Implications for the Writing Center," Daniel T. Lochman (1986) investigated such play. At first, when a student writes on an evaluation that he had "fun" when visiting the writing center, Lochman imagined an archetypal school administrator who would bristle at such a confession (p. 11). But, he surmised, the WC, where grades are absent and experimentation is promoted, "offers the ideal site and optimal methods for students to learn the value of play." Lochman's idealized administrator—and, for that matter, writing center staff—can take heart that "by discovering writing can be playful, [the student] has found what interests him, and he can learn that what interests him may be communicated all the more effectively to others" (p. 17). The presence of this aspect of play in the writing center not only makes our efforts more welcoming

> "The writing center, where grades are absent and experimentation is promoted, 'offers the ideal site and optimal methods for students to learn the value of play.'"

to writers—especially marginalized writers—but is also essential for the continued success of WCs. The NES was chosen as an activity aimed at engendering an association of writing with fun, an activity that may serve as a precursor to the play with language and convention that students may expect to engage in at the WC.

So it was as simple as that: offer incoming students an enjoyable activity that fosters the notion that the WC sees everyone as a writer with something to contribute to a project, story, or (eventually) discourse community, no matter if they would be likely to label themselves as such. What we have come to find, however, is that for the students who participated in the NES and the student tutors who staffed the tables at freshman Convocation, the project became much more than an entertaining promotion.

CALL AND RESPONSE, OR BLOW, MAN, BLOW!

One of the main reasons why the NES is a successful idea for an introduction to a WC is that it dispels the myth that writing is a lonely art, performed by tortured souls who lock themselves to desks and whiskey bottles. Many college freshmen have adopted the notion that writing is an art that can only be created through solitude, but the NES allows individuals to come into contact with a form of writing that requires them to interact immediately with others throughout the creative process, thusly introducing them to a social constructivist theory of writing.

During the course of the day, people would come up to the table and ask what the story was about. The usual response was along the lines of, "Read the last entry and tell us." Occasionally, people were very confused by the proctors' lack of specific knowledge concerning the direction of the piece. Those who were deemed by society to be leaders (writing consultants) had no control over the creative process. The real power is, quite literally, in the hands of those who come to visit the table. This implies a break from typical misconceptions attributed to writing, especially that there are certain people allowed to write and others who are not. Since all voices are considered equal in this exercise, this fallacy gives way to an opinion by Wendy Bishop (2000), "Writers are people who write. Just that" (p. 45). If we consider all people who write words to be writers, then the romantic notion of the lone writer breaks down, as there would be far too many solitary beings in the world for even a small society to function, let alone create a piece of work.

Playing off of the voice that came before them, the writer is allowed to add their own creative sense onto the NES and take part in setting up for the next voice to come. By reading the entry that comes before their own, the writer is able to directly interact with the piece as if she were sitting right behind the author who came before, egging them on into new and unexpected areas. Not surprisingly, people who came to the table together would often stand close to one another, reading each word as it was written, as if they were jazz musicians listening to a combo member's solo. As a person wrote out his or her piece, the observers were actively engaged with the creation and would laugh, shout, applaud, nod to show that they were with the person and wanted to add onto their work. Like members of a jazz combo, the NES authors listened to the individual so that they could (a) find ways to support the other's voice; (b) find ways to use their own voice; or (c) move the piece as a whole into new directions.

Continuing the thread started by a previous writer is similar to the way members of a jazz combo play chords that support the solo player's musical choices. While the "solo" is passed between writers in the NES, the thread keeps on moving within the agreed upon set of circumstances. This agreement follows the improv rule of "Yes and . . ." When a person onstage makes a statement, the others onstage treat this statement as being true. Through this agreement, the story is allowed to emerge unencumbered by disagreement on established circumstances:

> *But behold, something dark and sinister began to arise on the horizon.*
> *A GREAT and ABOMINABLE beast!*
> *Who had a severe allergic reaction to orange peels and jelly beans.*

The collaboration in these cases is clear, as the full picture of a character is only revealed through the entries of several contributors.

When these circumstances change, it is the result of a different member taking charge, offering a new tempo, new direction, new style. It is the start of a new musician's solo. The voice might be different in tone or circumstance, but there is still a link and a transitional element. The voice is still saying "Yes"; however, it comes out more so as "Yes, but . . ." For example, within two sentences of the NES, the setting of the story moves from the moon to China:

> *Due to the lack of available bachelors* [on the moon], *she died a lonely woman.*
> *Glorious sparkles emitted from her motionless body.*
> *And then somebody smoked them taking a brief hallucinating journey to China.*

The last writer does not dismiss what goes on before, but in fact uses the results of the death of a character to transport the story to China. The writer is still collaborating, seeing a new avenue in the story as a result of what went before. The author is saying, "Yes we were on the moon, but now we are in China."

In the truest sense of jazz, there are moments of sheer spontaneity that seem to throw the entire song into an unexpected area. For the NES, these moments arise from the seemingly unrelated non-sequiturs where the story jumps from the tale of a bumblebee to a commercial for one of the nation's largest banks. These moments could be considered moments of "No" within the shouts of "Yes," but even with these dissonant tones the piece continues onward. At the very beginning, the meeting between a bee and a prostitute is broken by a written commercial for Bank of America that simply ends itself. These dissonant moments are still part of the entire piece and are still parts to be used for collaboration. The "commercial" breaks the story out of a linear form much in the way that a blast of non-harmonic music within a solo can break an audience's expectations of where the story shall travel.

The interesting thing concerning this writing is that the collaboration is extraordinarily peer to peer. Within the NES, the voices have a truer sense of equality because the focus is on the process of the collaboration rather than the product that is formed from it. If the NES is unending, then the product remains unfinished and more voices can join into the text; the value of the NES is not the finished product, but the interplay of content, style, and language between authors. Often this equal collaboration is rare to come by in writing centers. In "Are Writing Centers Ethical," Irene L. Clark and Dave Healy (2001) mentioned that "collaboration in writing centers . . . often involves a writer who is not a full-fledged member of the academic discourse community. In fact, the purpose of the tutoring is often to help the author attain that status" (p. 250). The collaboration is used more as a technique to cultivate the writing of another rather than create a piece of writing. In the NES, all writers are assumed to be members of the discourse community, with no regard for whether or not they "should" be there, giving writers who are required to come to the writing center an experience of empowerment that we hope to see manifested in their session work.

READING MUSIC

When asked to express themselves through writing, many incoming freshmen consider that act of writing to be the catalyst of a rhetorical situation. That is to say, the order seems plain: a writer writes and then readers read. The NES flips this notion. The first step for those participating in the NES is to "backread," or read what the prior author wrote. This is when potential authors begin to determine the meaning of the text, when they draw on "textual information and personal knowledge to formulate their interpretations" (Golden, 1996, p. 95). Before putting marker on paper, the students in fact contribute to the NES by reading it. Only after being mindful of the context can the authors take the next step of the NES and write. Now the contributor to the NES has the opportunity to see that his or her writing is not an isolated, wholly spontaneous act, but is actually in response to a text and involves a series of processes.

Although the concept of writing as a process may be new to Columbia freshmen, the writing consultants staffing the table at Columbia Convocation are exposed to this theory in *The Allyn and Bacon Guide to Peer Tutoring* (Gillespie & Lerner, 2004): "We use three episodes in the writing process—planning, drafting, and revising—plus a fourth episode, proofreading/ editing . . . but it's important to keep in mind the nonlinear shape of the writing process (one that's quite hard to render on paper)" (Gillespie & Learner, 2004, p. 14). Another consultant resource, *The Little, Brown Handbook* (Fowler, Aaron, & Anderson, 2001), furthers the discussion of process by asserting that there is not a sole approach to writing:

> There is no *one* writing process: no two writers proceed in the same way, and even an individual writer adapts his or her process to the task at hand. Still, most experienced writers pass through certain stages that overlap and circle back on each other" including "Analyzing the writing situation," "Developing/planning," "Drafting," and "Revising." (pp. 2-3)

The different sets of authors' descriptions of the stages of the writing process are incredibly similar, suggesting that although there may be more than one way to engage the processes, these processes are indeed common to everyone's writing.

The reading that the NES participants do before they write is like the "planning" stage the authors describe in the writing process. It doesn't matter how much an NES participant reads before writing—a participant could read only the previous entry or the entire story—any amount of reading may be sufficient research to contribute. What does matter is that the contributor has some idea as to what he or she is adding onto—in other words, the context of the story thus far. While the time spent planning was not lengthy, the students, by familiarizing themselves with the project's context, were readying to draft. By understanding the rules of the game, a student became, as James Porter (1986) described, "part of the discourse tradition, a member of the team, and participant in a community of discourse that creates its own collective meaning" (p. 35). An individual's contribution, while an expression of that individual, came as a result of their immersion in the context of the NES.

To understand that context, the NES participant engaged in active reading. Louise Rosenblatt (1995) talks about how everything a person reads should be done actively:

> The reader's role . . . is an active, not passive, one . . . The greater the reader's ability to respond to the stimulus of the word and the greater his capacity to savor all that words can signify of rhythm, sound, and image, the more fully will he be emotionally and intellectually able to participate in the literary work as a whole. (p. 48)

NES participants who actively read before contributing are able to internalize the context of the story and in return "emotionally and intellectually participate" through their writing. In the segments of the NES written at Convocation 2004, authors were enthused about a character they had created, a woman of ill-repute named Backseat Betty. This character became the driving force of the story after her introduction to the text by its 16th author. Many of the subsequent 39 authors who contributed that day clamored to "out do" each other by thinking of a crazier antic in the life of Backseat Betty: Betty goes dancing and eventually becomes engulfed in a pillar of flames. As irreverent as this text reads, the competition to write the most outlandish Backseat Betty segment was serious business. During the authorship of this segment, crowds became almost slaphappy as they gathered around to celebrate the authoring of this devilishly fun character and to contribute to her hilarious demise. This game of one-upmanship focused on Backseat Betty came as a result of the engagement with the context of the NES that readers attained as a result of responding to the language that was present in the text prior.

Once one understands where the story has been, she is able to write her part of the NES. This stems from an idea that Rosenblatt (1995) stated well: "The reader, too, is creative. The text may produce that moment of balanced perception, a complete aesthetic experience. But it will not be the result of passivity on the reader's part; the literary experience has been phrased as a *transaction* between the reader and the author's text" (p. 34). The creative reader often reads "beyond" what would seem to have been the original author's intent, ascribing meanings in the text she read that showed up in her own contribution:

> *Carla wants to smoke, but she's afraid of getting cancer. Everyone in*
> *   her family has died from cancer, though never lung.*
> *The irony was killer . . . get it? Killer, cancer . . .*
> *Hey, that reminds me, the Killers are an awesome band.*

The second writer's self-effacing pun and the last author's digression—a replication of a conversational tangent prompted by the word "killer"—no doubt deviated from the intent of the previous author; these "Yes, and . . ." and "Yes, but . . ." moments are evidence of the active and creative reading on the part of their authors.

Additionally, the act of writing often served to help the authors further their understanding of the context, as Robert Tierney and Timothy Shanahan discovered: "Writing prompts readers to engage in the thought-ful exploration of issues, whether it be in the context of studying science, social studies, or literature" (cited in Gillespie & Lerner, 2004, p. 105). Yes, the NES is not a biology text, yet often a contributor would only fully engage in what they read when they wrote their own entries.

Since the NES authors were adding on to pre-existing text composed by writers with a variety of skill levels, it is probable that some encountered unfamiliar language or concepts that rereading did not clarify. Although few NES participants asked the writing consultants working the table to assist them with vocabulary definition or concept clarification, their authorship prompted them to engage with words and concepts they did not know. For the most part, these quick-thinking writers developed the tactic of working around unfamiliar items or beginning an entirely differ-ent story thread. In one instance, an author armed with an extensive vocab-ulary penned a segment that read: "*The combination of veal guilt and ennui . . . was almost unbearable.*" Instead of letting the unfamiliar term thwart her, the writer who stepped up next continued the story using only the concepts that were familiar to her, writing, "*Unbearable: a word that trans-lates as quickly as the passing fad.*" Encounters with new words and con-cepts and the challenge to elaborate upon them introduced student authors to the idea of writing to glean meaning from the text, and thus foreground-ing the simultaneous occupation of the roles of reader and writer.

As every reader-writer brought something new to the literal table, pre-vious entries from other NES reader-writers spurred uncountable possibil-ities. It was common after someone completed her entry to hear the per-son next to them say, "Oh man! I would have written 'xyz' if I would have had the marker!" And indeed the idea that person shared with the prior author was a completely different idea than what was just written down, yet it would have worked too. This is like in Van Ekeren's (1998) story "Crickets and Choirs":

> Harry and Florence sat on their country home porch nearly every sum-mer evening. . . . Not far from their home, a small creek flowed, and from the creek banks came a chorus of crickets. Harry listened to the crickets and said, "Crickets sure do sing." Florence agreed saying. "Yep, they sure know how to sing." Just then Florence heard the voices of the choir coming from the nearby country church and remarked, "Beautiful music, isn't it?" Harry responded, "Yeah, and to think they do it just by running their legs together." (p. 74)

Each one of the writers who added to the NES came from a different place. There were practiced writers—including fiction writing majors and journalism majors—and then there were contributors from majors with very little intrinsic writing, such as dance or photography. Many of these people would feel quite apprehensive about being able to write. "Oh, no," they'd say, "I'm not a writer." But the truth of the matter is they are both a reader and a writer. The NES invites all who simply read some of it to immediately begin the planning process, thus taking part of the discourse community while formulating a potential response. The context of the NES urged participants to assume roles of both reader and writer, and there was truly no black and white as to where one role ended and the other began. NES reader-writers executed overlapping tasks, making their beautiful music with the marker as they still pondered how the last author ran his legs together.

AND THE CROWD GOES WILD

Imagine: A brave student with marker in hand gently pushes her way through the giddy crowd of her peers who have gathered around the WC table to read the NES. When she takes her stance in front of the thick pad of butcher paper upon which the story is authored, the crowd hushes, watches, waits. She takes a deep breath, considering the last line authored, "*. . . and as we make our way we only find more to weigh.*" She glances at the group surrounding her and smirks as her desire to impress, to outwit manifests. She uncaps the marker, and scrawls in purple, defiant bubblegum script, "*But Backseat Betty likes to weigh everything.*" Before she can step fully away from her addition, the crowd is rejoicing, laughing, responding with playful banter, "Oh no you didn't!" and "You go girl!"

The NES prompted some student writers to consider the concept of writing for an audience because their readers were present, watching expectantly as the story was authored. Audience became more than a concept; it became a tangible force for writers to address.

Although the interconnectedness and collaborative nature of the reader and writer is undeniable in business writing (after all, who writes a résumé without thinking about the desires of its reader?), the relevance and virtue of consciously considering one's readers as they write is frequently disputed in academic and literary communities.

For instance, Aristotle maintained that audience is of supreme importance. Aristotle states, "of the three elements in speech-making—speaker, subject, and person addressed—it is the last one, the hearer, that determines the speech's end and object"[7] (Porter, 1986, p. 2). Like many authorities on writing, Raymond Obstfeld (2001) assumed an Aristotelian reliance on audience when he encouraged writers to carefully consider—even woo—their audience. In his book, *Novelist's Essential Guide to Crafting Scenes*, he wrote, "One way to look at the beginning of a scene is to treat it as if it were a blind date. The reader is the date sitting at the table waiting for you. He or she is gorgeous—your dream date—and you want to make a good impression as soon as you meet" (p. 10).

On the other hand, many authorities on writing concur with Plato when he asserted an "asocial mode of invention" in which the creator expresses ideas that are uncontaminated by the presence—actual or theoretical—of another (LeFevre, 1987). Author Milan Kundera (1998) presented an extremist Platonic argument when he implied that collaboration between creator and audience is akin to followers of Hitler. Kundera writes, ". . . in the course of the war against Nazism, the word 'collaboration' took on a new meaning: putting oneself voluntarily at the service of a vile power" (p. 125). As harsh as Kundera's assertion may read, the wary eye that many writers have been instructed to turn upon their readers can be found in the exclusive reliance upon style handbooks in the classroom. In his book, *Audience and Rhetoric: An Archaeological Composition of the Discourse Community*, James Porter (1992) suggested that this reliance on style guides results in writers overlooking their audience: "'clarity' is not 'clarity to somebody'; 'clarity' becomes an objective standard" (p. 35).

Even when instructors forego a heavy-handed approach to style guide training in favor of a more Aristotelian method, writers are given little guidance as to what it means to "consider" their audience, aside from the occasional soft suggestion to make assumptions of their target reader's demographic (Porter, p. 3). Porter stated, "If the audience has not yet convened, in any sense, as readers, how can the writer picture [them]"? (p. 4). With these conflicting theories of audience influencing academia, it is no wonder that it took the literal presence of an audience participating in a social dialogue for many of the college freshmen who wrote the NES to recognize that they actually had "real readers" to consider.[8] Once the student writer recognizes that readers of their work actually exist, they find different ways to approach the reader in their writing.

Karen Burke LeFevre (1987) asserted that "invention is a didactical process in that the inventing individual(s) and the socioculture are co-existing and mutually defining" (p. 35). In other words, even as Kundera—an author renowned for his philosophical stories inspired by his struggles living under totalitarianism in central Europe—asserts a Platonic view, he is collaborating with his internalized view of society (a form of audience according to LeFevre) to compose it. Porter concurs with LeFevre when he discusses the concept of "intertextuality." Porter asserts that no text has one exclusive author and "the very notions of author and reader . . . are regarded as simply convenient actions for domesticating discourse" (p. 68).

While observations of students like the purple marker-wielding female author reveal that many students developed an awareness of their readers simply because the audience had a physical presence, other students seemed to be oblivious to the crowd. NES participant Trent Zuberi was one such author. Although Trent claims to have been unconcerned with the crowd around him, he talks about his recognition of others during his authorship in a very didactical way, similar to the internal digesting of culture that Kundera exemplifies.

In an interview conducted by a NES coordinator, Zuberi—a sophomore marketing major—stated that he had no recollection of learning about audience in his English classes and that prior to the NES, he never usually thought of anyone but himself when he wrote. Zuberi stated, "I had to step outside of my own little world when I began my section of the [Never-Ending] story. Since the section of the story before mine was written by someone else, I had to get into their head—think along the lines that they were thinking—in order to segue properly into my bit." Trent, while unaffected by the actual crowds around him, was influenced by his internalized concept of an "other"—in this case, the author who wrote the segment before him.

Both the NES author who is aware of her readers and the NES author who is oblivious to the readers' physical presence are engaging with audience on different levels. LeFevre wrote about these two types of audience awareness, which she terms "the other." This other can be either "an internalized construct that she makes from social experience or it may be a perceived audience of actual others" (p. 38). Porter (1986) pushed the notion of "the other" further, suggesting that refined writers are wise to consider three main types of "reading presences": those whom the writer desires as her reader, those who will actually read the text, and finally those whom the writer addresses—directly or indirectly—in the text.[9]

Regardless of how the NES authors arrived at their understanding of "the other" while composing their segment of the story, the lesson is one of substance that translates well into more refined arenas of writing. To develop an awareness of the reader is to allow the writer to develop an "inner critic"—crucial for thesis development and revision. An awareness of audience also prepares students for feedback that they will receive from peer critiques, teachers, and editors in the drafting process (LeFevre, 1987, p. 42). Most empowering, the NES's commitment to continuation and its live, performative approach demonstrated to writers that the items they compose will not only be read by the crowds surrounding them on the day that they write their section, but may be read by others years from now; NES authors were shown that new ideas are built from the words they write, and that their writing is responsible for fueling a new generation of thought.

READING BACK

It is hard to say if the NES was successful as a recruitment tool. To encourage spontaneous, creative thought, the NES proctors did not inhibit students by requiring them to identify themselves in any way. However, the proctors provided students with an opportunity to leave their e-mail address to be notified about Writing Center activities and events, if they so desired. Out of 76 e-mail addresses acquired at the WC table during Convocation 2005, approximately 12 enrolled in weekly tutoring sessions at the WC. Although the success of the NES is difficult to quantify, this friendly introduction to the writing center may well have also encouraged many drop-in sessions and one-time appointments.

Perhaps a better lens for viewing the NES can be found in student testimonials of the project's overall success. One student commented that she was inspired to start her own NES on her blog. Another student, commenting on the NES, practically gave a commercial for the WC: "It reminded me I enjoy creatively and spontaneously writing and that I like sharing my writing and collaborating with others." According to another participant, the NES prepared him for the off-the-cuff responses that were required of him in the classroom.[10]

These testimonials and the observations made by the writing consultants who facilitated the NES suggest that the NES was not only fun, but it introduced the incoming freshman to concepts of composition that they will be expected to negotiate in their tenure at Columbia. Without explicit statement, the NES prompted participants to consider writing as a collaborative art, the production of writing as a response to active, creative reading; and the importance one's audience plays on what one writes. The pedagogical potential of these concepts—and others—will need to be more fully researched and explored in future additions to the NES, as we strive to help new students come to grips with the writing they do at the college, no matter if it's within our center's cubicles or under a loud, congested tent.

YES, BUT . . .

While the NES was popular with students, the new WC administration has recently made an executive decision to regulate "indirectly academic endeavors" to the confines of student run organizations. In other words, not only will the NES not be a WC function at Convocation, but it is also no longer permitted to be displayed on the CCCWC's Web site.[11] The potential damage to the WC's public face is obvious, as students who were recruited at Convocation were promised that they were participating in a published work. By not making good on the promise, the credibility of the CCCWC is justifiably circumspect. In a broader sense, as the decision made by administration has had other victims as well, including the light-hearted center newsletter, *Between the Margins*, the culture of levity, of play, that existed in previous years is dissipating, perhaps not by accident. The most disconcerting, however, is the fact that just when we realized what we had—the potential of the NES as a pedagogical tool—the rug has been yanked. The story seems to be coming to an end.

But while this removal of "play" from the WC is unfortunate for student writers who reap rewards from such activities, there remains an inlet of hope for the NES. A Columbia student group called the Writing Arts Community Organization (WACO) is eager to support this area of academic development. WACO, whose ranks, truth to tell, are swollen with WC staff, has expressed interest in publishing the NES online in a "forum" version where writers can add on to the story via the Internet. The NES will no longer mainly function as a recruitment tool, as authors will no longer be solely new Columbia students, but this should be a benefit for other writing centers. The NES's accessibility on the Internet should make it a rhetorical situation capable to be weighed by centers far and wide, by their tutors, and by their students. No markers, no artist's tablet, no hot dogs, no stilt walker. But a virtual Burkean Parlor with an invitation to engage as a reader and writer in a text that just won't end.

NOTES

1. A bank representative wrote: *"Bank of America is your #1 choice for Columbia. We offer free checking, as well, as many other offers! Please visit one of our ATM's on Campus!."* The next student followed *". . . said the corporate whore to the innocent bystander."*
2. Of course, because of our project's lack of terminus, one could say that the NES is, in fact, an exquisite zombie.
3. As a testament to the artistic *gravitas* the Surrealists put in such a spontaneous and collaborative exercise, they named it after the first sentence the game bore: *"Le cadavre exquis boira le vin nouveau"* ("The exquisite corpse will drink the new wine"). The game is also played by drawing separate parts of a figure.
4. And those numbers are substantial. In Fall 2005, for example, nearly 400 students were so required to attend weekly sessions at the WC.
5. This question was posed by one of the students who we surveyed on his involvement with the NES. When he showed up for the focus group, he expressed interest in joining up with the writing "club" that sent him the survey.

6. All scholastic accomplishments—conference presentations, publications, schol-
arships—of the CCCWC staff are detailed in a designated area of the WC's
monthly newsletter, *Between the Margins*.

7. From *Rhetoric*, 1.3.

8. Porter (1992), summarizing W. Daniel Wilson, defined "real readers" as "any
actual flesh-and-blood persons outside the text who reads it" (p. 65). Porter
suggested that when writers and readers participate in a social dialogue, writers can begin their analysis of audience by listening to them. In this way, "[t]he
writer learns from, not just about, the audience" (p. 138).

9. Porter (1992) summarized W. Daniel Wilson when he discussed the three types
of reading presences: the "real reader," the "implied reader," and the "characterized reader" (p. 65).

10. All testimonials were acquired through an online survey prepared by NES
coordinators.

11. Students who participated in the NES at the Fall 2005 Convocation have yet
to see the story as a whole as of this writing.

REFERENCES

Bartholomae, D. (2005). *Writing on the margins (essays on composition and teaching)*.
Boston: Bedford/St. Martin's.

Bishop, W. (2000). Is there a creative writer in the house? Tutoring to enhance creativity and engagement. In B. Rafoth (Ed.), *A tutors guide: Helping writers one
to one* (pp. 44-54). Portsmouth, NH: Heinemann.

Clark, I. L., & Healy, D. (2001). Are writing centers ethical? In R. W. Barnett & J. S.
Blumner (Eds.), *The Allyn and Bacon guide to writing center theory and practice*
(pp. 242-259). Boston: Allyn & Bacon.

Devlin, F., & Schultz, N. (1996). The writing center and the good writer. *The
Writing Center Journal, 16*(2), 144-163.

Fowler, R. H., Aaron J. E., & Anderson, D. (2001). *The Little, Brown handbook* (8th
ed.). New York: Addison-Wesley.

Gauss, C. E. (1943). The theoretical backgrounds of surrealism. *The Journal of
Aesthetics and Art Criticism, 2*, 37-44.

Gillespie, P., & Lerner, N. (2004). *The Allyn and Bacon guide to peer tutoring*. New
York: Pearson.

Golden, J. M. (1996). Reader-text interaction. *Theory into Practice, 2*(25), 91-96.

Grimm, N. M. (1996). Rearticulating the work of the writing center. *College
Composition and Communication, 47*, 523-548.

Kundera, M. (1988). *The art of the novel* (3rd ed.). New York: Harper & Row.

Lefevre, K. B. (1987). *Invention as a social act*. Carbondale & Edwardsville:
Southern Illinois University Press.

Lochman, D. T. (1986). Play and games: Implications for the writing center. *The
Writing Center Journal, 1*(7), 11-19.

Murphy, T. (1989). Bad poems/good poems: How do I know what I mean till I see what I say? *The English Journal, 2*(78), 24-29.

Obstfeld, R. (2001). *Novelist's essential guide to crafting scenes.* Writer's Digest.

Porter, J. E. (1986). Intertextuality and the discourse community. *Rhetoric Review, 1*(5), 34-47.

Porter, J. E. (1992). *Audience and rhetoric: An archaeological composition of the discourse community.* Englewood Cliffs: Prentice-Hall.

Rosenblatt, L. M. (1995). *Literature as exploration* (5th ed.). New York: Modern Language Association of America.

Van Ekeren, G. (1998). *Words for all occasions: Quotes, stories, anecdotes, poems, fables, proverbs and one liners.* Englewood Cliffs, NJ: Prentice Hall.

ABOUT THE CONTRIBUTORS

Derek John Boczkowski is the Assistant Coordinator of the Writing Lab at The Ohio State University at Newark. His article, "Swordfish: On Writing Centers and Speakeasies," was published in *The Writing Lab Newsletter*. He also co-authored "Writing and Reading Community Learning: Collaborative Learning Among Writing and Reading Students, Teachers, and Writing Center Consultants," a chapter for *On Location: Theory and Practice in Classroom-Based Writing Tutoring*. In Fall 2008, Derek will enter The Ohio State University's PhD program in Adolescent, Post-Secondary, and Community Literacies. In his rapidly fleeting spare time, he enjoys writing the occasional mash note to his wife, Victoria.

Elizabeth H. Boquet is Professor of English and Associate Dean of the College of Arts and Sciences at Fairfield University in Fairfield, CT. She is the author of *Noise from the Writing Center* (2002) and a co-author of *The Everyday Writing Center: A Community of Practice* (2007), both published by Utah State University Press. She served as co-editor (with Neal Lerner) of *The Writing Center Journal*.

Harry C. Denny directs the Writing Center at St. John's University (New York, NY) and is an assistant professor in its Department of English, where he teaches courses on composition studies, writing center theory, and research methods. His earlier research has focused on the rhetoric of social movements and identity politics around AIDS and sexual minorities. Harry's recent scholarship explores those issues in relation to writing centers, writing program administration and writing assessment initiatives, particularly as sites for community-building and for cross-cultural/disciplinary dialog. He is also active in the Northeast Writing Centers Association and a planning committee member for Metro-New York City Writing Center Professionals, a mini-regional collective. Harry's roots in writing centers extend back to his start at Temple University's Writing Center and subsequent directing positions at Long Island University, Brooklyn, and Stony Brook University (SUNY).

Michele Eodice is the director of the writing center at the University of Oklahoma. She is a co-author with Kami Day of *(First Person)²: A Study of Co-Authoring in the Academy* (2001) and a co-author of *The Everyday Writing Center: A Community of Practice* (2007), both published by Utah State University Press. She currently serves as associate editor of development for *The Writing Center Journal* and is co-editor of *Kansas English.* Michele is currently the president of the International Writing Centers Association (2007-2009).

Dawn Fels began working in writing centers as a graduate student tutor over a decade ago. As an English teacher, she set up a high school writing center and peer tutoring program, working closely with faculty and community volunteers, including professors and pre-service teachers from nearby universities. In her most recent post at a private Catholic university, she secured grant funds to launch another collaborative effort between a university and area high school. She currently serves as the Executive Board secretary for the International Writing Centers Association and is a regular presenter at IWCA, NCTE, CCCC, and regional writing center conferences. She now attends Indiana University of Pennsylvania, where she is a doctoral candidate in the Composition & TESOL program and the assistant writing center director. Dawn resides in Indiana with her two favorite writers, Cameron and Zada.

Anne Ellen Geller is currently Associate Professor of English at St. John's University, having previously taught at Clark University for eight years. She teaches undergraduate and graduate courses in rhetoric and composition and writing studies. As Director of Writing Across the Curriculum in the St. John's University Institute for Writing Studies, she works with faculty from all disciplines to support the teaching of writing at all levels of instruction in all departments.

Wendy Goldberg is a Lecturer in the Program in Writing and Rhetoric at Stanford University, where she has taught since 1984. In 2001, she helped to found the Stanford Writing Center, serving as Assistant Director of the Center from 2004-2007. She has played a major role in fostering the performance of writing at the Center, overseeing the development of a vibrant spoken word community. Wendy received her PhD in English from Yale.

Sandee K. McGlaun is Associate Professor of English and Director of the new Writing Center at Roanoke College. Formerly, she directed The Writing Center @ NGCSU. An instructor of rhetoric, composition, and creative writing, her essays have appeared in *Dialogue, The Writing Lab*

Newsletter, and *Southern Discourse.* A lifelong stage performer and professional dramaturg, she is also author of the one-woman show *What a Doll.* She holds a PhD in English (rhetoric and feminist theatre) from The Ohio State University.

Timothy A. Miank is a Professor in the Department of Communication and the Department of Language Skills at Lansing Community College. He teaches developmental writing and first-year composition courses, directs one of the composition program's portfolio programs, and is past coordinator of LCC's WAC program. He has presented at numerous conferences and is the author of a customized textbook, *Writing Essays: Audience, Purpose, and Process,* currently used in LCC's top-level developmental writing course.

Scott L. Miller has been working in and around writing centers during his entire career, stretching from 1985 until the present, and he currently directs the writing center at Sonoma State University in northern California. He earned his PhD in 1995 from The Ohio State University. He has authored or co-authored works appearing in *College Composition and Communication, Pedagogy,* and *The Journal of the Association for Business Communication,* and he is currently working on a book on writing centers and the liberal arts tradition. In the summer of 2006, he served as a co-leader for the International Writing Centers Association's Summer Institute, which was held at Stanford University.

sj Miller is Assistant Professor of Secondary English Education at Indiana University of Pennsylvania. sj has published widely in journals and, most notably, won the 2005 Article of the Year Award from the *English Journal* for "Shattering Images of Violence in Young Adult Literature: Strategies for the Classroom." Most recently, sj co-authored *Unpacking the Loaded Teacher Matrix: Negotiating Space and Time Between University and Secondary English Classrooms,* which received the Richard A. Meade award from NCTE, and co-authored *Narratives of Social Justice Teaching: How English Teachers Negotiate Theory and Practice Between Preservice and Inservice Spaces.* Current research interests are in unpacking English teacher identity in spacetime as pre-service teachers experience the larger matrix of the teaching world. sj is the co-chair of the CEE (Conference on English Education) committee for Social Justice, the secretary for NCTEAR (National Council Teachers of English Assembly for Research), and is a consultant for the College Board, providing best practices to secondary Pre- and Advanced Placement English teachers.

Cinda Coggins Mosher is a full-time lecturer in the University of Iowa Rhetoric Department and directs the Speaking Center. Her scholarly interests include composition, speech, hypertext fiction and theory, disjunctive poetry and prose, writing center pedagogy, censorship, and academic freedom. Since joining the Rhetoric faculty in 2001, Cinda has taught many Rhetoric courses, led the Department's teaching practicum, tutored in and served as acting director of the Writing Center, been a commenting mentor for Writing Fellows, and advised Rhetoric TAs.

Hans Ostrom is Professor of English at the University of Puget Sound in Tacoma, Washington. He is the author of *Three To Get Ready* (a novel) and *The Coast Starlight: Collected Poems 1976-2006* (Dog Ear Publishing). With Wendy Bishop and Katharine Haake, he wrote *Metro: Journeys in Writing Creatively* (Longman, 2002). With J. David Macey, he edited the five-volume *Greenwood Encyclopedia of African American Literature* (2005). He has also taught at Gutenberg University in Germany and Uppsala University in Sweden.

Derek Owens directs the Institute for Writing Studies at St. John's University, and is author of *Composition and Sustainability: Teaching for a Threatened Generation* (NCTE Press).

Jill Pennington is the founding Writing Center Coordinator and a writing professor at Lansing Community College. She has worked in writing centers since 1991 and has served as Chair of the Michigan Writing Centers Association, President of the East Central Writing Centers Association, and Community College Representative and Secretary of the International Writing Centers Association. Pennington has twice been a leader in the IWCA Summer Institute for Writing Center Directors and Professionals.

Ian Randall graduated from Columbia College Chicago with a B.F.A. in acting. A true Illinois nomad, he continues to work as a consultant at the college's writing center while serving as the co-artistic director of the Immediacy Theatre Project in Belleville, IL. He also plays the larynx for the spoken word poetry/funk band Farmer's Tan Market.

Julie Reid is a graduate student at Sonoma State University. Her poems have appeared in *lungfull! magazine, Skanky Possum, Crowd, zaum* and *em*. She is the author of a chapbook titled "Different Exercises With Dumbbells." Her artist's book and faux duden of poems, "The Keeping of Wild Bees in the Middle Ages" is forthcoming from Blue Barnhouse Press.

Truly Render tutored for two amazing years at the Columbia College Chicago Writing Center before moving on to the marketing department of the Museum of Contemporary Art, where she wrote copy and planned special events. In 2006, she moved to Glasgow, Scotland, for a year to coordinate marketing efforts for the nationwide Six Cities Design Festival. She currently lives in New York City and manages public relations for

Gotham Writers' Workshop. Truly looks forward to returning to Chicago—where she plans to stay put—to pursue another bachelor's degree in English Secondary Education.

Carol Severino is Associate Professor of Rhetoric and Director of the Writing Center and Writing Fellows Program at the University of Iowa. She teaches courses in tutor education, second language writing research, and travel writing and serves on the editorial boards of *College Composition and Communication*, the *Journal of Second Language Writing*, and *Writing Center Journal*. She has published numerous pieces about ESL writers in the writing center.

Sarah Sinovic calls Omaha, Nebraska home, but ate up big-city life when she moved to Chicago for her undergraduate schooling at Columbia College. Five years later, Sarah is still living in Chicago and currently works in the non-profit field. Sarah's weakness continues to be anything Italian, so it's no surprise that she dreams of moving to Italy one day (hopefully sooner rather than later).

Chad Verbais is the Coordinator of the Writing Center at Southern Illinois University Edwardsville. His research interests include digital technology and its impact on literary studies, visual rhetoric, various ESL issues, and minority language in the academy. He is active in numerous writing groups and is currently collaborating on several creative projects. In his spare time, he enjoys spending time with his boys and playing as much as possible.

Lisa Zimmerelli is Assistant Professor of English and the Director of the Effective Writing Center at the University of Maryland University College. She has taught a variety of writing courses and is co-author of the *Bedford Guide for Writing Tutors*. Lisa is a PhD candidate in English at the University of Maryland, specializing in Rhetoric and Composition Studies. Her particular interest is in nineteenth-century women's rhetorical practices. She has presented at conferences on both writing center and rhetorical theory topics.

AUTHOR INDEX

SUBJECT INDEX